**CARLISLE
DIOCESAN
TRAINING
INSTITUTE**

ARCHBISHOP
JOOST
DE BLANK

ARCHBISHOP
JOOST
DE BLANK
Scourge of Apartheid

John S. Peart-Binns

First published in Great Britain in 1987
by Muller, Blond & White Limited,
62–65 Chandos Place,
London WC2N 4NW.

British Library Cataloguing in Publication Data

Peart-Binns, John
    Archbishop Joost de Blank (1908–1968):
    scourge of apartheid.
    1. De Blank, Joost 2. Church of England —
    Bishops — Biography 3. Bishops — England
    — Biography
    I. Title
    283'.092'4 BX5199.D373

    ISBN 0–584–11130–4

Typeset by Action Typesetting Limited, Gloucester
Printed and bound in Great Britain

Contents

Acknowledgements

If biography is a journey then all manner of people have joined me on the way, clarifying, explaining, expanding and illuminating different aspects of Joost de Blank's life — from his childhood to his last days at Westminster. It is always difficult to know who to thank. I am bound to omit some names either by unintentional oversight or because people, particularly in South Africa, did not wish their names to appear in print. I hope that those people whose names do not appear here will be indulgent and accept both my apologies and my gratitude.

First, a word about Bartha de Blank. I recall exploring the possibility of a biography with her when she was writing her Memoir of her brother and I was writing a biography of Ambrose Reeves, one time Bishop of Johannesburg. She was quite sure that she was writing a Memoir and not a biography, a Memoir on which I based an article for *Church Times* (30 September 1977). The material she used was given to the Centre for Southern African Studies at the University of York. It is now lodged at The Borthwick Institute, York. All this material was placed at my disposal and I thank Dr. David Smith, Director of the Institute, for temporarily releasing this into my custody. Correspondence, transcripts of interviews and material used for the Memoir have been valuable for my purposes.

A large part of Joost de Blank's papers was not used and probably not seen by Bartha. There is a valuable collection in the archives of the Church of the Province of South Africa at the University of the Witwatersrand in Johannesburg. I record my gratitude to Mrs Anna M. Cunningham, the Curator of Manuscripts, for her advice and assistance and for arranging for me to have copies of a mass of papers by and relating to Joost de Blank.

de Blank is already becoming part of the University thesis circuit. One particularly good and enlightening thesis is that by the late Victor C. Paine on 'The Confrontation between the Archbishop of Cape Town, Joost de Blank and the South African Government on Racial Policies (1957–1963)', (M.A. Thesis — Faculty of Arts, University of Cape Town). I am grateful to Mr. Paine's executors for letting me refer to this work.

Acknowledgements

Then there are those people who have contributed by furnishing me with their recollections of and reflections on Joost de Blank. Many of them have written confidentially to help with a sense of perspective rather than for quotation. All have illuminated what they described. Amongst them I mention three former Archbishops of Cape Town — R. Selby Taylor, Bill Burnett and Philip Russell and a former Archbishop of Dublin, Alan Buchanan. Bishops have included F.A. Amoore, John Carter, Roy Cowdry, Lakdasa de Mel, Evered Lunt, K.C. Oram, Stanley Pickard, L.E. Stradling and Philip Wheeldon; Dean E.L. King, Archdeacons C. Griffith Green, H.A.S. Pink and George Sylvester; Canons J.W. Aubrey, K.A. Chaffey and Jack Roundhill; the Revds. John Andrew, B.M.W. Berdoe, Rupert Bliss, A.T. Burden, J.C. Collins, R.A. Cowling, John Foster, Michael Hamilton-Sharp, Arnold Hirst, A.G. MacGregor, 'Peter' Priest; Messrs John Baden, J.W. Birch (Old Merchant Taylors' Society), D.J. Collings, Bastiaan de Blank, Martin de Blank, S.A. Fuller, Andrew Knox, Alan Lindsay, T. McCallum (Chief Press Officer of Unilever PLC), W. McE. Bisset, A.D. Porter, James P. van den Bergh. Mr. & Mrs. S. Woodford, Mrs. Justine Allison-Beer, Mrs. C. Baden, Mrs. L.J. Banbury, Mrs. Monica Furlong, Miss M. Leuzinger, Miss Ella R. Snow, Mrs. M. Swanson, Mrs. Dorothy E. Whitfield.

Joost de Blank was an entrepreneur in religion. His nephew, Justin de Blank, is an entrepreneur in food with shops and eating places of distinction revealing all the flair of his uncle. As Bartha's executor he has been responsible more than anyone else for acting as midwife in bringing a laboured pregnancy to a satisfactory birth. He has done this most of all by arranging the wherewithal which has enabled the actual birth to take place. Let him explain:

'Episcopal biographies are no longer bought by parish priests across the country so the publishing of such books has become too perilous a commercial risk for a publisher to undertake on his own.

Thus in order for this book to see the light of day it was necessary to ask friends of Joost's and others whether they would contribute the funds needed to underwrite its publication.

It is not without significance that every person so approached responded positively. Some asked that their names should not be listed and I would like to put on record my gratitude to them as well as to the following people who responded so generously:— Mrs. Justine Allison-Beer (niece), the Revd. John Andrew (St. Thomas's, Fifth Avenue, New York), Mrs. Co. Baden (sister), John Baden (nephew), Revd. Peter Michael Baden (nephew), Jennifer Banbury (niece), Mrs. Lou Banbury (sister), Martin de Blank (nephew), Mrs. Priscilla Meek (The Sam Meek Trust, Greenwich, Conn.), Revd. Robert Parks (Trinity Church, New York), and the following two companies who in their different ways played not insignificant roles in Joost's life — Anglo-American and De Beers; and Unilever.

Finally, there are the people of my own family, particularly Annis, my wife, to whom Joost appears to have been a permanent guest in our midst. For her forbearance, patience, encouragement and prodding I am, as always, grateful beyond words. Without her love there would be no book.

List of Illustrations

Preface

Mountains more than most natural phenomena have the ability to enlarge the feelings, widen the vision and diminish the person. To feel 'on top of the world' and only a little lower than the angels is also to feel minute, 'as nothing worth'.

Writing this preface whilst on holiday in the mountains of Austria with the baroque splendour in villages below seems an appropriate place to close, or rather to open, this biography of Joost de Blank. He would have approved of both setting and circumstance and the feeling each conveys. They engender a sense of perspective which is an important ingredient in a biographer's quest.

There are two things I wish to record at the beginning of this book. One is the *joy* of researching and writing it. If I did not feel that Joost de Blank's life and work did not have permanent merit and abiding interest I would not have lifted my pen. I have seen him as Bishop Suffragan of Stepney at mass rallies, not exactly swaying crowds, but arresting, sustaining and convincing large numbers of people. The language used went 'dart-like' into the minds as well as piercing the hearts of the audience. He had the capacity to commend, convince and convert. Many of my countless correspondents owe their faith to him.

I also have to record the *agony* of researching and writing this biography. I do not want to anticipate what follows except to say that when one hears glib talk about a 'crucified life' or the 'difficult path' the life of Joost de Blank is a reproach to such glibness. Spectacular success and abysmal failure are not usually revealed in a single life. When it is, why should a Christian be surprised? One perspective is that Jesus Christ was the biggest flop of all time — claimed to be Messiah and ended dead!! And yet — and yet! As the tale unfolds we will see success and failure, glory and forsakenness. And yet — and yet!

I feel I have walked along many a *via dolorosa* with my subject. There have been times when all seemed lost and the ink in the pen would not flow. But the 'blockage' passed and flow resumed. When I reached the end of Joost de Blank's life the former glory was not far removed from the present agony. I recall a Watchnight Service at Westminster Abbey; also a reception in the Jerusalem Chamber which showed two undiminished sides of his nature. One the preacher still reaching for souls and minds; the other, the party giver, hosting a gathering of people, drawing out from each what each had to give (as well as emptying a few pockets for a good cause) and enabling a sense of stimulating joyfulness to permeate the occasion.

Betwixt the joy and the agony is the life. This is the biography of a leader and man of action with a tortured soul. It is the story of triumph and failure, of limelight and shadows. Was the subject of this biography a frustrated impressario or a confessor of the faith; poseur or prophet; proud prelate or humble servant; bon vivant or monk manqué; Christian statesman or revolutionary leader? In small or large measure Joost de Blank was each and all of them.

The Times obituary writer noted: 'He had few of the physical attributes that tend to bring ecclesiastical preferment. He was small in physical stature, quiet in voice, at times almost sinister in appearance as a result of wounds received in Hitler's war. Nor was he a scholar. But he was possessed of personal qualities that made him an impressive figure in every piece of work to which he was called. Always an indefatigable and imaginative worker, a preacher of simple, yet powerful eloquence, a facile writer with a flair for religious journalism, he developed at Stepney qualities of leadership to which in South Africa were added gifts of statesmanship, so that he became one of the most dynamic leaders in the Anglican Communion in the present century.' (2 January 1968)

Around such a figure, myth and reality merge. It is no surprise that the reflections of the recently retired Archbishop of Cape Town, Philip Russell (1980 to 1986) illustrate this point. He reflects, 'It will possibly sound odd for me to base my comments on that truly illustrious predecessor of mine, Joost de Blank, on three "events/sayings", none of which I can prove; and yet each I believe is completely consonant with the character that I have come so much to respect and admire.

'The first is his alleged statement that "apartheid South Africa was 'expendable' in the total African context" — or words to that effect. What he meant, I believe, was that if the soul of the *whole* of Africa was to be saved for the Christian faith, the presence of racism in a declared Christian country, South Africa, would be a

xi

major stumbling block. Here was something of the greatness of vision of the man. He could see all the forces which would pull Africa away from a true relationship with God; animism, Islam, Nationalism etc. He was not prepared to see Africa turning away from Christ because of any mollycoddling of white Christians in South Africa.

'The second "event" is his alleged refusal to conduct a single "segregated" confirmation service in any of the parishes of this diocese. In the nature of things, I do not know precisely which church or churches he had in mind; I certainly can well imagine they may have existed.

'But how could he conduct a segregated confirmation service — which would simply be part of the whole racialistic intransigence to which I have been referring; and which he saw as a major obstacle towards the evangelisation of the African continent?

'The third "event" is the alleged response of apology he extended to those members of the Dutch Reformed Church who were present with him at the never-to-be-forgotten Cottesloe Conference. He had not, and note this, wavered for one second from "the great vision" for Africa; he would not under any circumstances return to his diocese to conduct segregated confirmation services. Through personal contact hitherto denied him, he had come to see in those to whom he had been opposed, something of the "men" themselves, and his was the true greatness to be able to say, "Sorry, let's get closer together".

'Note how in each of these "events/sayings" his greatness had shone through. This is not surprising; for that is the word above all others that I use to describe him.'

To comment on these reflections at this stage is inappropriate.

There was ever present in Joost de Blank, along with so much that was extravagant, enigmatic and paradoxical, a practical shrewdness which would have been noticeable in any career, but his gifts were given to the Church. The directness of the man of action comes out in his style — expressed in language of extraordinary force and felicity. What he had seen he could remember and utilize.

Joost de Blank wanted to be a leader. But the leader's crown is ever in some sense a crown of thorns. The suspicion of egotism, of some private interest concealing itself beneath the public procedure, of some streak of self-seeking in the crusade, can kill the life-blood of authority. Joost de Blank must have been aware of this.

His diaries carry many expressions of self-doubt and self-tormenting questioning.

It would have been utterly impossible for him, with his charismatic gifts, with his dramatisation of himself and situations, to have gone to South Africa as an unassuming pastor and fence-sitting leader. Private anguish and public silence were not his metier. He once said to a friend that he did not know whether he would be able to get back. He tended to go to absolutes and rarely had second thoughts because action followed quickly, often too quickly. Yet he was an inspiration to a whole host of people in Africa and throughout the world.

A discerning friend observes: 'If Joost had had the same sort of experience as Thomas à Becket, that kind of dramatic approach, forcing and constraining issues, it would in a curious way have been a fulfilment for him.'

There was another side too, 'the dark night of the soul' at which Bishop William Wand hinted in his Address at Joost's Memorial (or Thanksgiving) Service in Westminster Abbey on 26 January, 1968. '[We think] of the inner struggle that went on throughout his life ... to know and understand what was God's will for him. Man, we are told, is born to trouble as the sparks fly upward. Sometimes we are tempted to try to jump off our own shadows and think ourselves in an imaginary life where troubles will cease to harass us. That is impossible. Life is not a sentimental sphere in which we can lose ourselves in happy and pleasant thoughts without fear or trouble or anxiety. We have to take life as it is — the trouble with the happiness. Sometimes we can be so happy that we become afraid of our own happiness. Sometimes the trouble is so great that we wonder whether indeed we have lost sight of God or whether He has actually forsaken us. Of all this stress and trouble Joost had his fill.'

Joost de Blank — man of action with a tortured soul is in the future. To write more now would be to prescribe the conclusions and that would conclude the scribe. I did not set out on the journey with pre-conceived conclusions. A journey of joy was constantly surprised by the companion of unexpectedness and agony joined me on the way. Let the journey begin.

July, 1986

Archbishop Joost de Blank (right) at the Consecration of Bill Burnett as Bishop of Bloemfontein, November 1957.

CHAPTER ONE

Bible and Cointreau

Joost de Blank was born in Rotterdam on 14 November 1908, a month when the world year by year rolls through an exceptional rain of shooting stars or meteorites. These meteorites come in from outer space and get burned up in our atmosphere as they tear through. They create an impression, leave a trail, make an impact. Some finish up in museums.

This is the story of a living meteorite whose flashing progress across the world lightened many a darkness and touched, even changed, many lives before burning itself out.

There was nothing special about birth in Rotterdam, that noisy, busy, commercial city located on the delta of two great river systems, the Rhine and the Meuse. But the fact of a Dutch parentage and long traceable ancestry was important. It shaped many of de Blank's convictions and explains many an apparent paradox. Flamboyance, wit, imagination and inventiveness are not words which leap to the mind when thinking of Dutch men and women. Are they not a little stiff and unromantic despite their enjoyment of music and adoration of painting? Do you not find Calvinistic attitudes sharing a platform with enjoyment of the good things of life? A law abiding people who are also liberty loving has led to some strange moral acrobatics today. The Protestant ethic of hard work and rewards found fertile foundations in the dykes.

1

Some of the conflicts in de Blank's own character can be traced to his Dutchness although he left Holland whilst still a baby.

Joost de Blank's father, also Joost de Blank, was born at Dordrecht on 24 March 1871. From at least the sixteenth century his forbears had lived in and around Rotterdam and the fifth century town of Tiel in Central Holland. Joost de Blank senior's own father, Bastiaan was a merchant seaman and travelled throughout the Middle East and Africa. Travel and wanderlust was a family trait. In 1887 Bastiaan took his son, Joost, then aged sixteen, out to the Belgian Congo. Here primitive conditions, hard work, long hours and a punishing climate that claimed many a victim toughened the son's exterior and strengthened his interior. At the age of twenty-five Joost returned to Europe, sought a job and was engaged as a book keeper by Van den Berghs in Rotterdam. He studied before leaving home for a long day at Van den Berghs and resumed his studies until late in the evening. He was determined to succeed. He did, and his abilities were quickly recognised. In 1902 when Van den Berghs acquired a small margarine factory in Gildehaus, Germany, just across the Dutch border, de Blank went there as the confidential representative of the directors in Rotterdam and London.

Joost de Blank had developed an analytical mind, was not given to easy optimism and was always suspicious of facile solutions to complex problems. These were ideal character testimonials for book keeper turning accountant. From an early age he had wide interests and became much more than the talented amateur in literature and music.

On 25 May 1899 he married Louisa Johanna Quispel (born in 1870). On her father's side, she came from a family of sailors for at least seven generations including sea captains, a lighterman pilot, a chief-officer of the herring fleet and a sail maker.

Louisa Johanna's mother's Christian names were Jacoba Gwetray and her maternal grandfather was a goldsmith named Massieu. Three generations further back, the Massieu line came from Normandy which seems to confirm family tradition of this line being French Huguenots. French was apparently the first language of the Massieus until very recent generations. Although Louisa Johanna knew no French her halting English was spoken with a French accent. But Dutch was her own language. The family name Quispel was that of the largest piano manufacturer in Holland, but it did not belong to her immediate family. She herself

2

had trained as a milliner.

We shall hear more of this couple. They were very different. He was a man of extraordinary capacity and brain power, gentle in character and an excellent linguist. She was formidable, lively, spirited and, though charming, could have a biting tongue. She had both presence and dominance, always creating a feeling of the matriarch until in later life that is what she became.

There were six children of the marriage, Willem (Wim) 1900; Jacoba Geertruy (Co) 1902; Louisa Johanna (Lou) 1904; Bartha and her twin Sebastian (Basty) 1906; and Joost 1908. Joost was not the only child to find these Dutch names a handicap. The English pronunciation of his name was Juist rhyming with boost so he had to correct people. When he became Bishop of Stepney he wrote to his clergy, 'I am sorry about the name JOOST! No one can cope with it, but it reveals my Dutch origin, and has been anglicised for several nephews to JUSTIN. To pronounce it correctly the best I can do is to give it its phonetic spelling, which is YOAST.' He contemplated changing *his* name to Justin but when he discussed this with the Bishop of London (J.W.C. Wand) they came to the conclusion that to sign '✝ Just-in Stepney' might provoke more mirth than understanding.

In 1909 the family moved to London where Joost's father became the pivot of the London office and of the entire Van den Berghs' organization. He was the financial expert, and he put into operation a modern administration, proper controls and participated in most of the private discussions with the directors. Not only was he considered an expert on many subjects in his own business, but the British Government also recognized his expert knowledge and later, in the early nineteen thirties, he was consulted when the pound sterling was about to be devalued.

After the formation of Unilever he became the head of its financial department in 1931, until he retired in 1935, although he continued to advise on financial matters until 1943. Together with Dr.G.H.Gluck (also of the Unilever Treasury Department) de Blank wrote many articles for *Progress* (the Lever Brothers' Magazine), on such subjects as *The Economic Rise of Tropical Africa, The Economic Unity of Europe, Germany's Economic Policy* and *The Standard of Living in Russia*. His last article *Money — a Measure of Value?* appeared in the Winter 1951 issue when he was eighty. The articles are notable for their sound research, clarity of thinking and high moral tone.

The de Blank Family, Hindhead 1939.

Standing: John Baden, Joost, Bartha, Sebastien, Jacoba, Bray Banbury, Louise,
Percy Baden, Edith de Blank, Agnes Frances de Blank, Justin de Blank.
Seated: Joost de Blank senior, 'Mama', William de Blank.

All these interests and activities did not make Joost de Blank an absentee father. He was away quite often but when at home was accessible to his children and he particularly enjoyed planning outings and holidays and any route of travel in intricate detail.

And what of the subject of this biography? Bartha de Blank remembered her brother Joost as 'a shy and serious small boy with big, dark eyes and a winning smile. He was also sensitive and had a well developed sense of right and wrong. — He was generally sweet tempered and outshone us all in the personal charm he had inherited from both his parents. There was also, of course, the opposite side of the picture; a self-willed child with a quick temper who screamed if he did not get his own way. But people chiefly remember the solemn and attractive little boy who, even in those days, could wheedle anything out of anyone; this facility of getting what he wanted or what he thought needed doing remained with him until the end of his life.'

Joost's own earliest recollections were later committed to some unpublished autobiographical notes. 'Consciousness awoke I suppose when I was about five years old. I remember walking with my Father over the cliffs at Southbourne near Bournemouth on the day war was declared in 1914. Although my father's English was impeccable there was no doubt that he was a foreigner and I was quite certain in those early days that my Father was a German spy. No one loved this country more than my father and no one saw the advent of the German menace more clearly than he did in the years between the two wars, but as a small boy I was quite confident that he was in the pay of the enemy. It took me a long time to realize that I was quite wrong. — The fact that I was not English (the family were not naturalized until 1921) made me feel in some way not quite as involved as my school friends — as a small boy at school it made a profound difference to my early years.'

The chief influence in the de Blank home at Ealing was mother's. And that meant that the practices and attitudes of the Dutch Reformed Church were paramount. Joost's father had an independent, even detached, view about religious allegiance. If one had to fix a label on his outlook it would be Unitarian. But he did not object to his children being brought up as Presbyterians which was the nearest Mrs. de Blank could get to the Dutch Reformed Church near their home. (Joost had been baptised at the Dutch Church in London). The family attended St. Andrew's Presbyterian Church, Ealing, as Joost recalled. 'I was a very devout little Presbyterian. Just before eleven o'clock the church officer would come in and place the Bible and the Minister's books on the desk in the pulpit which stood in the centre of the north end of the church. At eleven o'clock precisely the curtain at the side of the pulpit was raised and the Minister, the Reverend Herbert Wylie, came through. At that time he was a rather theatrical figure who, I was convinced came immediately from the very presence of God and the gates of heaven to deliver God's Word to us.'

Inspired by this ministerial figure little Joost de Blank played a sermonical game at home. 'I can still remember the thrill of mounting the kitchen table with service book in hand, and with histrionic force and elaborate gesture, preaching sermons that had no intelligible words but imitated the sounds heard from the pulpit Sunday by Sunday.' Bartha remembered the same game played at the seaside where a pulpit, complete with steps, would be built in the sand and where similar noises and gestures would be made by Joost while bemused onlookers formed an interested, puzzled and non-participating congregation.

The overall picture is of a religiously devout home, a happy family with no financial anxieties. Nevertheless, there were the natural anxieties of wartime with food shortages, air raids and a festiveless Christmas one year when Joost de Blank senior was missing for about a month when on a business trip to Holland. The trouble was fog outside the Hook of Holland but he was unable to get news home.

Haberdashers' Aske's Girls School at Acton was attended by the de Blank girls and at the age of five Joost joined them there. In later years if the occasion and company were right he revelled in revealing that he had been to a girls' school. From Haberdashers' he went to Hillsborough Preparatory School and then in 1919 to Merchant Taylors' School which at that time was in Charterhouse Square in the City of London. de Blank travelled by the then Great Western Railway from his home in Ealing to Paddington and on by Metropolitan or Inner Circle to Aldersgate. He wrote a few of his memories for a special issue of the school magazine *(The Taylorian* – June 1961) commemorating the Quarter-Centenary of the School.

'From November to February there was always the chance of a good fog, often a real 'pea-souper' and this meant that one could arrive late with impunity. — A second, closely-associated memory takes me back to high summer. The asphalt jungle of Charterhouse Square was so exhausting in the heat that when the temperature rose above eighty degrees Fahrenheit we were given a half-holiday. This was an unlooked-for relief from our labours and a great treat.

'— We had to work hard. We travelled long distances wearing, as smaller boys, Eton collars and, when older, ordinary starched collars, with satchels on our backs; and when we reached home we were expected to settle down to several hours of study. The train journey was naturally a very useful time for making up arrears but when these arrears were most pressing, the train was always too crowded to be able to extract the necessary books. Frustration has seldom since reached a higher pitch.

'Two outstanding events, I recall, were the opening of the new buildings by the Prince of Wales, and the General Strike in 1926. Some of the monitors volunteered their services in the Strike but no boy, so far as I know, had any awareness of its political and social implications. This was perhaps the weakest part of our education. The nearest we ever reached to current affairs were general talks to Sixth Formers by H. L. Hutton. His name deserves mention for he managed to raise our sights beyond the normal examination curriculum to other things, including architecture, politics, and literature for its own sake.

'Because we came from such a widely scattered area, there were not many voluntary societies. Spasmodic attempts were made to start debating clubs; the Christian Union persevered: the photographers, the model railway enthusiasts and one or two other groups eked out a fitful existence.'

de Blank also referred to the 'unchanging monotony of a time-table over a stretch of thirteen weeks at a time that got us down, not the work itself. And anything that upset the regular routine was therefore welcome.' It is a telling observation, for de Blank needed constant change and variety. His life and ministry can be divided into five year cycles. He needed to move on, and prefer-ably up. Was it that he needed fresh challenges in new settings? Or did he get bored with the familiar scene? We shall see.

de Blank was no longer burbling imaginary sermons from the kitchen table but witnessing for Christ following a conversion at the age of twelve. 'I really "got" religion. I was invited to a school-boys' mission in the Christmas holidays, and as a result I joined a "boys" Bible class. The teaching was forthright and definite. You were either saved or unsaved — the choice was yours. And so I was converted — not just once but every time I was submitted to a "Gospel appeal" lest I had not done it properly the time before.' It was hook, line and sinker Christianity. Later he acknowledged, 'it was an incredibly bigoted, partial and puritanical religion with which we were presented — but as with so many at the time of adolescence it spoke to my needs, and I responded to the best of my understanding and ability.' Nevertheless, 'the reality of Christ was brought to me then and has never left me since.'

But in these candid reflections from a mature age he could see the limitations of his youthful faith. 'Alas, my Bible class experience militated against my church allegiance. Unless the church one attended was 'fundamentalist' in its attitude towards

7

the Bible, unless the challenge to be saved was sounded weekly, unless the substitutionary atonement of Christ on the Cross was proclaimed without compromise — unless all this, one's church was not really a church at all: God had no pleasure in it and it was extremely unlikely that even the Minister was "saved" much less any member of his congregation.'

So young de Blank became bigoted in his religion. Yet converted commitment not bigotry was how it felt to him at the time of his youth. He and those who thought like him were redeemed and saved.Without that inner light of certitude other people dwelt in outer darkness. Churches were full of unbelievers. The only true way was the one he had found. 'Thus my allegiance was weaned away from the Church to the company of the like-minded who set themselves up as a church of their own in everything but name — although there was no ministry and there were no sacraments.' And there was no fear of doubt creeping in through the ventilators. Neither was there drinking, smoking, dancing, theatre or cinema going. It seemed more a death pursuing than a life enhancing commitment to his friends.

It was an uncritical and unwholesome brand of Christianity saying 'No' to death but not as clearly 'Yes' to life. To some extent it was a reaction against the organisational life of the Churches which appeared to be formal, faithless and futile. de Blank's way was the way of Calvin and the strength and the weakness of Calvinism lay in the fact that it was a fighting creed. It raised the infallible Book against the infallible Church: the sure guarantee of an 'effectual calling' against the external pledge of a valid sacrament: the dynamic force of individual conviction against the corporate strength of immemorial orthodoxy. It was clear in its premises, inexorable in its logic, remorseless in its conclusions. There was always a streak of Calvinism in de Blank's character. There were even times, particularly at the end of his life, when he wished for a little of the old certitude.

Calvinism was ever a fighting creed and de Blank frequently referred to the Church and the ministry, ordained and lay, in fighting metaphors. Confrontation was equated with witness and therefore with strength. Battling for Christ was all that mattered.

If this was the complete picture of his character it would be a frightening depiction of an arrogant, unyielding even unpleasant youth. It is only part of the picture. The de Blank children had hot tempers which flared up and then subsided rapidly but which

8

when coupled with a biting and fluent tongue like Joost's, could hurt and wound. Yet after his conversion he became more thoughtful and tried to curb his temper if not his tongue. His boldness in professing his faith did not extend to his personality for he was shy and solemn. Other traits emerged including an impish sense of fun, a quick wit and a gift of repartee. One friend referred to it as a whimsical irreverence.

Gradually de Blank's leadership of Bible study groups became more relaxed even though his fundamental approach to the Bible was unchanged. There was a text to answer all of the world's problems — and Joost's!

At Merchant Taylors', de Blank had the kind of intelligence that approached examinations with confidence. His brain was not of the highest kind, not even first class, but it was an agile one. Although he considered many careers including the normal childhood ones, full time service or evangelism in one of the Churches lurked at the back of his mind. The nearest he got to an alternative was a mining engineer. This was impossible for he was colour blind. Those people who remember his love of colour and good taste in style and fashion were astonished to the point of disbelief when they learned of his colour blindness. 'I am sorry for myself because I am partly colour blind, that is to say I cannot distinguish between reds and greens and confuse blues and pinks and purples. It is an hereditary complaint which descends through the daughters to the sons. My maternal grandfather was colour blind and so am I. Both my brothers suffer from a similar affliction to a greater or lesser extent, but I am, I regret to say, the worst. It does not mean that I do not appreciate good art and it is worth remembering that a great French painter, I forget which, was himself colour blind. Again some of Van Gogh's creations are, or appear to be, designed for appreciation more by the colour blind than by those with normal vision. But it is a definite disadvantage.'

Leaving Merchant Taylors' in 1926 de Blank spent a year studying journalism at King's College, London, before going to Cambridge where he had obtained admission to Queen's College. It was not a strenuous year and it was only later that de Blank realised how much he had gained from learning some techniques and disciplines of journalism. He would have been a first rate journalist.

He went up to Cambridge in 1927. It was a time of unceasing activity. After one month he wrote to one his sisters, 'One gets no time here at all. If one isn't writing letters, one plays games, and

9

if one isn't playing games one eats.' There was much sport. At Merchant Taylors', his size was against him when playing Rugby football. At Cambridge he steered a crew of eight stalwarts day after day up and down the River Cam. There was one memory when they hit an iceberg and ripped the bottom out of the boat, 'to say nothing of the language of the crew which melted the ice for yards around.' Golf was a favourite sport and he became treasurer of a hockey club called the Dodos.

de Blank's natural shyness was covered by a layer of *bonhomie* which, though not false, prevented people from getting close to the real Joost. He wrote to a friend: 'My private opinion of myself when I am among people I do not know or scarcely know is that I am so insignificant and inoffensive that I am not worth speaking to.' This was not mock humility or humbug but plain muddle. Already de Blank was developing a personality of contradictions and paradoxes. They were there in the youth, they became paramount in the man. Consider the contrasts at Cambridge.

There was the deceptively shy student who did not make friend-ships with ease. Some people thought he went about in armour as thick as a tank. To get at the man inside you had to crack that crust. Of course with such people, once inside there may be little there. That was not the case with de Blank but few people penetrated to the pulsating heart of the interior.

Then there was another person developing at great speed. This was a worldly Joost correctly recalled by his sister, Bartha: 'By nature he was extravagant, loved colour and flamboyance in his clothes and in his belongings, and appreciated modern art and modern design. He was fortunate in that while he was at Cambridge his Father's financial prosperity enabled him to indulge an expensive taste in clothes, in cars and other luxuries of life. He wore the baggiest of plus fours and the widest Oxford trousers; he liked brightly coloured pyjamas and neckwear, modern paintings and unusual ornaments. His rooms were comfortably furnished. He was an omnivorous reader and had a mass of books dealing with a wide range of subjects.' His tastes were like his attitudes to food. He liked costly gastronomy, not mass mediocrity. The latest play or film was a 'must' and there were dashes to London to see them. Nothing shy about this extrovert! Yet as with many people with flamboyant characters the outer display concealed a private interior of travail and torment. It may not have been so with de Blank at Cambridge but he developed in this way in the future.

There is the suggestion of a young man spoiled by his father as he had been pampered by his mother as a child. de Blank bought a car in 1926 with a loan from his father's sister and it was the first of a succession of cars. He drove fast, even recklessly. His lifelong lust for speed and travel had taken root. Some of his travel diaries are not only excellent journalism but also a reflection of a man with a zest for movement.

This may suggest the religious fundamentalist had left de Blank. Not so. He faced his fellow Christians in the tone of man who had a unique and infallible assurance of truth, whose witness could only be rejected by those who were blinded by prejudice or enslaved by sin. Writing from Queen's to a friend who had fallen under the spell of Dr. W.E. Orchard he said, 'my position is that of the definite conservative evangelical — the fundamentalist if you like — who doesn't believe that we can collect every form of doctrine to suit all tastes. It seems to me that a man like Dr. Orchard must be a man of no personality — otherwise he could not be a Congregationalist as well as an ordained Romish priest, or he must be a man of tremendous personality which entirely swamps his religion. Are you sure he is helping you from the spiritual point of view — is he telling you to follow a God or to follow a Dr. Orchard? Don't mistake me. I believe these men may do good to some extent but I think this "good to some extent" is a definite evil if it blind's man's eyes to ultimate truth — and what is ultimate truth? That "God was in Christ reconciling the world to Himself" — that somehow on the Cross of Calvary Christ bore away my sins — the evil in my life, "He bore my sins in His own body on the Tree." Do you see what I mean? And then He calls to a life of victory over evil, of victory over the world, the flesh and the devil, a high ideal you say to which no man can attain. No, I know that He gives the power — He Himself comes in the Power of His Holy Spirit to live in the hearts of those who trust Him and His Power can keep them from sin.

'Absolute cant you may say! But yet I believe it to be true and in some measure I have proved it to be true in my own life. But you see it immediately blocks out the other side. This is a definite communion with God which needs no candles, no vestments — a belief which can be held only while the Word of God stands firm and hence every man who is not a fundamentalist is a danger to the Church of Christ.'

This extract presents de Blank's belief in its Cambridge fullness

11

— or shallowness — depending on one's view. No matter, it stayed with de Blank for a long time. Cambridge was a time of fervent activity with the Cambridge Inter-Collegiate Christian Union (CICCU). It was a diet of prayer meetings, Bible study groups, open air and indoor evangelism, accosting the sinners and self-satisfying the righteous. There were meetings to be addressed and Conventions to attend and at one of the Keswick Conventions he offered himself for missionary work.

de Blank may have been strong on fundamentalism but he had no theology. Where was this frenetic activity leading? 'I decided,' he wrote, 'that God wanted me to go into the Ministry — but the Ministry of which Church? As I surveyed the spiritual landscape o'er it seemed to me that the Church of England had advantages that outweighed all its Romanizing tendencies and ritualistic dangers. These advantages were pastoral. No other Christian body in England had the right to work the parochial system — and that parochial system meant that the Minister was not limited to shepherding the members of his particular denomination, but he had a right to confront [note the word] anyone in his parish with the claims of the Gospel. He had a right to go to those who went to no church at all but who still thought of themselves as ''C of E'' It was this desire that my ministry should be an evangelistic one that first led me to the Church of England. I was prepared for Confirmation during my second year [at Cambridge].'

Finally, at Cambridge there was de Blank the undergraduate. He did not need to push himself to get his degree. He absorbed facts quickly and had the ability to regurgitate them with fluency, cogency and power. His year's course in journalism helped. He was not a natural student and the academic life would not have suited him but his natural ability, coupled with developing skills pointed to an interesting future. For a moment that future hovered over the legal profession, and he would have made an outstanding advocate and Queen's Counsel. The law hovered and flew away. de Blank obtained his tripos in English and Law.

Visits to his home were always welcome even if there were a few tensions between him and other members of the family who did not share the proselytising ardour of his religion. It was some time before he learned that earnestness in the right cause is good, but laughter and love are sometimes better. The religion of his home was still flavoured with its Dutchness. There are two Dutch words which describe it: *Deftig* which covers such qualities as decorum, propriety, dignity, respectability; and *Gezellig* which reflects comfort and pleasure. The combination was usually in evidence, even at meal times. George Reindorp, one time Bishop of Guildford and later of Salisbury, remembers the combination of the Bible and Cointreau after lunch.

de Blank made many lasting friendships at Cambridge, with men rather than women. It would be tedious to list them but they represented many spheres and not merely religious ones.

He decided to go to Ridley Hall for his theological training. He entered the college in July 1930 and left in December 1931. He was well remembered by his contemporaries. Let two speak for all. The Rev. Rupert Bliss remembers him as 'likeable, amusing, mischievous, and above all *puckish*. Apart from that — very fundamentalist; prayed most fervently at Christian Union prayer meetings, missionary and others, of which he was a great attender. Regarded it as part of his Christian duty to torment Paul Gibson (the Principal) whenever occasion offered and deliberately and blatantly never took a single note at his lectures. He played scrum-half in the vicious and nearly always victorious inter-theological college rugger matches. The ones against Westcott were particularly profane and bloody. He regarded Anglo-Catholicism as fellow-travelling with the scarlet woman.'

Another contemporary, Rev. S.J. Berry remembers de Blank's sports car as did most people, for there were not many about in those days. Also, 'His attitude to the General Ordination Examination seemed to be that it was irrelevant, a waste of time. I felt that he was capable of a more constructive attitude as he had had the benefit of a wealthy background. At least that is how it seemed to me, a student of average means.'

What de Blank needed most at this time, and did not get, was sound theological training and a massive injection of Anglican teaching. That came later by reading and experience. Yet from such an unsatisfactory base he ultimately became one of the Anglican luminaries of this century.

Now the time for Ordination approached. A friend, Francis Lampen, was going to a curacy in Bath. Why didn't de Blank go with him for there was both need and vacancy for another curate? The decision was made.

How would this introverted extrovert cope with mundane parish life? His knowledge of parochial life was nil. He knew little about the various strata of society. Current affairs existed within

13

the folds of newspapers — not within his own experience. He had little idea how the other ninth-tenths of the population lived. Politics and economics had not captured much of his attention and certainly not his mind. But Bath was not going to get a pale young curate. The contrary is nearer the truth for it was a young man of energy, ideas and ambition who travelled to Bath.

CHAPTER TWO

Flawed Influence

de Blank was made deacon in Wells Cathedral on 20 December 1931 and ordained priest in the same cathedral on 18 December 1932. The late Patrick Cowley was priested when de Blank was made deacon and recalled 'vividly how solemn and withdrawn he [de Blank] was during the Ordination Service and also for the previous few days. It was obvious that something most profound was going on in him and being experienced by him. God and he were in encounter.'

He served as curate of St. Swithin's Church, Walcot, Bath. It was a large eighteenth century church with galleries of no aesthetic appeal. Within the parish of 13,000 people there were two daughter churches, St. Andrew's and St. Thomas'. The patronage of the living was in the hands of the Simeon Trustees, which decided its emphasis in churchmanship — low, if not rock bottom. The great Evangelical leader, Charles Simeon, founded his famous patronage Trust towards the end of the eighteenth century to ensure the Protestant aspect of the Church of England was maintained or developed in parishes. As the years passed the Trust, and others like it, tended to perpetuate a type of church-manship that was obsolescent. They attempted to rivet the limitations of the early nineteenth century on the neck of the ages. There is a case to be made for placing a certain amount of patron-age out of local hands, but the existence of party patronage has tended to be prejudicial to sound discipline and quickly comes into conflict with episcopal government. It can, has, and does occasionally inflict grave hardship on parishes and congregations.

I mention this here in view of de Blank's progressive programme for reform of the patronage system twenty years on. For the moment, at Bath, he was plunged into a fairly typical Evangelical parish. The Bible was at the centre of everything: texts for all

15

occasions. However, de Blank's colleagues were not as rabidly fundamentalist as he was on arrival in Bath. The staff comprised the rector, Francis E. Murphy; three curates (Francis Lampen, R.S.S. Head and de Blank); a lady worker and another full-time worker appointed by the London City Mission. Francis Lampen, who also arrived in 1931, went to the fashionable and well-attended St. Andrew's Church. de Blank was given charge of St. Thomas's, a little mission church in the poorest area of the parish. Perhaps de Blank's flair and ability to communicate with crowds would have told more at the flourishing St. Andrew's, but it was good for him that the hard uphill grind of St. Thomas's was to be his particular patch.

After only one month, he wrote to a relative: 'One of the saddest things about visiting round here is the amount of unemployment — the utter hopelessness of men, and materially one can give them very little comfort.' And the men were not much attracted by the thought of spiritual rewards in the hereafter, despite de Blank's forceful preaching. And he prepared his sermons 'for the man in the street' which was also the sub-title of his book *A Working Faith* (1963). Any young curate is an easy target for the down-and-outs. de Blank gave them each half-a-crown (thirteen pence) for a meal and a bed until he grew wiser when vouchers were given instead. Sometimes vagrants got a surprise when they were handed a shilling Bible. de Blank had bought one hundred of them but the majority were dumped unopened.

From the start, preaching was important. His method of preparing sermons never varied. Each sermon was written out in full and most of them survive. He did this as a form of self-discipline and to prevent deterioration of the literary style. He liked arresting titles or provocative texts. Having written the sermon he memorized it. He told a friend that he used a system of mental diagrams which he was able to retain photographically while speaking, to aid his memory. These were more than mental diagrams for each full text is supplemented by a diagrammatic sermon showing clearly that, unlike so many sermons, there was a beginning, a solid middle and, most important, an end.

de Blank's sermons never fizzled out. They ended with a flourish or a challenge. Only in later years when he was tired or exhausted did the quality of his sermons vary, when sometimes they remained earthbound, failing to 'lift-off' or 'lift-up'.

Reading the Bath sermons now, they compare unfavourably

with his later preaching. There is much fundamentalism, the infallibility of Scripture and an emphasis on 'Repent and be saved'. Yet in that place at that time it was effective. A youthful member of St. Thomas's, now ordained, recalls the preacher. 'In his early days his abrupt and even brusque manner was somewhat off-putting to younger members of the congregation, and to older ordinary folk, but such was his eloquence in the pulpit, that it became an important endeavour each week to find out where he was preaching the following Sunday.

'For most people the attraction of his preaching was that it was without notes. This made a tremendous impression and enabled him to make much of gesture and emphasis. I well remember a forthright sermon at a very formal Matins to a large and stuffy St. Andrew's congregation on the text, "When thou art converted, strengthen thy brethren". He was also in those days a master with the apt story or illustration and never hesitated to kindle emotion in what he said and the way he said it.'

de Blank's own ideal, which was increasingly less achieved in later years, was, 'Next Sunday's sermon must be started on Monday so that you can live with it for the rest of the week'.

The majority of the Bath sermons were preached in St. Thomas's, a church with an ugly three-bay front exterior at the upper end of a suburban terrace. Its exterior was matched by a dull, plain and depressing interior. There was nothing here to lighten or brighten the Gentiles. It was de Blank's task to breathe new life into this shell, and he did. It was hard, uphill work. As any young curate, he was brimful with ideas and the rector gave him complete freedom to implement them. Indeed, it does not appear to have been good as a *training* parish for de Blank was allowed to do what he wanted, unchecked. Perhaps the rector was interested only in results.

The 1932 de Blank was writing: 'The problem of getting hold of young people for the Church and Religion is an acute one. We are in the middle of our Young People's Campaign and we are very pleased that we are touching some 300 young people, but considering very nearly 8,000 handbills have gone out it shows the difficulty. One thing I'm certain of, and that is that to a large extent the way of the Future is by Open Air Meetings in different parts of the town, and we shall be starting those when the weather gets a little warmer.'

de Blank's impact on Walcot was threefold. He was an attractive figure amongst young people. By now he realised that he would have to acquaint himself with the passing fashions of the age in music and culture if he was to understand the young people amongst whom he ministered. He did so with some success. There was the impact of his preaching, to which reference has been made. A church notice board proclaimed the fact that the preacher in a certain parish the following Sunday was to be the Rev. Martin Jones and, so the story goes, someone had stuck the wayside pulpit slogan underneath with the words 'Don't worry — it may never happen'. Such a story could never have been told of de Blank. If anything, there was the danger that people went for the man rather than for the message. The saying attributed to Gandhi can be applied to many a preacher: 'What you are speaks so loud that I cannot hear what you say'. The saying is capable of two very different interpretations. If you went for de Blank the man, you were likely to get more than you bargained for. A popular theme of de Blank's from Bath to Cape Town was that Churchgoing is Dangerous. 'Sometimes as you go about the countryside you come across the Grid system, and you read the warning on the pylon saying DANGER HIGH TENSION CABLE. 22,000 VOLTS. The Church is like that. Don't touch it, don't touch it — it's dangerous. Don't come too near or you too will be linked up with the power and the love of God — and you will never get away.' Such was de Blank's challenge. Although the sermons carried emotional appeals there was also much for the mind. He was on guard that it may never be said of him as was said of a certain course of lectures at a certain university — that they were the sort of lectures where the material passed from the lecturer's notebook to that of the student without going through the mind of either.

So de Blank proclaimed the Gospel at Bath. Not for him the moral cliché of wayside pulpit from which all the genuine life had long ago been extracted, nor the sanctimonious exhortation that emasculated the Gospel, no longer anchoring it to the solid grounds of reality but on the shifting sands of sentimentality. It is interesting to hear him criticising some preaching of that period: 'It was fashionable to hang generally accepted bits of bourgeois morality on to texts convenient for the purpose with little or no enquiry into the theological significance or content of the words of Scripture.'

Finally, there was the very considerable influence of the Oxford

Group Movement, alternatively called Moral Rearmament. de Blank had first been caught up in the Group Movement at Cambridge. The founding leader was Frank Buchman an American Lutheran with Swiss ancestry. Like so many Movements, it began with a personal vision which was communicated to others by forceful enthusiasm and quickly spread throughout many countries. The principles of the Movement were absolute honesty, absolute purity and absolute love. There was a strong emphasis on listening to God for guidance.

The Movement was active at a time when a strange lethargy had befallen the Churches which then seemed bankrupt of faith and power. There was something really impressive about a Movement which plainly succeeded in stopping people in their tracks and giving them a life-changing religion. The Movement's acknowledged purpose was to adapt the message to the habits of the well-to-do, the 'key' men, those who counted for something in the world, whose behaviour therefore was likely to tell. It drew into its orbit the titled, the wealthy, the fashionable, the notorious in any of the known categories of notoriety. It sought them where they were found, in the fashionable hotels, in the seats of the mighty, in the centres of fashion. The Movement propitiated their prejudices by aping their manners. That was not all however, for after making a big impact in the universities it began to spread to the organised churches.

de Blank swallowed the Buchman bait completely. He had not been in Bath long before he introduced the Group and its methods. Blanko, as he was often called, created a few divisions by his advocacy of the Movement's ideals. All over the parish there were little groups meeting but the focus was the Oxford Group Movement, always in danger of becoming a sect, and not the parish. de Blank was impervious to criticism for he was head over heels a Groupist and spoke and wrote in a strain of ecstatic assurance which was perhaps pardonable in an enthusiastic neophyte. He even wrote a little booklet in 1933 *Will God Speak?* (The answer might well have been — If you will let Him and if you really want to hear Him). For Groupists were talkers. And this talking included the constant repetitive 'sharing' of past sins from which they had been redeemed. This practice is dangerous. The penitent may even feel a strange pride in the sins which he publicly proclaims as once his own. Moreover, repetition robs the testimony of spontaneity, and insensibly casts it into a rhetorical

19

form which is more effective and convincing. It is a long way from real repentance and lasting forgiveness.

For de Blank this was different from the testimonies he had given at Merchant Taylors' and Cambridge. This was regular repetition of particular sins. There is something distinctly unwholesome about this form of breast beating. Some people who were sucked into the Movement but who later left it, wondered if there had been an over-emphasis and over-interest in sexual sins — spiritual Peeping Toms with a lust for detail. It was far removed from the healthy and salutary avenue of sacramental confession before a priest, where God forgives and the priest forgets. In the Group Movement it was apparent that the sins shared in confession were not done with. They were 'shared' over and over again in 'witness'. 'Sharing' involved a concentration of the mind on former transgressions which was ever in danger of becoming formalized or exaggerated or dangerously morbid.

The Group drew de Blank away from Bath to Bredon in Worcestershire in August 1934. The rector, Bill Yerburgh, was an influential Groupist, and it was his intention that de Blank would be loosely attached to the parish — his main task being to act as liaison officer for the Group in the West Midlands. de Blank felt guided to undertake this work without payment and to live by faith. Bartha de Blank says this action 'worried my parents and consequently Father gave him an allowance during the two years and more that he was at Bredon. I am always slightly amused by this solution of the problem of Joost's finances but I suppose it is one way in which faith works.' Precisely! Yet it is always easier to go forward in faith in the knowledge that there is something to fall back on.

Joost was an influential organiser. It was a period of house parties, public meetings, sharing, guidance and witnessing (key words in the Movement). Joost delivered his own witness almost daily, for months on end. But did he retain any sensitivity of conscience, any spontaneity of testimony and sincerity of speech, any power of spiritual response?

If one judges this period of his ministry by results, the answer must be 'Yes' even if he himself did not always think so. Even in the small portion of his time given to the parish of Bredon his ministry was manifestly successful. It was good for him too as Bredon was not conservative evangelical but rather in the mainstream of the Church of England at that time. This opened de

Blank's eyes to a different, but equally effective, form of churchmanship.

Beneath the apparent success there were, however, inner conflicts regarding his faith and his future. de Blank was impatient, a man with ideals and ideas and in a hurry to implement them. But how, and when? By 1936 his Oxford Group work was not as satisfying. In one of his occasional private journals he committed the conflicts to paper. The following extracts reveal the aspirations and the agonies. In different ways and in different circumstances similar entries could have been written at many periods of his life. The views changed, but not the character. There was always the feeling of much to be achieved and little time in which to achieve it.

20 April 1936

I am aware that I have been essentially irreligious this last week in the way of Christian exercises as prescribed by authority, and yet I have been more Christian within myself than ever before. All my own humbugs I have stripped from me. The blether of so much that I have said and thought and prayed! Now I know, and the knowledge no longer depends on my own evanescent feelings, but on something deep within me, untouchable and alone. There — deep down in the abyss I know God. He is bigger, so much bigger than any experience of Him — so much more real in *spite* of experience than because of it. But I have still so little knowledge of God. I have still got to be buried and rise again in Him. I am not really ready for the Cross until I like the dark, and still there is fear of the dark ... fear of the intangible, fear of the unknown.

22 April

'At my back I always hear, Time's winged chariot hurrying near'. That is the atmosphere I'm breathing. 'So much to do, so little done.'

23 April

... now the time has come to focus: What is God's Will for me?

5 May

I am getting my views on money clear. Stanley Jones helped me tremendously in *Christ and Communism*. Roughly speaking it boils down to this: (a) we use the minimum necessary for the most effective way of spreading the Kingdom. (b) What is over we use through others for the same purpose ... We need to look at our

21

money in terms of the under-privileged. But this attitude definitely fights against saving for human security ... As I see it at this moment, it means using everything I have for the common good, e.g. if I get a rectory not to let it out but to use it for and with anybody who will use it with me. I am looking forward to that; may it come soon.

9 May

Are we working out our stewardship in the light of the conditions of the under-privileged? How much do we rationalise about getting hold of our crowd — as we hang on to our comfort? People we change must be challenged to see what might be involved in money, property, possessions, etc. I have to beware of thinking of smoking and drinking as self-indulgence — but not a five-course meal.
    ... Can Christianity flourish in a competitive system?
    Are we merely making the present system more bearable?
    ... Certain things have emerged pretty clearly. These are: I am more than ever certain that the Oxford Group principles are right — based on the New Testament and for everybody — but I am not so happy about the ways the Group is manifesting its activity ... We cannot as Christians coerce a man either by physical force, or by *the power of emotional propaganda*. The challenge of Christianity is always to the mind to think and the will to take action. Emotionalism (jelly-bellied flag-flapping) — unintelligent propaganda are not worthy instruments to bring in the Kingdom of God because they are transitory and not permanent. Any pageantry there is must be supra-national. (Doesn't national flag-flapping ask to be misunderstood in these days of nationalism?) It must be a challenge to vital Christianity, pure and undefiled — above party, class or creed.

16 May

I am like a car engine which is running with the clutch out and which never quite gets started. I admire other people. I am struck by the quality of their work — and I wish I were like them — and somehow I don't become any different. My dreams, my hopes, my visions for my life never get beyond that into real action — and now I am 27 and the years rush by, and if I don't hurry I shall do nothing worth while. Somehow I need to develop the *power of application*. Maybe that's the real thing I've got to learn in a parish, but why wait for that? It can begin here and now. I know for me it means two things: (i) Putting God's will first in what I do. There are so many sentimental desires to see my people and my friends that I am often in the grip of the next thing and not really applying myself to the job in hand. (ii) Learning to work hard. I need to be willing to be really tired — dead tired — going on till the job is done.

8 June

How pagan am I? How much do I honestly believe just now? I believe I am still Christian. I am certainly terrified of what my friends would say (especially my pre-Group friends) if I were not. And the Oxford Group, what about that? Actually I think I believe in all the principles of the Group but am not very keen on its present manifestations. Rather a tricky position and probably due to me . . . I must record for my own sake that . . . seven Bishops have lately come down against pacifism. So often I feel like resigning my Orders!!

9 June

I am completely up a gum tree and have no idea what to do next. I realize this evening more than ever the need for guidance. Doesn't that alone make it worth while being a Christian? Of course it does. I should like the knowledge of a definite job in September and a rest till then.

10 June

I am still uncertain what to do. I suppose I should like to know much more about the future:
(a) Am I willing to work in a parish?
(b) Am I willing to work in a team?
(c) What is my attitude to the organized Church? Could I honestly work in a parish?
(d) How — if I am not absolutely guided — am I going to earn my money?
(e) How far does being identified with the will of God mean being identified with a church, a group, or what?
(f) What sort of message have I to proclaim?
(g) Doesn't it mean a whole new attitude to sin — what is sin? — and far greater liberty in God's service?
If only I knew a definite job ahead. Surely I do know that — even if it isn't the paid, respectable job I'm looking for. Somewhere I need that drive within me to creative work — whatever that creative work may be.

16 June

'Whosoever will save his life shall lose it.' It is only as I lose myself in the lives of others that I shall really find myself. 'To give and not to count the cost.' As I look at my life these last weeks it covers me with shame to see how selfishly I have been thinking. Now to live for others — to burn out for God. Of T. E. Lawrence it was said that 'he refined his life to a flame'. May my life be a flame for God. May

23

I always, always, always be relaxing in the hands of God so that He through me may work the good purpose of His will.

19 June, in Holland

To-day I began to feel homesick for house parties, office work and what not — but I am more than ever convinced that for me to draw out of the apparent main stream of Group activity is the best thing that could possibly happen. I need time to think. I need to give God time to develop my personality. I find I have been little more than a chameleon. The seventh commandment or principle in Italian schools is: 'Mussolini is never wrong'. My guiding principle has been: 'The Group is always right' and because I wanted so much, so very much, to be accepted by Group leaders, I have always obediently toed the line. But these next weeks I am not going to care a hang what any Group official thinks, only what God thinks, so that I may be able to say with Martin Luther: 'Here I stand, I can do no other'.

I am already feeling something of that new release. A book is beginning to take form within me on *Christ's Ideal Church*. I have always wanted to write — I have always wanted to use my preaching, and both those gifts, if I dare call them gifts, have been atrophied through my unintelligent acceptance of a Group dictatorship. The fault has not been the Group's. It has been entirely mine, my chameleon-like character and my desperate inferiority. Thank God I believe that that inferiority too is beginning to clear up ... Now I realize God has a plan for my life as an individual and not as one of a team, now I am willing to think for myself — I am beginning to be ready to face the world.

19 June, Evening — firework display

... and the noise was the noise of the guns in the next war. I was afraid. But the evening was an allegory. There just behind the visible — beyond the touch of the tangible — just inaudible — stands God, but to-day He showed the hem of his garment in the wonder of the evening sky, but as always the crowd preferred the tinsel offerings of the world.

> 'They hurl their pretty worthless fireworks
>   bright against the sky
> In whose unspeakable and unnoticed beauty —
>   draped AM I.'

21 June

My religion is completely in the melting pot just now ... What do I believe? Do I believe that world-changing through life-changing is the only hope? I don't know the answer myself except that I consider so many 'changed' people unchanged, and also that so many fall by the wayside. I am still desperately keen on world-changing, enlightened internationalism, the freedom of the individual, the outlawing of war, the banishment of hate and fear and poverty. Is the Group doing that? and even if it is, is it doing it the quickest way?

... Couldn't I get into Parliament and put these matters across? Is the Church the right vehicle for this? Does Christianity mean anything when people don't stick and when I have no ultimate answer to inferiority? Isn't guidance ninety-nine times out of a hundred ordinary thinking in which God need not in any detail have taken a hand? I have proved before and am unfortunately proving again that I don't miss quiet times when I don't have them. I am finding that my enthusiasm to change people is waning as so few seem to last; I don't know where I am, and I don't know what to do.

And yet I believe in Christianity. I see the four absolutes radically applied as the only hope for the world. I believe I demand more of a programme and a lot less loose talk about guidance in matters that rarely affect social life. That is why I still believe in the book I want to write — *Christ's Plan for the Church*. I may find my own answer to my future there. Certainly just now I have not the least idea.

I wish I were a barrister or something so that I could do a secular job. It's being tied up with the Church ... But what else can I do? O God — so badly I want to change the world — How can I do it? There I need and must have guidance. And how much is personal ambition mixed up with it all? ... I must answer the question: What part have I for the world? That seems to me to be the question I must give time to these next weeks — and my ambition flies so high. I want to be able to wield the forces of goodwill, which seem to live so undirected.

29 June

It has been a weekend of mental turmoil. What I need to realize is that, for me, mental turmoil is sin — sin chiefly because of its selfishness. My mental turmoil which may result in depression or anxiety affects those with whom I live, and that being so it is a form of self-indulgence which has no part or lot in the Kingdom of God. And yet somehow I feel that the turmoil has not been altogether wasted. This morning I woke up close to God. It was as if the fogs and tempests of the last weeks had cleared; I could see clearly; I could go straight. Yes — I know, Devil, that I have had spiritual catharsis before and after a few days you have laughed at me — but this is not so much a difference in degree as a difference in kind. It is as if I have flicked my fingers at the world. Nothing matters but what God tells me, and if God tells me nothing — why that doesn't matter either! 'God's in His heaven — all's right with me.' What a selfish misquotation, but absolutely right and unselfish in this instance. It is as I recapture that certainty of being permanently yoked to God that I shall be enabled to lose myself in the lives of others.

5 July

It's curious that I came up to Edinburgh rather wondering how much I really believed in God and was going to spend time working that out here. But actually God seems to have a fast hold on me here. He is more real than I have known Him for a long, long time. Nevertheless, I want the assurance in my own mind that my faith is genuine and not just auto-suggestion. I still undoubtedly long for special revelations — but at the same time even though these do not come, I find myself wanting to pray and trusting for guidance.

. . . I do want that assurance and knowledge of what God wants me to do. I thought in my quiet time this morning that I spend all my time crying for the moon. Rest in the Lord; rest in the Lord. Wait patiently — wait patiently — wait patiently for Him and He will give you your heart's desire. Help me to learn to wait.

These extracts cover a rainbow of de Blank's pre-occupations. He could not abandon the Group's conception of 'guidance' even if it was the root cause of his temporary spiritual paralysis. He wanted a 'sign'! Something precise, concrete, calculable. It was as if a sign would exclude or override conscience and reason. de Blank had been sure that God was an accomplice of his wishes and interior experiences. Now he was not so sure. He felt periodically empty and lost, but still he looked for a sign. 'The difficulty is not to find something to do — but to find the *best* thing to do. The world is so needy. Where can one help most?'

de Blank's experience with the Oxford Group Movement did not liberate him as its leaders claimed it would for people. It was a flawed influence. Plato was right — people who are good at setting people free are also good at enslaving them.

Some of the agonies of the summer of 1936 recurred in different guises during de Blank's life. For the moment it is best to let the extracts stand without further exploration or explanation.

During the Autumn of that year he was approached by the Vicar of West Ham in the Diocese of Chelmsford who enquired if he would accept a parish of which he was Patron. The parish was Emmanuel, Forest Gate, in London's East End. The Oxford Group was looking after its own, for the patron was a prominent Groupist. To de Blank, this was the sign.

CHAPTER THREE

Dynamism

de Blank commenced his ministry at Emmanuel, Forest Gate, in January 1937. Aged twenty-eight he was perhaps the youngest incumbent in the London area. Before accepting the living — and before the living accepted him — he had appeared before the Parochial Church Council. Some older eyebrows were raised when faced with this very young man. He seemed full of confidence, energy and ideas — but oh, so young! Perhaps a mature incumbent would be better suited for the parish. Fortunately another view prevailed and de Blank was warmly welcomed. At a party to follow his Institution a rhyme was quoted:

> 'If you do not like your vicar
> Never advertise your view:
> Pray the Lord to make him
> quicker
> And perhaps to quicken you.'

The penultimate line could not have been more inappropriate, for within weeks the parish found it difficult to keep pace with the innovative energy exuded by its new vicar. And de Blank had to be recognised for the man he was as a clerical collar was not much in evidence. 'It sets up a false mark of difference between the clergy and the laity. You would be surprised to discover how few people can be natural with a clergyman. They seem to think that Ordination has turned a very ordinary sinner in a moment of time into a very extraordinary saint, and that the clerical collar is actually a halo which has slipped out of position a bit.'

In his first sermon at Emmanuel on 24 January 1937 de Blank challenged the pew few to cease being respectable: 'We have compromised with the world so far that we are no longer distinguishable from it'. He saw the Church (not just Emmanuel) as weak, failing, losing grip, ignored, forgotten. He intended

27

transforming it into a Church full of power, of life, of vigour, growing in quality and influence.

Challenge was the keynote to his ministry. Emmanuel was a parish of 12,000 people: a predominantly middle class area with a large Jewish and Roman Catholic population. There was little opposition to the Church of England. For some people there was even a feeling that an occasional dose of piety was good for them. Of course that had nothing to do with the growth of God's Kingdom. It belonged to those whose religious belief was essentially something between a bet and a prayer. At life's great moments — birth, marriage and death — they welcomed the Church's ministrations, provided that it soothed and did not disturb their religious equilibrium. It was sympathetic magic they invoked.

Into this setting de Blank dived with vigour. Here was a man with a plan of campaign. In one respect he treated Emmanuel as a run-down family business. It was founded in 1852. Its fortunes had varied but by 1937 it was ready for new management. As an ecclesiastical managing director, de Blank showed that he combined a capacity for producing new ideas in rapid and endless succession with the organisational ability to bring them to birth and reality. 'He was inspiring' was the comment of one parishioner. He had been stung by H. R. L. Sheppard's angry book *The Impatience of a Parson* a decade earlier and now, having a patch of his own, he was determined to act. 'There are times today when a man has to decide between the shackles of ecclesiasticism and the freedom of the Spirit,' he said in an early sermon. Little has changed. The Church often hides Christ. People who hunt for the pearl of great price are offered a paste necklace.

Within two months de Blank had scrapped the existing parish magazine and started a new one called *Review*. It had a professional touch about it which was to be the hallmark of all that de Blank edited, guided or sponsored. Only the highest standards sufficed. As with most of his stylish endeavours de Blank had the advice and help of friends. He always seemed to know an 'expert'. In the case of the *Review* it was Norman Sutton whom he had known in Cambridge and who died tragically young in 1939. He had worked on the staff of *The Times*, *The Daily Mail* and *The Daily Sketch*. He gave enormous practical help as de Blank recalled: 'He set up dummies of the kind of magazine we wanted, interviewed printers with me, went into advertisement details and thought out the right kind of type to use'. If it looked good, the contents did not let the appearance down. Not everyone realised that to achieve his required quality of excellence de Blank dipped deep into his pocket, or rather into the pockets of relations and friends from whom he borrowed money. In this sense he was often in debt. In short, there was a real cost for implementing his ideas and realising his ideals. As we shall see, this was not a trait which vanished with the years.

The *Review* was a platform for de Blank. At last his pen could be put to use, and what he wrote was read and frequently quoted in the press. He started by writing a series of articles on *The Mighty Army* in which he compared the Church's advance with the laborious crawlings of a tortoise.

'When this has been done, and when that has been corrected, then we shall act — is our all too frequent attitude. The brightness of our buttons is not the primary essential when there is a battle to be fought. Zero hour is not the time for adjusting our puttees.

'I can already hear the murmurings of my seniors:- 'How can one of the junior clergy realise all the problems and difficulties we are up against?' 'He has not yet developed the saving grace of tact.' 'He has no idea of the issues involved.'. It may be that this is precisely why I have felt called to write this series.Older, wiser and better men have often started with the same crusading zeal, but 'the lust of other things entering in' — those clerical committees, the parochial routine, the 'dead hand clutching at the heart-strings' — has choked the word before ever they could utter it'.

How he detested administrative obstacles and pastoral inertia. Dynamic action was needed if results were to be forthcoming. Instead, he found complacent contentment. It was like the man fishing in the local river who, when asked if he had caught anything, replied: 'No, but I think I created a climate of interest among the fish.' But that was in the wider Church. In his own parish he was his own master.

It would be tedious to chronicle the quickening of parochial life at Emmanuel. Although his popular book *The Parish in Action* was primarily based on his later ministry at Greenhill, Harrow, he acknowledged in that book that many of the experiments 'were first tested, often in an undeveloped form, in Forest Gate, and nobody seemed to mind.' Indeed, they did not, for congregations grew rapidly. This was as a result of de Blank's infectious vitality.

As one former parishioner recalls: 'He was enthusiastic in working for the Christian Faith, and his magnetic personality encouraged many of his congregation to follow his example'.

Although details of parochial life are omitted, a few innovative landmarks are worthy of note.

de Blank wanted Emmanuel to become *The Church of the Good Companions* and this is how it was known when he left. His *ideal* was 'to create a fellowship of people who have learnt the secret of living together and who, as a result of their spiritual unity, are effective in bringing peace and goodwill to our neighbourhood'. And the *idea* was, 'Every worshipper a worker'. There was a piece of work which was waiting to be done by every person who regularly or occasionally entered Emmanuel. Some of it would lead to the limelight, more of it would be behind the scenes. 'The societies of the world are always fencing themselves around with rules and regulations so that the publicans and sinners shall be excluded. Moreover, in the world at large there is still unemployment and masses of unwanted material. In the Church of the Good Companions there is no exclusion and there is work for all. No exclusion — we are a fellowship of sinners, not of saints, and the only difference between the publicly condemned and ourselves is that they have been found out'.

Within a short time more than one hundred people felt themselves motivated to represent, or rather be, The Church of the Good Companions in every part of the parish. It was a kind of voluntary coercion. Then two members took responsibility for a road, not only or merely as parsonical *oculi* but also as living organs of the Body of Christ in that place. In 1938 this was radical. They were not simply fetchers and carriers of messages to and from the vicar — but Good Companions who wanted to increase the effectiveness of the work of the Church.

One innovation which attracted a good deal of publicity was the formation of *The Spiritual Clinic*. The idea was a uniting of three strands in de Blank's experience. First there was the sharing and healing experiences he had witnessed with the Oxford Group Movement, of which he was still a member, though not so active. Secondly, he had developed an interest in Jungian psychology. Thirdly, he was struck by the phrase 'the cure of souls' used at the Institution of any new vicar which emphasised the most important part of a priest's work. If souls were not being cured through his ministry, his work was a failure. Every priest ought to be a general

practitioner in the things of the spirit rather than a general
factotum in the things of the world. As a beginning, de Blank was
available at the vicarage for a 'spiritual surgery' one evening a
week for consultations. There were also cards in the church for
people who wanted to make appointments at other times. And
people came with their personal problems, secret fears, inner
defeats, seeking and feeling a need for adjustment. Again the
fighting metaphor: 'The Spiritual Clinic exists for all who feel they
need personal help in the battle of life'.

de Blank was desperately serious about the clinic. He was not
providing shoulders to cry on but real assistance to people. He
wrote: 'Those who link themselves up with the Clinic will be
followed up and helped to the limit of our ability. The value of
such experience as we have had as well as training in pastoral
work and psychological skill will be at their disposal, and more
than that — a link has been forged between ourselves at
Emmanuel and experts in the field of medicine and psychology
who are willing to help us in this work. Ideally, a parish should be
manned by a priest, a doctor and a psychotherapist.' He
emphasised that no one would be passed on to the West End
experts without consultation with his or her local doctor. de Blank
had frequent visitors from other parts of England and from Europe
to enquire about the Clinic. For parishioners of Emmanuel many a
bruised and troubled soul sought advice and received sound
counsel in their confusion and moral mess.

de Blank's greatest initiative, and one which attracted national
attention, arose out of his deep sense of patriotism (not territorial
patriotism) and the conviction that the gathering world crisis of
the late nineteen-thirties needed a drastic remedy. His view was
that democracy had grown weak because it had failed to capture
people's imagination: and his answer? 'We need to form a
Christian Front across the world — an international Army of
Goodwill'. In April 1938 he declared: 'The first essential in the
formation of the *Christian Front* is that the Churches get together.
The second essential, that the imagination of the world be
captured by this movement. A simple means to that end is some
recognisable symbol which all members of the *Christian Front* will
wear. [He favoured the wearing of an armlet.] It does not matter if
we are stealing ideas from Fascism or Communism'.

The *Christian Front* was based on basic Christian principles, and
this is how de Blank defined them:

31

1. The universal brotherhood of man, of all colours, races, classes and creeds.
2. The most valuable possession a man has is his own soul. Any attempt to bludgeon a man's soul is contrary to the teaching of Christ.
3. True patriotism is to the kingdom of God, and this world-wide conception of Christ's kingdom is the highest form of collective security.
4. A determination to make individuals, homes, industries, countries and the world to approximate to the picture of the Kingdom of God laid down by Christ.

Within a few months, de Blank had worked out a basis for membership. There were three classes of membership: The Fighting List (for those who were prepared to make the *Christian Front* the first call on their time outside working hours); The Active List (a firm commitment but unable to give more than one or two sessions a week); and Reservists (those who supported the *Christian Front* but who were unable to undertake definite commitments). Its work would be done by meetings , personal work, literature and propaganda. There were training sessions covering the fundamentals of Christianity, their personal and social applications and the practical expression of one's faith.

Naturally, a movement aimed to mobilise Christians of this and other countries was bound to catch the attention of the press. After all, de Blank wanted the *Christian Front* to influence public opinion and members of parliament. Conscience not whip should be the decisive factor in parliamentary voting. Although de Blank was not advocating a new party, he did not rule out the possibility of a Christian Democratic Party.

A member of the *Christian Front* recalls studying articles and news in the national press and writing his own views on current affairs. These were gathered together by de Blank, edited and produced in a news sheet called *Dynamite*. Interest was growing all the time and in different parts of the country. If war had not intervened it is interesting to speculate what would have happened to this initiative. There seems little doubt that de Blank saw himself operating on a larger stage and a grander scale than as a parish priest. He was making new contacts and renewing others with people of talent. He knew how to use natural gifts for the glory of God and, a cynic remarked, 'it didn't do Joost any harm either'. For the moment I will leave the observation unchallenged, but I shall return to it.

What of the worship at Emmanuel? de Blank did not radically alter the pattern of existing services but enhanced their dignity and increased their popularity. The first was achieved by de Blank's meticulous care for detail and reverence; the second by encouraging congregational participation wherever possible and by his powerful preaching. Two innovations reflected two aspects of his thinking. Emmanuel stood at the corner of Romford Road and Upton Lane, which was also the main road to Epping Forest and the east coast. de Blank saw its commanding site as an evangelistic opportunity. Once a month in summer he held an Epilogue on a Sunday evening and this became a traffic stopper. He also arranged for discussions to take place after sermons each month. The other innovation was less evangelistic than meditational. The Evening Watch was kept weekly from ten o'clock until eleven-fifteen at night. The church was in darkness except for the flickering candles on the altar. It provided an opportunity for stillness.

From the outset of his ministry at Emmanuel, de Blank made it clear that the vicarage should be open house. His housekeeper may not have approved of the constant stream of people using the vicarage, but it was the way de Blank wanted things. Young people were always in the vicarage. Again, this illustrates an important aspect of de Blank's character — the need to be surrounded by people even if and when he was emotionally remote from them. After one year on his own he acquired a curate, A. T. Burden, who was familiar with the area as his father had been vicar of a parish in Forest Gate. Burden was de Blank's first curate. He writes: 'I was only at Emmanuel a year before going on to Dagenham where I was much happier and not the only curate! Much as I valued my experience at Emmanuel — and thank God for it — at times I felt I might break down under the strain. Joost was a strict disciplinarian and everything was timed to the minute. The cup of tea was brought up to him at exactly 7 am — breakfast was at 8 am. The old English sheep dog was taken for a walk around the block (there was also a Dachshund called Adolph!). Work in the study began at 9 am — and so it went on through the day. I made the mistake of living in the vicarage where I felt he watched my every movement.

'He was very keen on psychology and though I never saw this happen he said he could, under hypnosis, put a patient to sleep and reach his unconscious mind in order to counsel.

'He was a brilliant preacher and his sermons always began with some topical reference. For example at the Munich crisis I well remember him beginning, "Mussolini is never wrong".'

Many individuals were helped and inspired by de Blank. Occasionally the financial cost was exacting. Bartha de Blank recalled one incident involving a member of Emmanuel who was in serious trouble. 'Joost with his compassion for others wanted to help but a considerable sum of money was needed to put this man back on his feet. There was only one thing to do — sell his car — which he did, and the proceeds were used to try and rehabilitate the offender'. Unfortunately the sequel was that the man returned to his former ways.

Parish priests cast in de Blank's mould seek and need outward success in order to sustain and renew them. Although inner tensions and conflicts remained, the sole charge of a parish had given de Blank great confidence. de Blank's mind was always on the move and he considered this lust for activity and movement to be what Christ required for a successful Church. In 1937 we find him writing: 'As I read and reread the Gospel story I am always struck by the intense activity of Jesus and His disciples. They were busy all the time, but not busy in an academic way or in administrative work or running from one committee to another. They were busy all the time meeting people and supplying the answer to their deepest needs. Jesus and His disciples constituted a travelling clinic, and the evidence of satisfied and cured patients brought them more custom than they had time to deal with.'

Again de Blank proclaimed: 'Anything less than a victorious message which defeats the pagan world cannot be called success' and 'no church is successful unless it supplies the needs of the world.' The 'success' is overplayed, even dangerously applied. For there is a sense in which people are only fit to join the Church when they know that it is now, always has been and always will be, a failure. To realize this is to prepare ourselves to confront a part of the suffering to which we, as Christians, are called in this world, and converts must also be prepared to face it; for evangelism should not be an invitation to become one of a spiritual elite for one's own spiritual satisfaction, but a call to surrender oneself into a company of sinners. It would be a healthy symptom if the Church would admit its failure and learn to live with it, instead of running after so-called success which is the way of the world. The Church should be a living protest against such a way. de Blank's view and the contrary one each carry subtle temptations and distortions for Christians. At Emmanuel the former obliterated the latter view. And success carried its dangers for it is the food of pride, and pride is the assurance of superiority. There were still many traces of the Oxford Group in his theological stance. But ecclesiastically he had broadened. The function of the Church of England was not only as an instrument of evangelism but also to be the ark of the faithful and the servant of society.

de Blank continued to have exciting plans for the future but they had to be abandoned at the outbreak of war in 1939. He lost no time in volunteering for service as an army chaplain and eventually left Forest Gate in July 1940. He had arrived at Emmanuel a pacifist. Hitler's abominations in Austria and elsewhere reversed that conviction. So far as the *Christian Front* was concerned he wrote in April 1938:

> There remains the vexed problem of war. Whether in any circumstances the *Christian Front* would take up arms would have to be left to the individual's conscience, but certain principles can be seen:—
>
> 1. In no circumstances would a member fight to assist in a war of aggression. Many might feel it right never to fight.
> 2. If ever a member felt it right to fight it would be to defend the principles of the kingdom of God and for no other reason. With his new patriotism therefore he should be willing to fight for these principles *anywhere*, and not only for the sake of his own territorial fatherland, and the international police force of many an idealist's dream would become a reality.
> 3. Such decision to fight could only be envisaged as the lesser of two evils. All members of the Christian Front would recognise the horror of war and try by all means of conciliation consonant with Christianity to maintain and secure peace.'

His ministry at the Church of the Good Companions came to a close after only three and a half years. In that time the parish had seemed to change at break neck pace under a disciplined hand. *Dynamism* is the appropriate word.

CHAPTER FOUR

Courage and a Scar

de Blank was granted an Emergency Commission as Chaplain to the Forces 4th Class with effect from 1 July 1940. Three weeks later he was posted to Western Command for duty with HQ 33 Anti Aircraft Brigade in Cheshire. A fellow chaplain, the Revd. 'Peter' Priest, who was to become de Blank's chaplain in Cape Town, was also in Cheshire. His view after their first meeting was that de Blank was, 'very stand-offish, more than that, rather distant, slightly arrogant.' However, they soon became friends and 'Peter' Priest puts the initial impression down to de Blank's shyness.

Like any chaplain, de Blank wanted to be where the war was being waged. In March 1941 he was attached to 73 Medium Regiment RA, posted to Northern Command in June and embarked for the Middle East a little later. The convoy of troop ships spent a week in Durban which was a welcome respite from ship life. There were three thousand men on board quartered in very cramped conditions. de Blank was made head of all the sports and entertainments on board. He presided over the control committee and formed four sub-committees — one to deal with concerts, another with bands, another with deck games and sports and another with debating and discussions. Again he proved his powerful ability of organisation. He knew how to achieve specific goals in the quickest possible time.

This position enabled him to establish a quick rapport with the men. His wit, sense of fun and earthy humour were evident and appreciated. Yet there was never any doubt of his firm faith. de Blank himself was uneasy with 'this beastly war' which he hated. He detested the C.O. and was not happy with some of the officers and his own assistant deputy chaplain-general who appeared to glory in the war, like soldiers who had been starved of combat and killing for years. Although by rank he was an officer, he found

*First steps in South Africa, with Royal Army Chaplain's Department.
Durban, September 1941.*

himself taking the soldiers' side against officers on many issues. In
times of war it can be the little irritations which, if left unchecked,

lead to great frustration. One of many incidents is recorded in a diary note:

23 August 1941

Also I ought to record a battle with a certain objectionable major which I won. One day after lunch I was on deck with one of our subalterns and found that although most of the chairs were empty, all of them had hats and books on them to keep them. I removed these from two and sat down with the other fellow. Soon after the Major returned very angry and turned the subaltern out. I told him this attitude was fantastic, brought the matter up before the authorities and a notice was issued forbidding the reservation of chairs. It was all quite funny and I'm pleased I won.

A number of men were prepared for Confirmation, and when the ship docked at Durban a Service took place in St. Paul's Church. The confirming bishop was Gerald Vernon, Bishop of Madagascar, who was prevented from returning to his diocese during the war. There was a tea party in the church hall and de Blank asked a group of sailors how they had enjoyed the Service. 'They told me that they had appreciated it greatly, but the effect was rather spoilt when one of them went on to ask: "But who was the old beggar with the boat hook?" I like to think he said "beggar!"'

Eventually the convoy arrived in Egypt. Here there was a mixture of high life and sightseeing before the bombs arrived. An old Cambridge friend, Geoffrey Warner, now a chaplain, was in the area and so was 'Peter' Priest who had a flat in Heliopolis. There was good food at various clubs and, if not up to French cooking standards, it was very palatable. He saw the pyramids and the sphinx 'which to my surprise completely satisfied me. They were far less spoilt by anticipation than I expected'. He visited the Roman Cathedral in Ismailia 'for a service which was very enjoyable and beautiful' — a comment which would have been unthinkable in his earlier years. Then all that was Roman was evil. By now he had enlarged his view of Anglicanism. And 'Peter' Priest was the first real Anglo-Catholic he had met and liked — not that he had previously put himself in the position of meeting many.

To date there had been no danger. The nearest he got to an injury was one evening when he came out of a cinema, did not look which way a tram was moving, bounced off it and bruised his right buttock. His lovely hat was run over and irreparably damaged.

In November 1941 the troops passed through the wire into Libya. For de Blank war had begun. One of his first sights was a sergeant lying dead by his tank. 'How hateful war is,' he wrote in his diary. Before the war ended he had buried hundreds of men. The sickening horror of war always appalled him. Strangely, one thing he was 'rather squeamish' about was searching for identity discs on dead bodies.

There was one incident when Rommel was retreating. de Blank and the doctor had been to look for one of the batteries that had been mauled. They did not find it, but on the return journey they found a bridge had been blown up by the Germans. de Blank decided to cross the river bed when the car got stuck in the mud. They could not free it but although it was dark de Blank would not abandon the car to the marauding Germans. 'We will defend it', he announced. 'What with?' the doctor asked. 'With this', was the reply, and de Blank pulled out of the back of his car his batman's Lee Enfield rifle. 'But', said the doctor in amazement, 'chaplains are not permitted to use arms'. 'No,' said de Blank,'but M.Os are when it is to defend their wounded'. 'Wounded?' queried the doctor. 'Yes,' was the reply: 'My pride is hurt by being such a B.F. as to get stuck in the bloody river bed.' So the doctor watched all night with a loaded rifle in his hand while de Blank slept calmly beside him until, after summoning aid the next day, they and the car were rescued.

Contrasting pictures of de Blank in the desert reveal two characteristics. One is of the chaplain amongst the men, at once a morale booster, grief sharer and priest. The other is of the stylish chaplain travelling around in the largest camouflaged black and yellow staff car. He loved it. These pictures will remain, though the backcloth is to be dramatically different.

In the retreat from El Alamein, de Blank was in charge of the stores vehicles of the regiment. It was a perilous journey but he was a very skilled navigator and missed the fall of Tobruk by four hours. He knew there was one unmined way through the wire defences and he took the upwards of thirty trucks along the coast road for three days towards El Alamein.

de Blank expected and wanted promotion. In August 1942 he was transferred to the headquarters of the Ninth Army in Syria, near Beirut. He was a staff chaplain but it was not promotion. Another chaplain, K. C. Oliver, (later Warden of the Royal Army Chaplains' Training Centre and Department, Bagshot) met him there. He was travelling up from the desert to man the Syrian-Turkish frontier, reporting to Army Headquarters on the way. There was often tension between Headquarters' chaplains and those of the fighting divisions. Oliver was welcomed by de Blank. 'He [de Blank] showed a complete grasp of all the practical problems that a chaplain's work involved. This, combined with an air of serenity, a charm of manner and a delicate sense of humour, completely won us over and made us realise that here was a friend to be cherished.

'Joost's relationship with his chief, the assistant Chaplain-General, was a typical example of both his competence and his humility. His chief was an old-fashioned regular chaplain, kindly and good-hearted, but with very limited ability and a stickler for regulations. Joost managed him beautifully. He took complete charge of the whole situation and unobtrusively made all the decisions and ran the office with the greatest competence and charm and yet enabled his chief to gain all the credit for its successes and feel that he was in command.'

One soldier who kept in touch with de Blank until the end of his life writes cogently of de Blank's gifts: 'The situation was not one of a bleak training camp, a battlefield, or a casualty unit. It was in a remote Eldorado called IXth Army HQ in the hills just outside Beirut. Here the sheer exuberance of the landscape, and the comfort of the billets made wartime England seem strangely remote and unreal. So too the staff worked in civilised comfort and at a leisurely pace.

'In these conditions a group of the lower ranks, of which I was one, had established a variety of activities, bridge playing, satirical theatre, safari expeditions and so on. Joost quickly established his particular ability for being an entrepreneur of talent. He quickly united a body of individuals into a coherent group all filled with a corporate enthusiasm. There was no question of rank, race, religion, political interest or prestige. The only criteria was one of a person's ability to add stimulus. This motley body formed a club called 'the Rogue Elephants'.

'Looking back at this epoch I am sure it was this brilliant 'awareness' of individual character that was the inner talent Joost possessed.'

All this activity was not sufficient to satisfy de Blank's fertile mind. His plans for *The Christian Front* had been snuffed out by the onset of war. Something else was needed *now*. What part should the Church play in social, national and international affairs? A new vision was needed! Why not start a pioneering group which would rebut the dead hand of orthodoxy and the impersonal claims of ecclesiastical authority? de Blank acted, and with a few others chaplains formed *The Forward Group*. He drew up a memorandum which was circulated to chaplains in the Middle East and in England. It was an entirely private matter and nothing to do with the Chaplains' Department. The three main planks to the platform were: (1) *United Action*. The need for all Churches to work together was paramount — 'a pious hope for union sometime in the future is not good enough'. He urged Inter-Communion and a co-ordinated policy of action between the Churches wherever possible. (ii) *Social Responsibility*. The *Forward Group*, 'stands for the Kingdom of God and is willing to condemn, challenge or support any policy according as it rejects, or ignores or abides by the principles of the Kingdom'. It would involve itself in politics. (iii) *Christian Mobilisation*. This was the spiritual counterpart of a country mobilising for total war. 'The old accusation made so often that those who go to church are no different from those who do not must be proved demonstrably false. This will mean more study, greater discipline and a more loyal consecration on the part of church people everywhere, for the Church of Laodicea must cease to cumber the ground.'

de Blank had plans to publish *Forward Views* from time to time, containing members' ideas. First, he had to awaken the itch of cupidity in people to join him. He saw the Movement spreading quickly. It must do so for the times were urgent. On 16 May 1943 he sent a copy of his memorandum to the Archbishop of Canterbury, the Moderator of the Church of Scotland and the President of the Free Church Council. The reply of William Temple (Archbishop of Canterbury) dated 17 September 1943 is interesting:

Dear Mr de Blank,

I am grateful to you for sending me the paper describing the aims of the Forward Group. I am very glad to know about this group. It would, I think, be a very dangerous symptom if the experience of the Chaplains in the war were not leading to some such movement.

I should be grateful if I may be kept in touch with it, but I think it better that I should not comment unless I am specially asked to do so, and that you should develop your ideas freely. When, in the last war, I was concerned in the Life and Liberty Movement, we were

41

always emphatic that no one wearing gaiters could be a member of the Life and Liberty Council; in other words we were a group of unofficial clergy. I think we were the freer on that account and nobody was embarrassed by us, as some bishops or Archdeacons might have been if they had been associated with us — though I am not sure that any situation arose when they would in fact have found attachment to us awkward.

So while I hope you may believe in my genuine interest and sympathy, my silence is not to be regarded as necessarily representing approval of everything that you have put into your paper.

Yours sincerely,
WILLIAM CANTUAR

Before anything could develop with *The Forward Group*, de Blank was transferred to the Royal Dragoons in August 1943, joining them in Cyrenaica in North Africa before the Italian landings. The transfer was regretted by everyone at Headquarters. A private even organised a petition, collecting almost one thousand signatures, hoping to persuade the General to keep de Blank. It was unsuccessful. When de Blank left, a tribute in the Club's weekly bulletin referred to the community's 'irreparable loss'. 'Liked equally well by non-churchgoers as by those who have looked forward to hearing his brilliant addresses each Sunday, he has devoted his time here to the general welfare of us all'. 'His sparkling conversation and repartee have been the inspiration of many gatherings . . .'

In September 1943 de Bank went with his new regiment first to Italy and then in April 1944 back to England. He was promoted to the position of Senior Chaplain with the 61st Division. D-Day was approaching and all camps were sealed. de Blank, now with the regiment in Kent, had the unenviable task of keeping the troops happy at the same time as they were 'in the dark'. These were tense times when some of the men were suffering from nervous anticipation every bit as potentially depressing as nervous exhaustion. When D-Day came de Blank did not accompany the troops who went to Normandy. He had to content himself with a service of intercession and to receiving an account from the local organ blower, 'To blowing for the invasion: 5/-'.

In the autumn he was sent to Europe to work with the British Liberation Army. Danger was constant and increasing. Like many people in the war, de Blank was not by nature courageous but given the circumstances of war he showed exceptional bravery, caring little for his own safety.

In November 1944 there was a Confirmation Service in Antwerp which de Blank had to attend. He went to enquire the way at a control post. At that moment a V-2 rocket fell on the building killing all in or around it except four people. de Blank was one and he was badly wounded. He was seen wandering about with blood pouring from his head and one ear almost severed. 'I must find my driver. I must find my driver', he muttered. (His driver was in fact safe.) The injuries were serious and de Blank was unconscious for several days. He was then evacuated to England and was a patient in St. Hugh's Hospital, Oxford. In 1950 he remembered 'lying in hospital in Belgium quite certain I was going to die, finding myself as it were a dispassionate spectator by my own bedside and I remember quite clearly feeling some surprise that there was no consciousness of the glory of heaven,but at the same time I felt perfectly peaceful with nothing to fear or disturb.' He found it hard to retain his hold on God. When he had been in hospital in Egypt earlier in the war suffering from dysentery he experienced spiritual paralysis. It did not produce the agony of soul and sense of dereliction which occurred later in life. Nevertheless, when he expected a 'sign' from the heavens, home of many mansions, the rooms seemed bare. His faith was not as sure as his proclamations suggest.

It was several months before de Blank was fit and then at a cost. He had a metal plate inserted in his skull and bore the scars of a badly crushed temple all his days. That was not all. There were few days thereafter that he did not suffer pain and headaches, sometimes of excruciating severity.

On 2 April 1945, de Blank was posted to the Royal Garrison Church Aldershot and subsequently became Warden of the Chaplains' Training Centre at Tidworth.

The war years had not been doubt-free ones. Gone was the exhilaration of Forest Gate. He was a good chaplain but he did not find the padre's ministry deeply satisfying. Nor did he think there was enough to do. The old temptations surfaced. How should he really spend his life? Would the Church use his gifts? Why was his faith so feeble? Were his many doubts ideas that were still alive? He was not insulated from reality by the blessed assurance of his former Oxford Group friends. He was not in a parish where his life and ministry seemed to have purpose and meaning. How do you measure success as an army chaplain? When the lights went full on after the flickering doubts, his faith in himself and his God returned in full measure. He had something to proclaim, and in a big way. In 1942 he wrote: 'I have pretty well decided to become a barrister after the war with a view to a Parliamentary career as the best way of propagating Christianity.' He was also attracted to the Franciscan life, but that was romanticism. Again we see the contrasting aspects of his personality. His anxieties suggest more than a temporary unsettlement, more a deeply dissatisfied sense of unfulfilment. Yet out of the dark dungeon of discontent came an unshackled de Blank. At last he decided to say 'No' permanently to the law, and a renewed, enthusiastic 'Yes' to his priesthood.

Other influences had been at work. The war had of course broadened his outlook serving with other men: it had also widened his conception of the possibilities of Anglicanism. Other chaplains from different traditions within the Church of England showed him something of other treasures which were at his disposal. de Blank had started by making his appeal to Scripture only, or to the inner light of his individual conscience alone. Forest Gate had tempered these views. The war years had shown them to be inadequate. de Blank began to see the Church of England in a new and transfiguring light. What he had previously only known and rather rejected in theory began to seem quite different. Yes, here was a Church claiming to be both Catholic and Reformed. In its doctrinal position it was the heir at once of historic Christendom and of the Reformation. In the sixteenth century it did not, like the reformed churches of the continent, cut itself adrift from the past in order to go back to the Bible and make a fresh start from there. It retained not only its customary organisation, apart from the Papal jurisdiction, but also essentially the ancient rites and ceremonies. It claimed that the only elements of doctrine it surrendered were medieval accretions on the teaching of the Bible and the early Church. It gave a large place to the reading of the Bible in its public services, paid close attention to the liturgical year, emphasised the practical and moral character of Christianity, attached great importance to sound learning, and made no claim to be the only authorised interpreter of the Christian faith. *This* was a Church worth serving, and de Blank was suddenly excited about the future. He would never go back to his earlier understanding of the Church, even though some of the sin-laden aspects of his past convictions occasionally nibbled away at him.

The seeds of the future had been planted. Whatever de Blank

really wanted to do after demobilisation it was to be in London.
His father had his spleen removed in 1945 at the age of seventy-
five and there was always the chance of death or permanent
incapacity. de Blank was clear what should happen if his father
died. In a letter to one of his sisters in October 1945 he wrote:
'Quite definitely I shall be delighted if she [his mother] will make
her home with me, and I am limiting my choice of jobs to one in
London so that that may be possible.' Although de Blank was the
youngest child he was always concerned for the welfare of the
family, for example, in February 1946 he corresponded with his
brother-in-law making sure that Bartha was provided for
adequately if she remained unmarried and that she should not be
the object of charity from her brothers and sisters.

The job de Blank accepted in London was on the staff of the
Student Christian Movement (S.C.M.). He was released from his
Emergency Commission with the Army on 27 March 1946 and
started his new work immediately. It was never his intention to
remain long with S.C.M. but for the moment it was convenient
and congenial work. The General Secretary of S.C.M. was the
Revd. Alan Booth, a Methodist. He had to revitalise SCM after the
war and needed an organiser. de Blank was the perfect choice.
There were a few tensions at first amongst SCM intellectuals who
did not like having their philosophical and theological meander-
ings cut short by de Blank. But what could not be resolved by
argument was concluded by friendliness and wit.

Alan Booth soon experienced planning on the grand scale, at
which de Blank was superb. Arranging a great Quadriennial
Conference in the Central Hall for two thousand students was one
of his jobs. Alan Booth recalls: 'The idea ... was an attempt to
overleap our membership and reach a new one; to do something
on a dramatic scale. Joost simply took over; partly administrative,
propaganda, getting us known, and doing all that while at the
same time in a not too aggressive way constantly saying to the
'think boys', look I'm not going to kill myself doing this if it's only
going to be about your cleverness and not about the Lord Jesus.'
The Quadriennial was an impressive achievement.

Alan Booth also remembered a visit to a meeting of the World
Student Christian Federation in Geneva with de Blank. They
stopped over in Paris and stayed with de Blank's brother. Alan
Booth packed some of his war rations thinking it would help with
the hospitality. But they were met at the station with a magnificent

car and enjoyed the best food, wine and entertainment available. This was to be Joost's approach in the future too.

de Blank's experiences of speaking to student audiences were mixed. He was usually recognisable by his distinctive appearance with purple choker in place of tie. He was pungent and witty even when giving out notices: 'Will the gentleman using the first floor in the Garden House kindly desist from throwing spent razor blades onto the path below the front window . . . [pause] . . . It is not the ecumenical thing to do!'

What he had to say was always challenging. Some student audiences preferred the brilliance of, say, a Ronald Preston, who was radical, anti-establishment, politically aware and an intellectual. de Blank failed with such audiences. The impression of him which remained in Alan Booth's mind was of a 'strange mixture between very adult, sophisticated knowledge of the world, a way of approaching people and a kind of intellectual simplicity which was almost childlike. He was a man who made things happen'.

Unfortunately for de Blank, SCM was more concerned with ideas and speculation. By mid-1947 it was clear that de Blank's time with SCM was limited, although there was a plan that he would become Editor of *The Student Movement*, (the SCM magazine) which would have given him an outlet again. That was what he really wanted — another platform, preferably of his own creation. He liked teams, provided he was leading them. Alan Booth was aware of de Blank's desire for change and recognised real leadership qualities in him. He telephoned the Bishop Suffragan of Willesden (Michael Gresford Jones) and told him that there was a good man who should have a good job.

About this time the Vicar of St. John the Baptist, Greenhill, Harrow, (George Ernest Ingle) was appointed Bishop Suffragan of Fulham. George Ingle had been at Greenhill only three and a half years but into that space he had crammed the work of a decade with the restless, tireless energy of a reformer. He would not be an easy man to follow and a priest of distinctive and varied gifts was needed. Joost de Blank was that priest.

CHAPTER FIVE

Parish of Action

After the War there was a growing conviction amongst many radical clergy that the Church of England was shackled by an organisation designed to serve the wrong places and by a legal system incapable of stomaching significant change. People no longer lived, worked, played, worshipped and died within the same small area. The Church no longer embraced the whole social and cultural life of the nation. No longer were the clergy the ones who thought, administered and disposed; while the 'laity' were meant to listen, to accept and to obey.

If the Church had not been so blinkered it would have realised that the break up came with the twentieth century. In its sociological and cultural setting, both national and local, the Church had been thrust (sometimes by default) from the centre to the circumference of affairs. In the social welfare and cultural context the excessive distance between the world and the prevailing outdated ecclesiastical structure and mentality could only be crossed if there was a revolution in thought and action. Or so the radicals said!

The parson had become an increasingly meaningless figure in the community, and appeared incredibly remote from his own parishioners. He had a completely secure job; he managed his own time-table; and much of what he did was mysterious and unreal; his approach to practical problems, as viewed by the laity handling similar problems, appeared amateur. In just over one hundred and fifty years he had lost, sometimes by default, the greater part of his visible function in society to educationalists, assistance board officers, probation officers, national insurance workers, psychiatrists and a host of other professional workers. It was small comfort that the Church worker pioneered in handling problems in many social fields and that Christianity itself had

47

provided the climate of opinion in which it became necessary for these functions to be taken over and dealt with on a far greater scale by the State.

What was left? The parson's function appeared to be leading his people in worship and offering on their behalf the praise and intercession they were unable or unwilling to give. In addition, society still expected him to add a touch of respectability and easy comfort to the landmarks of life such as birth, marriage and death. The parson should be able to help his laity to show Christ to the world in the places where they live and work but unfortunately in many cases his isolation from the world and also from his own parishioners' lives, ended instead in a spiritually impotent pastor, left in charge of a decaying fabric, disguising his ineptitudes by devices that concealed a flight from reality. Consequently, the Church of England seemed to be out of date, her voice muted and apologetic, with reform stuck in her gullet. Or so the radicals said!

It was easy and popular to agitate for reform. There were the vocal agitators who made a brief appearance on the ecclesiastical stage, roused their audiences, took their bows and disappeared from the radiant present into the dark future. Less flamboyant but more influential, and thus more dangerous to those cautious of reform, were those who reformed by stealth, creeping from one committee to another, shadowy figures, dimly discerned. A study of the Minutes of many Church Assembly committees, subcommittees, ad hoc groups and working parties of the post-war years would reveal a small but interesting number of radical clergy whose names appear with amazing frequency. Their thinking and contributions resulted in some of the reports which appeared during the nineteen fifties and sixties and which subsequently changed the direction of the Church. Naturally there were diehards who opposed change on principle. That was easy to do and saved them from the tedious business of thinking at all.

But there were other clergy who, whilst being energetic innovators and impatient reformers in many ways, yet believed in the potential of the parochial system. Moreover they showed that the parish church could still be the beacon of any community. By their own ministries they showed too that it was possible for the Church to make an impact on the community and influence large numbers of people and that it was possible to pack their churches!

There were some outstanding parish priests, not in the theological first team intellectually but men who used their natural gifts with energy, imagination and determination. In the immediate post-war years these included priests such as George Reindorp (later Bishop of Salisbury) at St. Stephen's, Rochester Row, Westminster; Mark Hodson (later Bishop of Hereford) at Poplar in London's East End; Edward Henderson (later Bishop of Bath and Wells) at St. Paul's, Knightsbridge; — and Joost de Blank at St. John the Baptist, Greenhill, Harrow.

A durable and strong tradition of parochial life and spiritual vitality already existed to some extent, at Greenhill. The Church was set at the central cross-roads of Harrow. To this place de Blank was instituted by the Bishop of London (J. W. C. Wand) on 9 February 1948, the fourth incumbent since the foundation of the church in 1896.

de Blank believed that great things could be achieved or perhaps it is more accurate to assert that he believed he could achieve great things in Greenhill. It was not arrogance but dedicated conviction. He knew what he wanted and was determined to succeed. Suddenly he knew all about the glory of being an Anglican priest. As Vicar of Greenhill he was responsible for everyone in the parish — that is what the 'cure of souls' meant. 'The Church of England is rightly proud that its life for centuries has been organized on a parochial and not on a congregational basis,' he asserted. 'The parish church, by its very nature, exists to offer to Almighty God the worship of the locality for which it is responsible.'

de Blank was not on his own at Greenhill. He had the strength he received from his family, for his parents moved into the Vicarage at Greenhill. In the parish there were usually two curates and a Church Army sister who was youth leader and parish worker. One of the outgoing curates, Jack Roundhill, who served only a few months under de Blank, draws an interesting comparison between his old and new superiors. 'George Ingle was a hardworking priest who had a passionate concern for individuals and for social justice (he supported the Industrial Christian Fellowship enthusiastically and collected huge parcels of clothes in his vestry for displaced persons in Germany and elsewhere) and who seemed to care little for order and tidiness. He threw himself into things energetically and one got the impression of 'impulses'. Joost de Blank came with a contrast: everything was smooth and orderly and (so one gathered) under control. He appeared to have adequate funds which he used for the benefit of the parish and the entertainment, parties etc., were — so it seemed to me — much more sophisticated. He gave the impression of one who was not "wearing himself out" — one imagines that he saw all the West End shows as they appeared — but certainly there was no suggestion of idleness, more I think effortless ease. He was able to delegate work to people in the parish and put it to them in a way that gave one confidence that the task would be properly done.' These memories may only contain a fraction of the picture but they are interesting for the impression created by the new vicar.

Another curate, Roy Deasy, who served several years with de Blank, makes a similar point on delegation, referring to it as: 'sheer professionalism and efficiency ... making the best use of one's time and energy, seeing a job to be done, defining it and then getting on with it and not hanging about. This is one of the things he gave me more than anybody else did.

'We used to dread him coming back from his holidays with his little black loose-leaf note book. He would open it and there would be a programme for the next three months in outline. Interestingly it was not for discussion.' This is usually the way with men of action. There is something dictatorial in their approach, although it may be benevolent, a kind of unspoken 'Father knows best'!

Within a few months Greenhill felt the dramatic change, and from then onwards it was change, change, change. One of de Blank's most used sayings at Greenhill was: 'You so easily get into a rut and before you know where you are, a rut becomes a grave'. The ultimate failure would be if the parish got stuck in a rut. Roy Deasy notes: 'He always examined quite critically and coldly anything that we ever did in the parish, regardless of whether it was a success in terms of people coming or not. Sometimes I think he subjected the things to which people came to a more rigorous examination than the things that you could write off as failures. This I'm sure was the reason why year after year he did something different that called for more effort in a different direction and built in more people.'

The story of de Blank's experiments was subsequently set down in *The Parish in Action* (1954) which one critic described as 'a tonic for the manic-depressive mentality which has invaded large areas of Church of England life.' The book showed how de Blank led his congregation to share in the mission of the Church, and find its fellowship not in irrelevant week-night meetings but in doing the job of Christian evangelism and service.

Most of the experiments have now become part of the regular life of parishes throughout England, but they were neither numerous nor popular in 1948. It is worth glancing at a few aspects of the Greenhill 'revolution'. The word is not too strong for that is what it was. The changes were not ones of emphasis but of direction. Moreover, they reveal more of de Blank's character as the whole parish began to buzz — but there was never any doubt as to who was Queen Bee.

First, worship. In the nineteen forties and early fifties there was the stirring of liturgical renewal in the Church of England and the best ideas — and results — came from the French Roman Catholic Church. An influential book was *Revolution in a City Parish* by Abbé Michonneau (1949), parish priest of Sacré Coeur de Colombes in the suburbs of Paris. Abbé Michonneau saw a stream of priests from France, England and elsewhere coming to his parish to witness the liturgy come to life and learn how this had been brought about. de Blank had visited the church and *experienced* the liturgy. He realised how much in Church of England services was static. There was no 'lift-off' and thus no penetration. Prayer was from the lips outward. 'Lift up your hearts' was intoned on note G and the response remained on that note too. Somehow the liturgy had to balance the need for dignity in the presence of God, the joy in worshipping Him and the real strength one received from the fellowship of God's people worshipping together.

Abbé Michonneau returned to basics: took nothing for granted. A 'Feast of the Mass' was used to make clear his constant effort to make the Mass 'everybody's Mass'. 'As a crowded church watched, more of the parish brought forward three benches: these were to be the altar. An altar boy carried in the altar stone. Skilled and willing hands had made the crucifix, candelabra, the altar cloths and vestments, and even had written and designed the missal. As all these were brought forward, a priest in the pulpit described each article. To make the Mass more personal, everyone brought up at the Offertory an envelope containing a list of his or her own special intentions. The children each brought up a piece of coloured glass; when the pieces were fitted together, the phrase "The Mass is the centre of our lives" was spelt out. As each child came up with his piece, he said aloud, "This is to make my Mass mean more." The evening service is used to develop the same idea. Up to the altar are brought the tools of the workmen, household objects, school books, children's games, and bread and wine.

51

Meanwhile a long chanted prayer fits all these things into the harmony of Christian living and unites all the crowd in an inspiring prayer. The ceremony closes with veneration of the altar stone.'

Words such as these were intoxicating to de Blank. Before the War they would have been meaningless, even offensive, something that Roman Catholics get up to on the Continent.

His approach to the liturgy and its central place in the Church's worship had changed. During the War, de Blank had celebrated Holy Communion at dawn, late at night, in the open air or in a hut. Maybe a white linen cloth had been spread on the square bonnet of a truck that stood pulled closely into a hedge, and that was the altar on that day. 'We bowed before it, perhaps with a deeper reverence than one we used even in church, because there we felt a tremendous sense of the presence of the Divine in and through the ordinary business of our daily work, there we realized how the ordinary things of everyday life could be consecrated to the service of Him who is the Lord of all life.' Again, de Blank remembered a celebration on board ship. Very early in the morning, an altar was set up on a ledge of the ship; and men, surrounded by the tools and implements of their trade, received the Bread of Life. Then again, he had preached during Holy Week at St. Bartholomew's, Dover, at which his former chaplain friend, 'Peter' Priest, was vicar. If the parishioners were impressed at de Blank's powerful preaching, he was struck, moved and influenced by the Holy Week Services which were undilutedly Anglo-Catholic.

de Blank took the best from his experiences and started a Parish Communion first once a month, then every Sunday. The liturgical pattern was that of the Book of Common Prayer and the manner in which the Service was performed underlined the fact that it was both an act of Fellowship and an act of Consecration. de Blank explained it thus: 'A simple and plain nave altar is set up in front of the screen; and this altar is a real carpenter's bench used by many of our boys; and nothing could be more fitting — for the Lord is at home at a carpenter's bench. The Celebrant stands behind the altar, facing the congregation, just as a father sits at the head of his family table — and this is a return to the custom of the Primitive Church. The Gospel — the proclamation of the Word of God — is read with due solemnity from the pulpit; and minds and hearts turn to Him Who is the Word made Flesh as the account of His words and actions is declared to those who hear.' The Offertory Procession of alms, bread and wine was symbolic: the alms symbolizing the giving of all effort and work that had been necessary to earn the money; the bread and wine as symbols of man's material needs for God to bless and return to His people. Wheaten bread was brought from a loaf used in one of the homes of the parish. These, together with the sacred vessels, were carried to the altar in a procession. This represented the life of the family of God in Greenhill.

And the family of God in Greenhill grew and grew. There was something exhilarating about the liturgy in action there. Few parishes had experimented to the same extent at this time. The word that more than one parishioner has used of these services is 'arresting'. Yes, they stopped people in their tracks. The church was usually packed and at festivals such as Easter and Christmas over a thousand people were 'arrested'.

de Blank's preaching continued to attract large congregations. Queueing for church, extra chairs in the aisles, was commonplace. His sermons whether at packed Parish Communion or overflowing Evensong, for the morning innovation did not eclipse the evening star, were powerful. He may have moved away from his earlier Evangelicalism to a Catholic conception of the Church, but not, and never, at the expense of evangelical preaching.

de Blank used any and every method of 'getting the message across' — visual aids, journalism, epilogues ('for people in plain clothes, by people in plain clothes'), open-air services, festival weeks and much, much more. He even had a slide on the screen of the local picture house, the Coliseum, shown during the interval, and a page in 'Tittle-Tattle', the cinema's monthly circular. As with so many initiatives, de Blank financed this latter project from his own pocket (£100 a year in this case) and appealed for the money afterwards. A seemingly endless flow of leaflets was distributed in the parish which housed 20,000 souls. A poor parish magazine was transformed into something special — *Greenhill Challenge*. Note the word 'challenge'. Everything about de Blank's Greenhill ministry was constructive and challenging. A series of meetings was held on the theme 'A Faith That Works'. *Leaves from a Diary*, in the parish magazine, was eagerly awaited each month by both parish and press. de Blank was at his journalistic best. There was a good deal of chaff and humour but it was always more than structured gossip and there was always much wheat.

One aim of de Blank was to break down the organisational side of pastoral life and build up a corporate life. This is always difficult when people have allegiances to particular organisations, yet he achieved some success. There were many regular activities to which the whole parish went, a natural extension of worshipping together. But de Blank was after more than a 'successful' church in terms of numbers, he required the Church to make an impact on public life in Harrow. In him the Church in Harrow had an articulate and powerful voice and people listened to what he said. A local councillor thought de Blank combined, 'wisdom and matter-of-factness'.

There was no mistaking who the Vicar was, and for what he stood. On one occasion his car was being filled with petrol at a local garage and the pump attendant was blaspheming about something. de Blank got out of his car and said, 'we do not speak like that in this parish'. He was more often remembered for his wit and outrageous remarks rather than for his rebukes. Hilarity was associated with the 'Holy Joost' as some people called him behind his back, but with admiring affection. On one occasion the Women's Fellowship had a new banner and some alms bags to bless. Discussion with a curate in the vestry before the service led to something like, 'Bless this banner, O Lord, and these bags . . .'. The occasion was made even more delightful by a procession that inexplicably divided into two, and was then seen moving in opposite directions so as to present finally a confrontation of the women who ground to a halt at the west end!

For a parish in constant action, what was the quality of its spiritual life? A thermometer would have seen the spiritual temperature rising from 1948 to 1952. de Blank provided more opportunities for quiet contemplation and corporate prayer. He knew that the real battle of the spirit takes place in silence. There is a fatal fluency in praying as well as in preaching. de Blank himself rose early in the morning and prayed. He did not find it easy. The Church of England priest is more fortunate than he often realises in having the daily Offices of Matins and Evensong to recite. A mixture of daily prayer, intercession, psalms and Old and New Testament readings is a wholesome diet for a priest. When the soul slumps, the Offices may be little more than 'vain repetition', but perseverance usually restores the equilibrium even if the heavenly heights are reached but rarely. de Blank kept a prayer diary into which he put hours of love and care and so the needs of individual people were brought to the throne of grace. All this was a well-planned method of petition and intercession as one would expect from de Blank. But he wanted more. He explored the heart-searching and heart-expanding possibilities of adoration, thanksgiving, and confession. He studied the spiritual classics, including St. Francis de Sales' (a favourite saint of his) *Introduction to the Devout Life*, and St. John of the Cross's, *The Dark Night of the Soul*, a book which disturbed him. He never felt confident in prayer and often inadequate. Although he went through bouts of introspection and troughs of dereliction he was no contemplative. At Greenhill he tried to follow the spiritual exercises of the mystics but failed. The harder he tried the less it worked. That was the trouble. He tried too hard and felt guilty that his times of deliberate contemplation were crowded with the things of this world. Roy Deasy is correct when he says that de Blank's meditation and contemplation were done with his pen in his hand when he wrote. 'His devotion was bound up in his active life. He had not the stillness of mind to be a monk, but he had a tremendous awareness of the presence of God. He did not go through his private prayers as a matter of routine, but he really did believe that if he prayed for Roy on this day something would happen.'

'A man of prayer' is not a phrase that leaps to the forefront of one's mind when thinking of de Blank's ministry at Greenhill, but it was there that an increasing number of people came to him for spiritual counsel. This was surprising, for despite his popularity, many parishioners did not find it easy to approach him. Why? First, there was his physical appearance and manner. Though small in stature, he had a remarkable presence. He was always conscious of his dignity and he was always neatly attired, both in robes and in ordinary dress. His wartime wound and scar gave him a sinister look until he lifted one eyebrow in amused surprise. Moreover, he did not suffer fools gladly. One curate felt very inferior in de Blank's presence, to such an extent that he could hardly string his sentences together. Another curate, Michael Hamilton-Sharp, writes: 'Joost undoubtedly had a magic touch about him. But not with everyone. He was at his best with men. With women he felt ill at ease. Intelligent women respected his brilliance, but I doubt if they really liked him. But as I write this I can think of a mass of women who idolised him — but he never seemed to get *through* to them as he did with men. "Those young men he always had around him", was a comment one woman graduate gave on his inclinations. It was a blind spot. He never seemed to understand the emotional make-up of women.'

There were many women acquaintances but few close women friends. This is understandable as acquaintances have to talk; friends can sit quietly together. If only he could have — would have — allowed one or two close friends to share his innermost travails, delights and aspirations he might in the end have had less of a tortured soul.

Monica Furlong, the author and journalist lived in Harrow and was in her late teenage years when de Blank was at Greenhill. She was drawn into the life of St. John's Greenhill by de Blank and saw how friendly and outgoing he was with a group of people, but it was not necessarily so with individuals, 'women especially'. She felt frightened of him. 'He could hurt me all the way through almost more than anyone I have ever come across. But what to me is so interesting is that although he found it very hard to talk to me in an ordinary and informal way, he still nevertheless helped me at that point of my life more than anyone else. It shows how the wish to love and care for other people gets through absolutely everything.' At the age of eighteen she was going through a crisis of faith and told de Blank, 'I can't believe in God'. He listened without interruption and without expressing any surprise. 'He was the first person who had ever taken me as seriously as that.' He did not attempt to furnish cut-and-dried answers as he would have done before the War. At Greenhill he helped individuals who lived in the border country of faith and doubt. In countless instances he was able to guide and lead them to a reasonable faith yet one which made real and even costly demands.

Monica Furlong stopped going to church for a long time. Two years later she had a religious experience and again went to de Blank expecting a prodigal's welcome. Instead, 'Joost was offhand about the whole thing, and rather threw cold water on it', — but told her to start attending church again. His influence was to prick the bubble of ecstasy without blowing it away. 'It made it possible to digest the experience and not to expect to go on having grand experiences all the time'.

Had he lived longer he would have been bemused to find Monica Furlong as Moderator of the Movement for the Ordination of Women for several years, and 'tickled pink' as well as moved to learn that she would be talking on *Spirituality in the 80s* at St. Martin-in-the-Fields in 1985. But the girl of Greenhill was one of those who was with de Blank during his last illness, near the end of his life, when all that mattered was to hold his hand and weep with him a little.

The majority of individuals from whom this biographer heard, tell a different but not a contradictory story of the Greenhill years. With de Blank as Queen Bee there was only room for workers in the hive. He was difficult to work with because he only wanted his own way. When he left, a parishioner wrote an open letter to him remembering, 'the way in which you have made us all work, disarming our natural caution with the assurance that this new project, or that new theme for discussion, would really involve very little more of our time and energy. "It depends on what you make of it", as you have often said, with the cheerful assumption that we should welcome this invitation to serve in a new way.' In practice parishioners found that *all* their time and energy were caught, harnessed and used. Their talents too. de Blank knew how to discover a person's natural gifts and persuade the individual to use them for the glory of God and of Greenhill. Thus there was a standard of excellence in all his endeavours. People were not only recruited to serve but also were left 'to get on with it without interference' as one of them writes.

It is natural that someone with de Blank's flair and energy — and also ambition — would be drawn to and in to the wider life of the Church of England. His name and voice were soon heard in many places.

The great 'Mission to London', one of the Church of England's postwar landmarks, came in de Blank's second year at Greenhill. This was the kind of transforming event to which he could add dynamism and lustre. Conventional churchgoers became militant apostles. The circumference of the Church's influence on the community was pushed further out as the centre of faith was strengthened. In 1950 de Blank was elected Proctor in the Convocation of Canterbury and a member of the Church Assembly of the Church of England. He had no intention of hanging on to his Assembly maidenhood and intervened in a debate on his first attendance. 'I was accused by a later speaker of being — "a young man in a hurry".' That accusation, turned compliment, could be applied to him at any period of his life.

The Bishop of London enlisted de Blank in the planning of the Diocese's next great step forward, *Schools of Religion* during Lent 1952. This was to rectify one of the real weaknesses of Church of England members — namely knowledge of their faith, the why and wherefore of belief, why they are Anglicans and how it meets the needs and conditions of the age. 320 parishes enlisted in the diocesan course.

A man of de Blank's energy, fertile with ideas, was bound to have views on contemporary events and never failed to express them. He supported Proportional Representation in Government, considered most of Convocation's work irrelevant, denounced the Pope and the Cardinal Archbishop of Westminster on many issues whilst admiring the Roman Catholic Church in Belgium and France, condemned Malan's Racial Discrimination policy in South Africa, supported Trade Union rights . . . the observations flowed from his pen week by week and were good 'copy'. He knew that. His voice was also heard on the radio, but here as a defender and instructor of the faith.

This chapter can only give the flavour of unceasing and imaginative activity, of packed congregations, of parishioners who had been led from their dug-outs to join the *Advance* (that was a key word), of real impact on the community. There is no room for detail. We can only glance at his home life. de Blank needed the security, even serenity, of his home even if it was a place from which he was often absent as demands on his time increased. The death of his father in 1952 was a massive blow. The dominance of Mamma had been increasing and now it was absolute. But the vicarage was not a retreat. Here he entertained, from here he ventured to the West End for shows and french cooking. Amongst congenial companions where the scale of entertainment was often lavish and conversation always scintillating, de Blank was usually the centre of attraction, but not necessarily the most vocal. Everyone who knew him expected him to 'go far'. He was a leader.

Was there another side, too, more difficult to discern, a darker one? The *priest* had emerged. Was he a caring autocrat, a paternalistic priest despite the way in which he shared his ministry with the laity? Did he use the ordained ministry as a means of self-assurance? How far was there inner conflict between the evident need for the applause of the crowd and the knowledge that a priest should be more bothered about the things of the next world than the enticing tinsel and glitter of this world? These, and many other questions will be considered later. Most of them troubled de Blank at different stages of his life: a few he refused to face until the end.

By 1952 he had put St. John the Baptist, Greenhill, on the map.

It was a place where other clergy went to have a look at what a parish in action was like. They marvelled at what they found and went away and copied it. When one incumbent confessed to copying, de Blank said, 'Do not have any scruples about plagiarism if it is in the service of the Kingdom of God'.

In May 1952 the Bishop of London asked him to call at Fulham Palace. He did, and came away 'overwhelmed and humbled and grateful'. He had been offered the Suffragan Bishopric of Stepney.

CHAPTER SIX

Episcopal Éclat

The Suffragan Bishopric of Stepney, comprising London's East End north of the Thames, was created in 1895. Taking in Holborn, Finsbury and Stoke Newington its heart was in Shoreditch, Hackney, Bethnal Green, Poplar and Stepney itself.

It had been served by a galaxy of bishops. George Forrest Browne (1895) served for only two years before being translated to Bristol. Arthur Foley Winnington-Ingram, who became Bishop of London and whose whirlwind four years at Stepney until 1901 were remembered by his successor at Stepney, Cosmo Gordon Lang, 'in those radiant days he seemed to me to be the Bayard of the Church of England, the *'chevalier sans peur et sans reproche'.'* The Cosmo Lang of Stepney was completely different from the Cosmo Lang of Canterbury. In his Stepney days he was regularly seen with his priests among the prevailing poverty, squalor, worn-out mothers, ill-paid home workers, drab streets and dirty surroundings. He was at Stepney until 1909 when, at the age of 44, he became Archbishop of York. He was followed by Henry Luke Paget who gave ten years to Stepney. His style was very different from that of his two immediate predecessors. He was a pastor, a bishop known for his sympathy and wise counsel. He was effective, not least in raising money for the work of the Church in the East End. As a man he was content to be a public figure with a private face. But not so private a pastor as to escape translation to the See of Chester. He had been called the English Curé d'Ars.

Henry Mosley who was at Stepney from 1919 until 1928 had

St. Paul's Cathedral, after de Blank's consecration as Bishop Suffragan of Stepney, 1952. Left to right: de Blank; Francis Johnston, Bishop in Egypt; Geoffrey Fisher, Archbishop of Canterbury; Humphrey Beevor, Bishop of Lebombo; Kenneth Riches, Bishop Suffragan of Dorchester.

already served twenty six years in the East End at Stratford, Poplar and Hackney and well understood the problems and challenges of the area although he admitted that problems he had known were nothing compared with the misery of Hoxton, Spitalfields and Stepney. He was a good pastor and did much to encourage his clergy in the difficult post-War years.

Following him in 1928 was Charles Edward Curzon who moved from West End Kensington to East End Stepney. Again he was a bishop who served the East End without self-advertisement but with considerable influence. He did not lack administrative gifts which he infused with the pastoral office. It was no surprise when he was translated to the bishopric of Exeter in 1936.

61

Robert Hamilton Moberly, Principal of Bishops' College, Cheshunt, succeeded Curzon and there he remained through the years of the blitz — travelling round on his bicycle, always managing to appear where help was needed. He was a patient and gentle man.

In March 1952 it was announced that Robert Moberly would leave Stepney for the Deanery of Salisbury.

At Stepney he had seen much of the work to which he had devoted the best years of his life destroyed by enemy action, and many of those he had served lost in the wholesale massacre. The delays and frustrations of post-war reconstruction had taken their toll. By 1952 he and many of the clergy of the East End were tired, if not worn out.

Winnington-Ingram of London had appointed Lang, Paget, Mosely, Curzon and Moberly to Stepney. Now it was the choice of Bishop Wand. He knew the East End needed leadership and that de Blank would provide it. The Consecration took place in St. Paul's Cathedral on the Feast of St. James (25 July) 1952. Four bishops were consecrated by the Archbishop of Canterbury (Geoffrey Fisher); Francis Featherstonehaugh Johnston (Bishop in Egypt); Kenneth Riches (Bishop Suffragan of Dorchester); Humphrey Beevor (Bishop of Lebombo) and de Blank. Canon John Waddington, Vicar of St. Peter Mancroft, Norwich, preached a challenging sermon: 'The Church today needs many more great leaders. It needs to hear the throb and the beat of the march of those who are led by men utterly sure of themselves, because they are utterly sure of God. It needs to recapture the dynamic drive and infectious enthusiasm of the early Church . . . wherever there is leadership, great things are happening. It is the bored, depressed, half-hearted attitude that baulks the work of God, all along the line.

'Let the Church's leaders show that they have learned the first principles of advertising, by broadcasting less black-letter news about a failing Church and more red-letter news about an unfailing Christ.'

This was pure de Blank! In no other sphere of his life did he show so effectively that under his leadership the Church in the East End had a 'fighting chance' — No! It would win! He carried a banner like a Christian warrior with enthusiasm and originality. His episcopate was one of éclat and sparkle. He fired his dispirited clergy and lay people were drawn to him like moths to light. It was a time of unapologetic triumphalism, of open air processions, colour, flamboyance — all under inspired and 'tycoon' leadership.

de Blank knew that renewal would have to start with his clergy. In the bishop the apostolate inheres. He is the Apostolic Father of a See and he partially delegates his apostolic powers to the priests in the diocese. Bishop Wand of London had the great gift of genuinely delegating powers to his Suffragan Bishops so that they were Area Bishops in all but name. de Blank never tired of reminding his clergy that his throne was in every parish church.

de Blank had developed a 'high' doctrine of the Church and considered that the Church was weak where the place and purpose of the Bishop was not acknowledged. Stepney certainly knew it had a bishop now! A 'low' doctrine of the Church was marked by weaknesses. There was no diocesan sense of belonging, each parish was in a little watertight compartment living for itself and in the end dying on its own. There was no common sense of discipline. Obedience was held or witheld on private judgement. There was no feeling of being under authority, only aggressive self-importance. It is always interesting to observe priests exercising authority but forgetting that they too are under authority. Again, a mark of weakness is that there is no parochial sense of ministry. A congregational atmosphere pervades. And there is no awe-ful sense of divine action because there is a weak sense of history, continuity and tradition.

So de Blank commended episcopacy by his 'high' doctrine of the Church. And it was attractive.

de Blank wanted the clergy to know that their work was appreciated. He did this by personal visits of encouragement. He wanted the rural deanery to mean more so groups of clergy were encouraged to meet more often. The physical and spiritual isolation of clergy worried him. 'No one ought to be left on his own in a down-town parish. . . . The boundary walls that separate his parish from his neighbours' create a private world where he plans a programme designed to provide for his parishioners and his parishioners only.' He advocated the grouping of churches with a team of priests serving a number of worshipping centres but united as a working team. 'But this is not all. In a parish with several priests, it becomes possible to enlist specialists who can cover the different needs of the parish more adequately than can the single-handed priest who has to be a general "know-all"!' He saw each team of priests comprising men of different specialist training and skills. In his vision of the re-organised Church, de

Blank saw the importance of 'the neighbourhood church, within the area of the larger parish ... standing half-way between the house church and the parish church. The neighbourhood priest's work will lie largely within the homes and "secular" activities of his area. His aim will not be primarily to run a series of organizations for varying age groups, because his work is much more the training of his lay leaders, the guidance of vocational groups, and personal contact with the non-church-goer. A large proportion of the religious sevices he conducts will take place in the houses of the people, and he will spend more time outside the church building than inside it. He will be found most frequently in those places where the people gather — the "pubs" and the clubs, the factories and the market-place, the shopping and entertainment centres, and the political and social organizations. As a result, and to his great relief, the kind of headquarters he needs will be very different from the average church-cum-hall-cum-parsonage. I suggest he needs a building erected on the lines of a modern house with the following provisions. On the ground floor (as the most important room in the house) there will be a well-appointed and beautifully furnished chapel. Here the daily services will be held, and here, for many, the Blessed Sacrament will be reserved. When required it should be possible to open up the chapel to include the other ground floor room, enabling services to be held for fifty or sixty or even more. When this extra area is not in use as part of the chapel, it is available for meetings as required. The first floor should provide the living accommodation for the neighbourhood priest (and his family), while on the second floor there ought to be enough room to accommodate two other church workers — preferably a junior priest and, perhaps, a woman worker. Space needs also to be found for a housekeeper. A fair stretch of land should be kept around the house so as to allow for any possible developments in the future. Such a house could be built quite easily out of the money received for the old church buildings. It is designed to meet the real needs of the contemporary situation and it is economical to run.

'With such a scheme the district would have at its centre the old mother church, with as good and up-to-date a provision of modern buildings for all club purposes as possible. The incumbent would have the staff of the parish church near at hand, either in the parsonage or in some other suitable house. Included in the parish there might be as many as four or five neighbourhood churches each, ideally, with its staff of three, and the staff of each neighbourhood church, together with the staff of the mother church, would constitute the parish team under the incumbent.

'Such a revolution cannot be completed overnight ...'

These words were written in 1954 as *Episcopal Postscript* to *The Parish in Action*. Thirty years later the church is faced with an identical but more critical challenge and de Blank's vision repays another examination.

In order to show what he thought of East End clergy, de Blank threw a Christmas party in the Grocers' Hall in the City for his clergy and their families. It was a magnificent occasion. Warm-hearted gaiety and fun permeated everyone who attended — perhaps six hundred in all. The Bishop of London was there but so were celebrities such as actresses Margaret Leighton and Athene Seyler, Admiral of the Fleet Sir John Cunningham, Sir Henry Vaisey, the Lord Mayor of London, Sir Rupert de la Bere, T.V. cook Philip Harben, flyweight champion Terry Allen, radio announcer Alvar Lidell, actor David Tomlinson, cricketer twins Alec and Eric Bedser, author and commentator E.W. Swanton, England's rugger captain, N.M. Hall. The Rural Deans of Poplar, Stepney, and Bethnal Green put on false noses, spectacles and cowboy hats to become Father Christmases who had a present for everyone. Naturally the occasion was widely reported.

Here we see de Blank the entrepreneur and showman. He loved giving parties. There was a deeper aspect to them too. Edward Carpenter, until recently Dean of Westminster, who knew de Blank over a long period and who saw him at close quarters in the last period of his life at Westminster, reflects perceptively: 'I always felt in an odd way that parties were in some respects essential to Joost. He naturally tended to withdraw very often, and a party and the social obligations of a party if he was running it, tended to bring him out. He found it easier to relax with a lot of people. This was probably due to the fact that he was extremely sensitive; his basic response to living was probably artistic and certain kinds of relationships invade the territory of the self whereas you can be more protected in a curious way in a crowd.'

This suggests that de Blank kept personal relationships at a distance. Canon A. J. Morcom, one time chaplain to Bishop Wand and Archdeacon of Middlesex, considered de Blank attractive, charming and excellent company: 'but I should be very surprised if he formed any deep personal friendships. It was a measure of his foreigness that his family circle were the only people to be admitted to his fullest confidence ... He was a very complex character, perhaps due partly to the fact that he was only a first generation Englishman.'

Into this 'family circle' de Blank introduced one or two other people such as Alan Buchanan (later Archbishop of Dublin) and 'Peter' Priest whom he quickly persuaded to leave Dover for the Isle of Dogs. But even then there were limits to how much of himself he would reveal to others.

Becoming a bishop helped de Blank to realise to the full one large part of his nature, the public dimension, whilst neglecting some aspects of the interior life. That is a difficulty facing many bishops who are expected to stoke the spiritual fires of their clergy, which de Blank did in full and generous measure, but who are in danger of neglecting their own. Bishops should make an annual retreat and have a wise friend who can tell them frankly 'where to get off'.

de Blank was determined to make an impact on the East End. He wanted the Church in that place to see that as bishop he was a focus of unity. He altered the way in which people outside the Church thought of a bishop. That was done by frequent broadcasts and television appearances and particularly through his weekly column, 'The Bishop's Saturday Topic' in the London *Star*. These were evangelistic opportunities which he used to the full, often speaking and writing on topical events but always challenging people, presenting the Church as a living and virile entity, worth joining.

In the Church he showed that ideally the bishop is the President of the Eucharist. Too often he is merely a part of the finale, brought on at the end to give a blessing just before the final curtain. This is wrong. de Blank as bishop was a curtain raiser.

de Blank certainly had presence and this presence was quickly seen and felt. He instituted a whirlwind Lent Progress in which he moved through his area, spending about a week in each deanery. He shared in the activities of the parishes. A day may start at six thirty with sixty people at Holy Communion and then a punishing programme of visits to meet people at work in factory, school, hospital and at home. He shared in Sunday School preparation classes, study circles, discussion groups and parochial church meetings. There were addresses and sermons to give and ten Confirmation Services. These Lent Progresses were morale boosters and bound bishop, clergy and laity in a bond of confidence and affection.

Children's Pilgrimage at St. Paul's Cathedral, October 1954.

Yet de Blank felt that something more was needed, something dramatic. The East London Church Congress in 1954 was the . result. With a Congress committee bold plans were laid. The motif of the Congress was, 'The Church Rebuilds' and the badge showed the sun rising behind the spire of Shoreditch church. There was the imaginative touch as de Blank reminded people that · the sun rises in the east. In the autumn of 1953 the Bishop's Heralds were enrolled (six lay people from each parish) to act as liaison officers. The Congress lasted from 31 May until 4 June 1954. Exhibitions, a souvenir newspaper *Contact*, a Congress hymn, receptions, meetings, musical items, lectures, brains trusts, were amongst the varied fare. For what purpose? 'The object is quite simply to capture the imagination of the East Londoner, for practical action follows awaked imagination.' Five thousand people in Shoreditch churchyard at the closing service of the Congress pledged themselves to be builders of Christ's Church.

The lasting effects of the Congress and other imaginative endeavours associated with de Blank at Stepney are not easy to assess. But the immediate impact was very great.

de Blank's flair for publicity and propaganda developed further at Stepney. The title of his occasional newsletter *In Step* was indicative of this. There was something special to follow. He gathered round him expert typographers, writers and artists and together they produced a magazine called *Cockaigne, The Bishop of Stepney's Quarterly*. This beautifully designed, printed, and well-written and illustrated periodical was distinctly non-establishment.

In 1955 the Suffragan Bishopric of Stepney celebrated its Diamond Jubilee. There was an attractively published account of sixty years' history written by Fleet Street journalist George Rowles who had been the lay editor of the *Greenhill Challenge*. The real celebration was held in St. Paul's Cathedral on 17 June 1955, which was also Bishop Wand's farewell to the people of East London. Thousands packed every corner of St. Paul's. There were fanfares and banners — and devotion. Always the Church triumphant under de Blank, never the Church quiescent.

Yet the Church and its bishops cannot be saved by processions. The church building should not be a place where reality loses its sting on the way through the door, a place where the 'sacrament of disengagement' is celebrated. People should take with them through the door their imperishable problems and nattering neuroses and, equally important, their overwhelming joys, gaiety and happiness. Bishops too! There is a man under every mitre with his own problems, needs and temptations. Where does he get his strength? Clearly from God — but also he should be sustained and supported by others. At Stepney, de Blank's spiritual life did not suffer by endless activity. He had a strong prayer life. There were always family prayers with his mother. In his house at Islington there was a little chapel occupying a small room on the second floor close to his bedroom. He wrote: 'To enter the chapel is not to escape from the world (the row of London's traffic is clearly heard) but it is to see things in their right perspective; it ensures that the demands of the moment do not crowd out the still small voice of God.' Sometimes he would take his car to Victoria Park and there at four thirty in the morning he would say his prayers. He once said: 'The awful thing is that no one ever sees a bishop praying'. He always arrived early for church services in order to pray. When he wrote to a large number of bishops suggesting a retreat together he was horrified how few replied and how even fewer were prepared to join such a retreat.

A popular book at this period was *Saints at Sixty Miles an Hour* (1955) which was reprinted many times. It was written at odd moments — in buses, cars or trains — as he rushed from one appointment to another. In it he shared his search for the 'calm centre at the heart of the whirlpool'. In short, sharp chapters he developed a theme on the significance and influence of bodily postures — the joined hands, the bended knee, the closed eyes, the bowed head. The habit of consciously assuming this posture and of associating it with the act of prayer, will of itself direct our minds and thoughts. So, too, can the use of hallowed words and phrases, the Lord's Prayer of course and the sign of the cross, 'the quickest of all prayers'. Observations upon the discipline of the body, the use of silence, the sacramental value of daily work, problems of old age and youth and the mystery of ill-health and physical hardship were included. The purpose of prayer is to follow St. Augustine's great injunction, 'Become what you are'. de Blank offered his reflections and help to those who were tired or preoccupied: 'Both preoccupation and fatigue may be diagnosed as part of the spiritual malaise of the nineteen-fifties. Both are often due to our living at too fast a pace'. Do not bewail the pace and the fatigue, 'but try to deal with them in the light of our spiritual necessity and hunger'.

de Blank's 'sixty miles an hour' pace never slackened. There was rarely anything but sparkle. A few clergy found him overwhelming, but that was usually a rebuke to their own inactivity. But he could be daunting.

The late Mark Hodson was Rector of Poplar and had known de Blank at the time of the Mission to London and had a memory of a clergy convention. 'The clergy were divided into groups and their findings were brought to George Ingle, Joost and myself. Each of us had several group reports to summarise so that at the end there should be only three reports. I shall never forget the last session. Ingle and I tried faithfully to do our best with the material we received. Joost just did not try. Brilliantly and naughtily, for some conservative evangelicals were a trifle offended, he took the book of Job, which we had been reading at the Services at the Convention, and applied it to our situation: likening the Bishop [Wand] to Job and, I fancy, we three Summarizers to Job's comforters, he kept us in hilarious mirth for some minutes. The crowning piece of information was that although the Mission might be likely to leave the Bishop with the extra thousand she asses, he could not vouch for anything else. It was tremendous fun, but I remember feeling a little put out because Ingle and I looked such dull dogs. And of course we were compared with Joost.

'This in some ways is a typical story. How he loved to make people laugh. And he enjoyed being a little shocking too. Of a story at the Diocesan Conference a lively Rural Dean said to me, "I say, that would be all right for the Young Farmers, but in Church House . . .!"'

The majority of clergy grew to have a great admiration and affection for de Blank — love would not be the word to use.

London's East End has known some wonderful priests. A few remained of the calibre of H.A. Wilson and St. J.B. Groser, and there were newer men such as Maurice Wood, Edwyn Young, Mark Hodson. Some of the evangelical clergy of Islington were not happy with what they saw as de Blank's inclinations for 'smells and bells' in the Anglo-Catholic parishes of the East End — of which there were many. Most of the lively parishes knew incense when they smelled it and some of the hard-working priests in very difficult areas were accustomed to 'vesture and gesture'. de Blank felt he must ally himself with them.

He also identified with the area. The East End had changed after the devastation of war. 'An age builds cities; an hour destroys them,' said Seneca. The War had turned the rhetoric into reality. Many East Enders had been evacuated during the War and did not return. Before the War, tightly knit communities were a feature of the East End. Street life was strong and neighbourliness was natural. The people who cared were not people from a welfare agency who were paid to care but the people next door.

After the War waste spaces were transformed in fits and starts, by over-powering mammoths of steel and concrete. Buildings were beginning to take the place of people. Life was better for the East Ender in material terms but there was a cost common to most flat-ridden areas. Rootlessness had been born, a sense of belong-ing died. As de Blank visited his one hundred and twenty parishes he felt strongly that there was needed an architecture for the age and not one dictated by developers who were coining money as fast as they could. Through the co-operation of architects, designers, painters and sculptors skilled in the expressive nature of forms, a wealth of new architectural devices, colour and textural values could be brought into play. Every building should be expressive, not just by its material and structural principles but by the nature of the life it served. de Blank often discussed these matters with his acquaintances and had he stayed longer in Stepney would have acted as catalyst in bringing people and ideas together.

Identifying with the area and the people did not mean a patron-ising approach. A bishop is called to lead and to serve and de Blank would say in that order! Leading *was* serving.

A leader must be recognised. Although he wore gaiters occasionally, and suit and purple stock often, he was mostly con-spicuous in his purple cassock. He was regarded as having the 'common touch' which is strange in a man not always easy of approach. It was necessary for him to make the first move. When he did, the encounter was almost always beneficial, even memor-able. Walking into a public house and talking at the bar with a glass of beer in his hand was not a natural action for him, but it was worthwhile. Talking with passers-by at a street corner took effort, but the conversation was remembered. Visiting local street markets was not his natural shopping milieu (the West End was!) but he made some good contacts by so doing.

So the people got to know 'our Bishop' and listened to him with rapport and respect. There was a nice touch to his articles in the *Star*. He always ended them with the words 'Good Night is God's Night. God bless you and yours.' It seemed appropriate and was appreciated.

Through the *Star*, sermons, speeches and broadcasting, his views on a range of topics became well-known. He caused a furore with his strong criticism of the Lord Chief Justice (Lord Goddard) who advocated the return of flogging as a deterrent for crimes of violence 'as enthusiastically as any official of a Victorian charity school'. Strangely he criticised the setting up of the Nuremburg War Trials which, he said, was 'revenge dressed up in a form of justice.' Young people found in him a champion of their sense of

71

adventure (for this was before the word 'boredom' entered the twenty four hour vocabulary). His views on moral issues were on the whole traditionally held if freshly expressed. He welcomed television religion but pleaded for a dramatic presentation. 'Let us see a missionary hospital in action as we pray for the missionary work of the Church. Let us see a few feet of film of an international conference in session as we pray for peace. For the same reason I do not care much for long sermons on television. We have the vision and we should use it. Far better have a ballet of The Prodigal Son, say, or a one-act play which we can watch, than a sermon where, while we can listen, there is nothing to do but to look at the preacher's face.'

de Blank was a campaigner for the abolition of the death penalty. 'The sanctity of human life is an essential element of religious faith, as it is of any civilized community. And though wars may still have to be fought, men are then killed because the rule of law has been denied, not because it has been observed. Let the man convicted of a capital crime be prepared for final judgement even if years of remedial imprisonment be involved. If we dispatch him into eternity unprepared, our crime is at least as grave as his.'

And whilst the death penalty remained in force de Blank had the priestly duty of helping prepare more than one person for that journey. He wrote of a prison confirmation (published in *Cockaigne* and *Church Times*). '[Recently] I confirmed two men sentenced for a capital offence. During those last few weeks the chaplain ministered to them, each one separately of course. They asked to be confirmed; both made their confession, and the Rite of Confirmation was administered. As the Moffat translation has it, with reference to St. Peter's imprisonment, ''A light shone in the cell,'' so with these men in their extremity. The Light of the world shone in their darkness and showed them the way across the last river. From one I received this letter which I append, with great hesitancy, because every word is sacred. Perhaps you will read it on your knees — if not the first time, then certainly as you read it through again. ''Stranger, tread softly. For the contrite Jesus bled''.

'''Dear Bishop, The Chaplain tells me that you will be praying for me. I have been told that there is no reprieve for me. I am not sorry that it is like this. I would like you to know that I have found great peace and comfort since my confirmation and confession; and I make my Communion daily now. I am sorry I did not always see things like this, but I know it is never too late to begin. I thought you would like to know this. Yours sincerely ..." Requiescant in pace.'

de Blank also visited Ruth Ellis in Holloway Prison as she was awaiting execution. Afterwards he exclaimed that he 'was horrified and aghast beyond words to find that Holloway prisoners could hear hammering going on as a scaffold was being built.'

An East London churchwarden writes: 'The coming of Bishop Joost de Blank to the Stepney area jolted us into life — we rallied to his call and it was an exciting time for the Church.' There was something of the business tycoon about de Blank in the way he organised conventions, congresses and rallies with flair and flourish — perhaps an entrepreneur for God is the correct phrase. He may have been a populist but not at the expense of the Gospel.

He had grown to appreciate, even favour, the outward trappings of Anglo-Catholicism. That was not surprising as he had moved in that direction and the flamboyant side of his nature was attracted to and assuaged by dignified symbolic ceremonial. But he had absorbed the deeper side too which included sacramental Confession. Nevertheless he never lost from his Evangelical background the importance of the preaching of the Gospel. He had arrived in Stepney as a young bishop of forty three years with a personal mission to stir up the Church in that place. He asked Patrick Appleford, then a curate at All Saints, Poplar, to write a hymn for the Congress, the first verse of which was:

> Christ our King in glory reigning,
> All our strength from Thee proceeds.
> Born of Mary, not disdaining
> Work or pain to share our needs.
> Thou Who conquered sin's infection,
> Guiltless victim for us killed,
> By Thy mighty resurrection,
> Christ, in us Thy Church rebuild.

And de Blank never thought of the Church in the abstract but always as individual people making up the Body of Christ. To them he commended a personal faith not a second hand one. And the emphasis was always on *faith* — in the end faith! He showed he had turned his back completely on his earlier blind acceptance of the literalism of the bible when he said: 'Personally I am convinced that God would sooner have an intellectually honest atheist or agnostic than an intellectually dishonest believer.

73

Tennyson was right when he wrote: "There lives more faith in honest doubt/ Believe me, than in half the creeds."'' From these words it must not be thought that de Blank had intellectual doubts or at least not at this time of his life. His doubts came in a more agonising form much later. At Stepney he presented the firm faith which was his own. Then certitude was the true note of discipleship, not uncertainty, speculation and misgiving, which was beginning to stir in some quarters of the Church of England.

In the Church's relation to society he did not stress the Church as an ambulance or Good Samaritan deploying its forces and resources to allay or mitigate the ills of society. He stressed the Church as a fire engine. In short he saw the Church's task as not limited to those who had been burnt or wounded. It also existed to put the fire out. Not only did it minister to the injured traveller on the Jericho to Jerusalem road; it also worked for the provision of a proper police control along the whole length of that dangerous journey, so that bands of robbers would in the future no longer dare to show their faces there. This gave a sharpness and directness to some of de Blank's moral pronouncements.

de Blank's great gift of lucid directness in contrast to the fluent incoherence of some of his contemporaries made him a compelling Mission speaker. In 1953 he took part in the Mission to the University of Oxford at which the then Bishop of Durham (Michael Ramsey) was the chief speaker. In 1955, advertised as 'one of the most dynamic personalities in the Church of England', de Blank conducted a seven day Teaching Mission in Glasgow. His talks were subsequently published — *Members of Christ*.

Another book of the period was *Is it Nothing to You?* (1953 — dedicated to his father). It was a meditation for Good Friday on the Seven Words from the Cross, as if by the centurion at the crucifixion who traditionally became a Christian martyr. He caught his audience by adopting an unusual approach to his subject and whom he caught he taught.

de Blank had fanned the smouldering embers of Stepney into flame. And the sparks and brightness were seen all over the Church of England. It was inevitable that the Church would want to use one of its brightest sparks in wider service.

CHAPTER SEVEN

Buoyant Anglican

In 1954 de Blank seemed to have established himself as a stirring exponent and defender of Anglicanism. He was more Anglican than just Church of England. He had travelled a long way from his Calvinist roots and fundamentalist upbringing, although psychological aspects remained. The fervent Groupist had given way to the buoyant Anglican. What was it that appealed to him?

Anglicanism was and is at its best Catholic, for it holds the Catholic essentials. It is Protestant because it rejects the papal innovations in faith and order. It is traditional, for it looks back to the past for the body of its creed, for the great facts of the Christian revelation on which it is based, and to the great march of the Church's history, from which it draws its precedents. At the same time it is modern, for it seeks ever to make this creed and these facts tell with force in the minds of this modern age.

And, important for de Blank, it is a *worldwide* Church. The international stage suited him. He did much to propagate Anglicanism and Anglicanism did much for him.

If there is one person from whom de Blank caught the glorious vision of Anglicanism it was his own diocesan bishop, Bishop Wand of London, one of the great Anglicans of this century. It was Bishop Wand who ensured that de Blank would be one of the Church of England delegates to the first Anglican Congress held at Minneapolis, Minnesota, from 4-13 August 1954. It was de Blank's first trip to America and he sailed on the Queen Mary. Of all places in the world, America became his second home. On 26 July he had his first sight of New York.

... through the mist the Statue of Liberty (our steward pointed out feelingly that it was pointing to England!) It is the most hideous statue I have ever seen, but of course tremendously exciting to see it — bright green from the oxydized copper I'm told. Then,

Manhattan Island. Cecil Beaton has said that this is the finest man made view in the world. And it is absolutely breathtaking in its beauty. The skyscrapers seem to stand shoulder to shoulder and from this distance it is hard to believe that the sun can ever reach down to the streets. It is a forest of concrete trees and turrets of different heights and various colours, red as well as grey. Nothing but a picture can convey its magnificence.

This was his diary entry. From that moment he was captured and enslaved by America. Perhaps it was the feeling of size, larger than life, that first captivated him. Then there were the people. Their outgoing manner and overt friendliness appealed to him. Perhaps they seemed larger than life too. Certainly that was true of Russell R. Brown, President of the American Distilling Company, who adopted bishops — taking them under his wing and lavishing his generous hospitality on them. de Blank was a favourite. And how he loved the grand treatment!

27 July 1954

Then to the Distilling Office where the largest and longest and newest Cadillac in the world was waiting to drive the Bp. of Bath and Wells (H.W. Bradfield) and myself around New York and Manhattan Island. . . . went to Voisin for dinner, one of New York's smartest restaurants. . . . walked along Broadway and saw such a display of lights as to make Piccadilly Circus look dowdy . . .

28 July

To lunch with Russell Brown at '21' now a very smart restaurant but during Prohibition the most famous 'speakeasy' in New York. They have an electric lift from the basement into the ground floor where the drinks used to be kept and sold — only possible then because the authorities got a rake off. My host was then in the Alcohol Control Dept. so knows a good deal about it .. and so to Russell Brown's house. It is no use trying to explain it. This new one has been finished only just over a year and stands in 23 acres. It is rather a millionaire's labour saving dream. As you approach the garage the lights go on and the doors swing open by themselves. When you drive out of the garage the doors shut behind you . . . [after a description] . . . the whole [cost] must be unbelievable. But that's the odd thing about Americans — their standards are so different that they don't know what we mean by extravagance.

The following day Russell Brown was server to de Blank at an early morning Celebration. The extravagance and the humility were

76

one. That was Russell Brown. de Blank liked this genuine business tycoon.

30 July

[Russell Brown] is a most interesting character — has little opinion of Eisenhower who, he says, can never make up his own mind & is really not much good. He has little opinion of Chicago either, which he says is still a corrupt city politically. He told us that his annual income from the firm was 80,000 dollars. But he said he only took that for book-keeping reasons; otherwise with taxation it would not be worth taking. He does most of his business by telephone and the telephone interrupts every conversation again & again. This morning he discussed with a visitor the purchase of a large New York hotel, but the sellers had put the price up by a million dollars and so he was not interested! A little later he was rung up from Wall Street who had wind of the deal. Then someone rang up about 100,000 cases of whisky for Korea! Every day about 4 p.m. he rings up his representatives all over the States to hear what's happening. 'What's new?', as he says over the phone. And yet during all this business, he will be talking about Bishop This and Bishop That, & will be arranging reservations & so on & so on. He is the most fascinating and kind person, and nothing is too much trouble.

Is this the kind of person in the ecclesiastical sphere de Blank would have liked to be? He was always attracted to and by people who had the power to make decisions — and who did not flinch from making them.

31 July

To Chicago by plane. We were met by local worthies & clergy and we had our pictures taken again & again. Then in three motorcars in procession with headlights on to indicate it was a procession we roared the 20 miles into Chicago with a police escort on motorcycles blaring their fiendish sirens — & everything stopping for us as at 60 miles an hour we went in triumph to the City. This police escort & all the public welcome — TV & all — has been done to outwit the Roman Cardinal who has rather held the city in his hand so far as religion is concerned.

de Blank clearly revelled in this treatment. It was the excitement of a child.

His diary is full of graphic descriptions of people met, places visited, miles travelled, food eaten, films and plays seen. The un-relieved pace suited him. Yet it was the wonderment of a child —

so delighted at staying in an hotel with his own private bathroom; hardly believing his eyes at the sumptuous fare in restaurants; marvelling at being invited back stage. de Blank had a taste for simplicity and refinement. He never over-indulged himself even if some of his companions did so. It was a strange mixture. He enjoyed the deference shown to him (and he was only a suffragan bishop) yet tried to convince himself it was for the Office not the man. But the man predominated. There were times when he prayed for humility. He may have jested with a friend, 'Lord, I am not high-minded: I have no proud looks' but the enemy, 'pride', kept emerging.

Before attending the Minneapolis Congress, de Blank went to the Anglo-Catholic Congress in Chicago, where the twin high-lights were an Address by the Bishop of London and a Congress Mass attended by six thousand people.

Of the Minneapolis Congress he wrote an impressive if 'informal' (his word) account entitled *Mighty River*. The account conveys a feeling of exhilaration at being a member of the Universal Church. Of the opening service he writes: 'For a moment the Church Militant was expressing the unity and victory of the Church Triumphant as the delegates passed the last seats in the auditorium making a total congregation of 10,000 people ...'

And in similar vein: 'In Minneapolis we were united with the saints, the martyrs, the doctors and confessors — one with those who in Christ's Church in every age have worshipped the God of their salvation.'

The feeling of elation and excitement is well captured in this passage: 'But now the "Anglican Mississippi" was in full flood. In a picture more appropriate to the Egyptian Nile, it was overflow-ing its banks to bring the water of life to parched and arid areas, both here in America and throughout the world. It was as if the button that released this tremendous hydro-electric power was pressed on this opening evening. To one observer it brought an echo of the Day of Pentecost, when, overcoming the differences of language and custom, men heard — and experienced — in their own tongues the wonderful works of God.'

The Congress said nothing significantly new on basic issues but it was 'good to state publicly that the Church, by its obedience bound, can recognize no barrier of colour or of race and that the Gospel of the Incarnation demands an involvement, at least responsibly and perhaps directly in the civic and political hurly-burly of modern life.' This reference to the Incarnation with its implications for practical living is interesting as it formed the basis of de Blank's attack on Apartheid.

Those at the Congress were reminded, 'that the proclamation of the Gospel is falsified if the Church fails to stress the need for social justice in all walks of life and for fair dealing between peoples'. In a few years' time de Blank was to use this very point in warning the South African Premier, Dr. Verwoerd, that the continued existence of Christianity on the Continent of Africa was being jeopardised by the policies of his Government. This is to anticipate!

The following observations of de Blank are significant: 'Although this was not the kind of gathering which forwarded resolutions to governments, nevertheless everyone present came to recognise the Church's right and obligation to enunciate those Christian principles on which alone a stable and developing society can be built ... In the strength of their global fellowship men and women went back determined that their Church should move from defence to attack in the triumphant assurance that the Salvation wrought by Christ would honour their obedience here and bring men to find victory in the life to come.'

The relationship between Church and State, especially when the latter is felt to have acted contrary to the law of God was strongly outlined at Minneapolis: 'When the State denies or rejects the Sovereignty of God, its power becomes a menace to God's order and it then becomes the duty of the Church to affirm the rule of God. We deny that the individual exists for the State, but assert that one of the principle ends of the State is the development of personality, which requires man's freedom under God ... The Church at all times and in all places should be a fearless witness against political, social and economic injustice.'

Of the Congress delegates, de Blank did not rate very highly the American bishops who, '*en masse* behave more like a meeting of successful business men than the successors of the Apostles. Indeed I get quite puritanical out here — the Church is too comfortable & too prosperous & too efficient — & somehow spirituality is not much in evidence.' (Diary entry.) He was constant in admiring the American people yet being critical of some aspects of Episcopal Church life — but not so critical as not to feel at home in it. Later, a number of American bishops became his good friends.

At the Congress the Bishop of London's Address was, by

general acclaim, the most outstanding as, indeed, it had been previously in Chicago. *The Position of the Anglican Communion in History and Doctrine* was his subject. It was strong meat, claiming that the Anglican Church was positively and definitely nearer to the heart of the New Testament, and therefore, to the truth, than any other Christian communion. The Anglican way was not one among many equally satisfactory by-roads to the heavenly city, but was indeed the high road of salvation. Other Christian ways had their merits, their graces, and their saints. None had so rich a treasure, so full a truth as this. In 1954 it was possible to say this and receive the acclamation of the crowd. de Blank cheered. He was also much impressed by the Bishop of Johannesburg (Ambrose Reeves) speaking on *The Church and the Family* and he had private discussions on Reeves' 'difficulties in South Africa — a country with the racial policies of which America is now very impatient, even though segregation is only just coming to an end here'.

He was flattered when the Bishop of Sheffield (Leslie Hunter), speaking on *A Church in Action* referred to a certain success story of *A Parish in Action* 'in a newly built urban area on the outskirts of London'!

Immediately after Minneapolis, de Blank travelled to Evanston for the second Assembly of the World Council of Churches under the general theme, 'Christ the Hope of the World'. It was an anti-climax.

18 August 1954

... The more I see of the World Council the more I liked Minneapolis. The ecumenical movement survives better if you don't see too much of the separated brethren i.e. in the abstract rather than in the concrete. They are so remote and heavy and lack understanding.

This cynicism is not typical of de Blank. Indeed it is at variance with what seems a genuine desire to bring all Christians together, more in the concrete than the abstract. Perhaps the comment should be interpreted in the light of the frustration he felt in having, as part of a minority group, to come to an accommodation with people whose views differed so much from his own after the elation and euphoria of Minneapolis where all the delegates spoke substantially with the same voice.

What was also frustrating for de Blank was that the deliberations at Evanston seemed so removed from life. Extracts from his diary indicate his feelings:

16 August

Here we seem to have so many professional theologians from Germany and elsewhere who love talking stuff so involved and so removed from daily life.

23 August

We are a little impatient with the remote and abstract theology of some of the Continental Protestants and the Anglican and Orthodox Church delegates are not altogether happy about things.

26 August

. . . The general sense of frustration is growing. I think most feel that there has been much too much on the periphery and too many public assemblies in a kind of ecumenical circus.

The above sheds further light on why de Blank compared Evanston unfavourably with Minneapolis. At the Anglican Congress the accent fell on the practical implications of Christianity whereas at Evanston he thought undue and unnecessary attention was given to sterile theological debate.

27 August

We need more laymen & anyway working parsons who want practical action in small doses rather than a ton of theory which few understand and which divides those few.

de Blank, the bishop in action, was a practical man and thought the scandal of the Churches' 'unhappy divisions' could be solved in practical terms more easily than exploring the accumulated growth of centuries of misunderstanding and divided convictions. At Minneapolis there was the focus of unity in the occupant of St. Augustine's Chair. At Evanston there was not even a common table at which participants could share Holy Communion. There had been controversial topics at the first Congress but now at the second Assembly the divisions as deep as the Grand Canyon surfaced. On race relations in South Africa de Blank heard the liberal Alan Paton, author of *Cry the Beloved Country* and Dr. Ben Marais of the Dutch Reformed Church; the well-fed delegates from the West were faced with the poor and hungry from the East; the advancing materialism of some countries was challenged by the quiet but powerful spirituality of some Indian speakers; a few participants from behind the Iron Curtain found themselves defending some of their countries' policies in comparison with tyrannies of a different colour in other parts of the world.

It was de Blank's first experience of this kind of conflict, even confrontation. He found himself ill at ease with the overdose of Lutheran and Barthian theology, which he did not wholly comprehend. He was impatient with the intricacies of theological debate and with those who seemed to chase paper schemes for uniting churches. At this stage of his life problems were there to be solved. He had yet to be faced with seemingly insoluble problems. The aspect of Evanston which he disliked most was the democratic process. To his mind the Church was not a society for discovering the truth by a show of hands, but the Body of Christ through which the unalterable truth was proclaimed. The lust for unanimity at Evanston's end masked disagreement which had punctuated most of the debates and sessions. He was reinforced in his conviction that the Anglican Church had a special part to play in bringing about the union of Christendom and he was determined to explore practical 'possibilites' on his return to England. This first visit to America was 'a very, very wonderful experience'.

In 1955 the Archbishops of Canterbury (Geoffrey Fisher) and York (Cyril Garbett) had issued *A Short Guide to the Duties of Church Membership*. de Blank was invited to write a book expanding the Archbishops' list. The result was *Call of Duty: Church Membership Considered* (1956) dedicated to his Anglican mentor Johanni Gulielmo Carolo Wand. Bishop Wand would have appreciated the Latin dedication. It was a successful attempt to infuse depth and reality into the diffused Christianity that infected too many of those who described themselves as Church of England. Churchmanship was presented as an adventure of faith, discipline and love. 'People actuated by duty untouched by love have not yet drunk the new wine of the Gospel'. The reader was invited to 'discover what it means to live as the people of God, corporately as the Church, individually as His disciples'.

de Blank challenged the Church to take up 'action stations' as he surveyed in turn the call to discipline; to witness; to devotion; to service to Church, neighbour and community; to sacrificial giving of money to the Christian cause; to loyalty, with special reference to marriage; and to compassion for children, the elderly and those afflicted or distressed.

There was nothing new, not even profound, in what he wrote: simply a vigorous, straightforward and optimistic commentary on the Archbishops' list of duties. The Archbishop of Canterbury wrote a foreword to the book.

It may have been over-enthusiastically and over-optimistically written. The mid nineteen-fifties were bringing to the fore and near to the helm some radical thinkers in the Church of England. The institutional Church was being criticised from within. de Blank, the buoyant Anglican, was always and everywhere a champion of the Church.

By now the Bishop of Stepney was one of the most popular speakers the Church had amongst its purple ranks. As a speaker he used occasional gestures, weighted pauses and changed intonation. Above all there was an intensity, a searching sincerity, a disinfectant irony at times of voice and manner — in brief that elusive quality of 'personality' which is the secret of power alike in churches, parliaments and theatres.

What was the next step for this whirlwind bishop? Many people, not only admirers, hoped that he would succeed to the See of London when Bishop Wand retired in 1955. An earlier Bishop of Stepney, A.F. Winnington-Ingram, did just that. It was what de Blank himself most wanted. There is a diary note of 6 January 1956:

> Announced yesterday that Henry Guildford [Henry Montgomery Campbell, Bishop of Guildford] is coming to London. That is far & away the best possible choice.
>
> Unfortunately a few papers comment on his age [68] & say his is a caretaker régime until Stepney takes over. Lord Thy will be done.

It was not, 'the best possible choice'. Despite the diary entry, de Blank was disappointed. So were other people. The late Lakdasa de Mel, Metropolitan of India, Pakistan, Burma and Ceylon, had met de Blank at Minneapolis and later noted: 'Here was a man who had a vision for the Church of England in a new era. I was prepared to like him and noted his quick wit, humour and sharp intelligence. Being of strong character he was the kind of person who could rouse feelings among the less gifted!

'Then came Bishop Wand's resignation from London and our disappointment that the Bishop of Stepney had not been translated. There was the rather unworthy crack by some wag: ''Joost as I am, without a See'', which failed to amuse me.'

The Stepney years continued in full flight. Bishop Wand later wrote: 'The really significant thing about him [was] that he was an unexpectedly *vital* person, a really invigorating force. He lifted the Church in the East End out of the weariness and apathy left by the appalling war effort and placed it for a time on the crest of a new wave of enterprise. (If he had been in business he would have been a real tycoon, the builder of a financial empire.)

'I don't think anyone would have suspected this dynamism on a more casual acquaintance. I don't know where it came from. He took immense pains with his sermons, but I don't think eloquence alone could have done the trick. It was probably his supreme sense of vocation and his feeling that he was the instrument of a power from on high ... I am sure the *character* of Joost is the essential thing.'

In 1956 de Blank went on a preaching and speaking tour of Canada, the West Indies and America. 'I have travelled some 35,000 miles, slept in 28 beds, given and officiated at 84 services, sermons and addresses and travelled in 34 aeroplanes making 54 flights.' It was a demanding and successful trip. The newspapers were rumouring that he would be the next Archbishop of Canterbury!

Shorty after Easter in 1957 de Blank left for another extensive preaching tour in America.

Meanwhile, in Cape Town ... ...

CHAPTER EIGHT

The Dutch Archbishop

'We must not attempt to use the name of God in order to bring to fruition purposes of our own,' were the words of Geoffrey Hare Clayton, Archbishop of Cape Town, one of the Anglican Church's formidable and great archbishops. He has been described as having 'the rhetoric of Churchill, the depth of Temple, and the eyebrows of George Robey.' If two out of the three descriptions can be questioned it is nevertheless a sign of Clayton's stature that they are mentioned at all. He had what Plato said was the highest courage — the courage of the cautious. This arose directly from his conviction that the Church is not here primarily to serve society. Its prime duty is to worship God and obey Him.

Clayton had left England for South Africa in 1934 at the age of fifty to become Bishop of Johannesburg. Fourteen years later he became Archbishop of Cape Town. This fat, formidable, garrulous, tobacco addict was a pietist among activists. He usually disagreed with, even opposed, the passionate involvement of such people as Ambrose Reeves (his successor at Johannesburg), Trevor Huddleston and Michael Scott. History has yet to show whether the activists or the pragmatic pietists will achieve most in final terms for the people of South Africa.

But people like Clayton have a limit beyond which they will not go and they are capable of the most courageous action. That limit was reached when the Government intended implementing the Native Laws Amendment Bill in 1957 which threatened to deny freedom of worship in the country. The Bishops of the Church of the Province of South Africa decided to challenge the Government and four bishops met Clayton in order to draft a letter to the Prime Minister (J.G. Strijdom). The letter is a piece of history and is quoted in full for although de Blank was no party to it, it formed the immediate background to his archiepiscopate.

Dear Mr. Prime Minister,

We, Bishops of the Church of the Province of South Africa, are approaching you rather than the Minister of Native Affairs because we believe that the issues raised in clause 29 (c) of the Native Laws Amendment Bill cannot be regarded merely as Native Affairs. It appears to us that as far as the Anglican Church is concerned, churches and congregations in every urban area within the Union, even those mainly attended by Europeans, will be affected by this Clause. Further, it is our belief that the Clause raises the issue of religious freedom and more particularly that of freedom of worship, and we venture to submit that this is a wider issue than that of Native Affairs only.

We desire to state that we regard the above-mentioned Clause as an infringement of religious freedom in that it makes conditional on the permission of the Minister of Native Affairs

(a) the continuance in existence of any church or parish constituted after January 1st 1938 in an urban area except in a location which does not exclude Native Africans from public worship;

(b) the holding of any service in any church in an urban area except in a location to which a Native African would be admitted if he presented himself:

(c) the attendance of any Native African at any synod or church assembly held in an urban area outside a location.

The Church cannot recognise the right of an official of a secular government to determine whether or where a member of the Church of any race (who is not serving a sentence which restricts his freedom of movement) shall discharge his religious duty of participation in public worship or to give instructions to the minister of any congregation as to whom he shall admit to membership of that congregation.

Further, the Constitution of the Church of the Province of South Africa provided for the synodical government of the Church. In such synods, bishops, priests and laymen are represented without distinction of race or colour. Clause 29 (c) makes the holding of such synods dependent upon the permission of the Minister of Native Affairs.

We recognise the great gravity of disobedience to the law of the land. We believe that obedience to secular authority, even in matters about which we differ in opinion, is a command laid upon us by God. But we are commanded to render unto Caesar the things which be Caesar's, and to God the things that are God's. There are therefore some matters which are God's and not Caesar's, and we believe that the matters dealt with in Clause 29 (c) are among them. It is because we believe this that we feel bound to state that if the Bill were to become law in its present form we should ourselves be unable to obey it or counsel our clergy and people to do so.

We therefore appeal to you, Sir, not to put us in a position in which we have to choose between obeying our conscience and obeying the law of the land.

We have the honour to remain, Sir,

Yours faithfully,

(signed on behalf of the Bishops of the Church of the Province of South Africa)

† GEOFFREY CAPETOWN

Archbishop & Metropolitan.

Clayton signed the letter on the morning of 7 March 1957, the day after Ash Wednesday. A few hours later he collapsed and died.

On 24 and 25 April 1957 the Elective Assembly met in the Cathedral Church of St. George, Cape Town, for the purpose of electing Clayton's successor as Archbishop of the Province of South Africa and Bishop of the Diocese of Cape Town. The election required a two-thirds majority in both the House of Clergy and the House of Laity voting separately and, very important, the approval of the House of Bishops.

There are a number of observations to be made about both procedure and election. Canon John Aubrey, a priest of the diocese, who took part in the election writes about the procedure. 'If there are two outstanding candidates then it is unlikely, if the voting is honest, that either candidate will get the necessary sixty-six & two thirds per cent of the votes cast. If the field is ordinary, even after a succession of votes eliminating the complete outsiders, the voters will still have difficulty in choosing between the indifferent candidates remaining. In these circumstances, the introduction of a new name is warmly welcomed by weary electors, both clerical & lay, who, in spite of the invocation of the Holy Spirit for guidance and strength, are already worn out by the seemingly interminable speeches made by protagonists promoting the interests of their already 'chosen' successor to the episcopal or archiepiscopal See.'

This Election was unexpected. Clayton had decided to retire after Easter 1957 and had sent a formal letter of resignation to the Dean of the Province and notice to his fellow bishops. Although he had been seventy two in December 1956, the bishops had persuaded him to withdraw his resignation which they, or most of them, had hoped would settle the matter for a little time.

There was no obvious successor from within the province. One or two bishops had individual backers but rather more detractors. The bishops, with dates of accession to their Sees in brackets, were — Grahamstown, Archibald Howard Cullen (1931); Natal, Thomas George Vernon Inman (1951); St. Helena, Gilbert Price Lloyd Turner (1939); Bloemfontein, Cecil William Alderson (1951); Zululand, Eric Joseph Trapp (1947); St. John's, James Leo Schuster (1956); Pretoria, Robert Selby Taylor (1951); Lebombo, Humphrey Beevor (1952); George, John Hunter (1951); Kimberley and Kuruman, John Boys (1951); Johannesburg, Richard Ambrose Reeves (1949); Damaraland, John Dacre Vincent (1952); and Basutoland, John Arthur Arrowsmith Maund (1950).

The year was 1957. There was no black or coloured bishop in the Province. All the bishops had obtained their degrees at an English University and all had been ordained in England (although one was ordained for service overseas but not in South Africa).

There were the conflicting claims of the Diocese and the Province to consider. Some Cape Town clergy and laity wanted the reflected glory of having an archbishop for their bishop but were less prepared for the amount of archiepiscopal activity away from Cape Town that this increasingly necessitated. The diocese of Cape Town consisted of sixty eight parishes staffed by 136 clergy of whom 11 were Coloured and 4 African. This included a number of retired clergy and three retired bishops. Monks of the society of St. John the Evangelist (the Cowley Fathers) had a small Mission House in Cape Town and were in charge of some of the African work. The white and non-white communicants were about equal in number. The densely populated part of the diocese was around Cape Town, but the diocese extended east to Bredasdorp and north to include Namaqualand, four hundred miles distant.

The hierarchy of the diocese was headed by Sidney Warren Lavis who had served in Cape Town since 1898, ten years before de Blank was born! Lavis had been Coadjutor Bishop from 1931 and at the time of the election was aged eighty four and on the verge of retirement. There were three archdeacons (of whom Bishop Lavis was one) and the Dean of the Cathedral.

How could the conflicting claims of Diocese and Province be met? The persona of the archbishop had increased in weight under Clayton. Reeves of Johannesburg was the bishop most often in the news and the prickliest thorn in the Government's side, but the Church looked to its archbishop for leadership. And never was leadership needed more than now. On the first few ballots no one name captured the real interest of the Assembly. There was always the danger that someone would 'emerge' whose greatest strength — and weakness — was that no one could really object to him.

It was decided to consider further nominations. Advice had been sought from a wide range of people including the Director of the South Africa Church Institute in London (Revd. R.M. Jeffery). Suddenly the name of Joost de Blank was mentioned and proposed. It was not a name that had been talked about as a possible candidate before the Elective Assembly. Now it seemed like an act of divine intervention. Quickly, as it seemed, enthusiasm gathered as the facts were revealed. His book *The Parish in Action* was not unknown. The Bishop of Pretoria (Robert Selby Taylor) had met him in America in 1954 and remembered telling him that he ought to be in South Africa.

A number of clergy had read of his activities. His reputation as a charismatic, vital, efficient and effective Bishop of Stepney, who could both preach and administer, who was both Catholic and Evangelical, had a dramatic effect on the Assembly. He may have been educated in England but he was of Dutch descent. Might this help to bridge the gap between Briton and Boer, the Anglican and Dutch Reformed Churches? There was a feeling that the *vox populi* was the *vox Dei*. A two-thirds majority in both the House of Clergy and the House of Laity voting separately was quickly achieved and the House of Bishops just as quickly affirmed the vote.

The Cape Town 'constituents' may have been ecstatic at electing a young and vigorous man as Archbishop of Cape Town but could he be persuaded to accept? His exact whereabouts were not even known. Accordingly, two cables were sent on 25 April (1957) to de Blank c/o Russell Brown at the address of the American Distilling Company! One was from the Dean of Cape Town (Tom Savage):

Confidential. By decision of overwhelming majority of clerical and lay voters of Elective Assembly you have been elected Archbishop of Cape Town and we urge your acceptance.

The Dean of the Province (the Bishop of Grahamstown) cabled :

'Bishops of the Province cordially and unanimously approve your election and ask you to accept.'

This was a bombshell. de Blank did not even know that the Elective Assembly was meeting and had never contemplated his future outside the Church of England. He cabled Dean Savage on 25 April:

Overcome by honour Province does me. Please thank all concerned. Regret cannot take decision until after consultation on return home early in May. But apart from other considerations must warn that acceptance dependent on responsibilities undertaken and not yet discharged.

Almost his first thoughts went to his Mother. Although she (and his sister Bartha) cabled on 26 April telling him not to 'let consideration of us affect your decision', he replied ominously: 'Thousand thanks but at present feel acceptance most unlikely and we shall stick together.'

There was nothing he would do until he returned to England and discussed the matter with his family and with the Archbishop of Canterbury (Geoffrey Fisher), the Bishop of London (Henry Montgomery Campbell) and Bishop Wand. There was a letter waiting for him from the Dean of Cape Town explaining:

This is a crucial time for the Church in South Africa, and the influence of the Archbishop extends far beyond the borders of our own communion. We are very conscious of our need for wise and courageous leadership at this time, but were also mindful of the fact that we were choosing a Bishop and Father-in-God for thousands of simple people, White, Coloured and African. A great deal of prayer has been offered, both in South Africa and in England, and of the many names considered yours commended itself to us the most strongly. We became convinced that you could bring to this office the gifts that the hour demands, and would also be 'a faithful pastor who shall . . . lead us in the way of holiness'. We fully realise that we are asking you to make a grave and difficult decision, and we pray that God will uphold you and lead you to knowledge of His will.

. . . The Anglican Church is very much in the forefront of the news at present, and in the conflict between the Church and the Government, it is regarded as the most recalcitrant of the Christian bodies.

... I am sure it is right to point out to you that if you accept the Archbishopric you are likely to render yourself liable to fines and imprisonment, but I do not think this consideration will deter you.

The Bishop of London and Bishop Wand advised acceptance. The Archbishop of Canterbury who was convalescing from a severe attack of bronchitis and was out of London until 13 May, wrote two letters (each dated 4 May):

When an invitation of this sort reaches one, the question is not whether one wants to accept it or thinks one ought to. The only question is, is there any reason so compelling that I ought to say no to it, and in my own judgement unless there is some personal reason known to you I doubt whether there is anything sufficient to restrain you from accepting a task full of terrible difficulties and fears, but not for that reason to be avoided.

The Archibishop's second letter was in the nature of a post script prompted by a letter received from de Blank, informing the Archbishop of 'quite serious domestic complications', a reference to his aged mother but 'apart from this and other personal matters I shall be glad if your Grace will be kind enough to tell me whether you think it is right for me to accept this call. I have no desire to leave my work in England, but I must be prepared to go wherever the Holy Spirit leads.'
The Archbishop gave this advice:

Obviously you must take into account the particular responsibility you have for your mother, but as a general rule even such personal ties as this should not be the deciding factor. I know something of the steps by which the authorities in Cape Town have reached this conclusion. I know with what anxious care and waiting upon the Holy Spirit they have guided their steps. In my own judgment there is no way of escape for you unless there is some personal reason completely unknown to me. I think you will feel that it is your bounden duty to accept the task since the call has come to it, and I pray that whatever labours and alarms may await you in the future you will never have any reason to doubt that your decision at this moment is laid upon you by God.

de Blank knew his advisers were right. He had received an exterior call which had come as unexpectedly as the position had been unsought. To say 'No' would be to deny the action of God in the matter. It may also be selfish even if the motive of devotion to family was praiseworthy. However, his mother and sister Bartha

Mama, Joost and Bartha, Bishopscourt 1957

came to a decision that they would go with him to South Africa.
'My last resistance was shot from under me.' Although his mother
was virtually crippled with arthritis and had not been outside their
Islington home for over three years she decided to go to Cape
Town. Bartha was doing invaluable work as Secretary of the
Magistrates Association and spent much time in visiting prisoners
in Holloway, yet she decided she would go with her mother and
brother.

On 7 May 1957 de Blank cabled Dean Savage:

92

Fully conscious of my inadequacy but relying wholly on God's grace I humbly accept honour conferred on me by the Church and pledge myself to your service. *Orate Fratres Pro Nobis.*

The Archbishop of Canterbury wrote again (9 May)

Now may I pray for you all those powers of wise judgment and quiet courage which the Church in South Africa so needs in these testing days. The situation there will not alarm you — the Christian need never be *alarmed* by anything in this sinful world. And indeed the conflict stimulates. The burden we bear is *first* to know what we ought to do after the mind of our Lord and *then* to find the *right* way of doing it when there are a hundred inviting wrong ways of doing it calling to us! Again 'burden' is not the right word. It is an absorbing occupation of all our faculties and certainly you will find happiness & strength in that.

de Blank was besieged by letters, telegrams, cables and the world's press. He was going to one of the toughest jobs in the Anglican Communion. He was determined to go to South Africa with an 'open mind' on the racial problems of the country and skilfully parried 'loaded' questions put to him. The South African Press welcomed the appointment and even the Nationalists were prepared to 'wait and see'.

de Blank decided to pay a preliminary and unofficial visit to Cape Town in June and July. His diary contains a number of interesting reflections and pointers to the future.

2 June 1957

[On 'Church Clause' in new Bill] The Bishops are certain that they must act as lightning conductors and draw the fire on themselves. Therefore a Sunday or two after the thing becomes law, a pastoral letter will be read in all churches saying that the Church's ministrations must on no account be refused to any bona fide worshipper of any race or colour. In other words this is definite rebellion — telling the church not to obey the law. And a dear old man like Grahamstown [Archibald Cullen] is quite ready for the consequences.

There is nothing to stop the Government from throwing all the Bishops into prison as a result — and the Bishop of Basutoland has already been told that he must be ready to take over the Province should this take place.

But most people think the Govnmt will go slow. They have put back the segregation of Cape Town & Witwatersrand Universities — probably as a result of public pressure — and it is thought that they want to make certain to win the Election next April.

Verwoerd [as Minister for Native Affairs] has built up a tremendous empire for himself, is the strong man of the Party, & clearly means to be Prime Minister one day. But he is cordially disliked even by a great many Nationalists.

14 June

... went to call on Bishop Lavis — a truly wonderful old man with a keen sense of humour & a terrific memory. He is famous chiefly for his work among the coloured population. One of their townships is known as Bishop Lavis township & he has established a wonderful maternity home, St. Monica's.

26 June

Visit from Mr. Albert Centlivres who has just retired as Chief Justice. A great man, Chancellor of Cape Town University — & very anti-Government. He believes that ultimately the Government will come down through economic reasons — but fears that may take some time. He believes public pressure overseas may have delayed action about apartheid in the Universities which shows a line of action for the Church.

29 June

One of the astonishing things here is how low Smut's reputation has sunk — on all sides — not only the Nationalists but the liberals too. They think he was always unsound on the Native question.

30 June

Of course it is all right our complaining of apartheid but our first job is to put our own house in order. At Groot Drakenstein for example they even have separate burial grounds for the white and the coloured so that even in death they shall not lie side by side. There is a mission church in the coloured area but a previous rector had a tremendous struggle to put on a Communion Service for coloured people in the parish church. The whites objected & appealed to the Archbishop who of course maintained the Rector's right to do what he considered to be right. As a last flying shot, having been defeated, some of the white women said that as the flowers at the eight o'clock Communion were put out by the whites for the white congregation they ought to be removed before the coloured services at nine thirty. There is clearly still much too much of this attitude — but it is, thank God, beginning to die.

1 July

... on 'plane. The journey was enlivened by having the R.C.

Archbishop of Cape Town (McCann) as a fellow passenger. He is a
South African — very anti-apartheid & very co-operative. I was
impressed to hear of one religious order here that has whites,
coloureds & natives — but he fears for its future. He also has a
couple of African bishops — one in Basutoland & one in another
strong African centre. At a consecration when the Basutoland
Bishop came to help, & the Mayor gave a reception afterwards he
would not have the native Bishop in!

During his visit de Blank had been taken on an unofficial tour of
his new diocese and his antennae quivered at what he saw. He
could not be drawn publicly on his initial impressions other than
to make courteous comments on the reception he was receiving
but his diary was recording what his eye saw and antennae
perceived.

24 June

The Group Areas Act is working great hardship both for Coloured
and Africans — and today we saw a coloured shanty town (called
Windermere) which beggars description. Just bits of tin and
corrugated iron in a water-logged area ... Unbelievable.

Of another African location:

27 June

The worst by far was Nyanga where an enormous area of veldt has
been cleared. Here the natives are sent ... without any provision at
all except a water tap every 200 yards and lavatories (earth with no
cesspit) every 100 yards or so ...

On his return to England, de Blank continued to refuse to
comment on what he had heard and seen during his short visit to
South Africa although in a sermon in Westminster Abbey he
referred to 'one persistent warning: the ease with which men can
be conditioned by their own situation if they do not get outside it
often enough to view it from the standpoint of eternity. And when
this happens prejudice can overcome principle and expediency
can put morality to rout.'

Before farewells and leaving for Cape Town there was a treat
provided by Russell Brown. de Blank had a three week trip taking
him to India, Burma, Thailand, Hong Kong, Phillipines, Japan,
Hawaii and America.

During September 1957 there were many crowded farewell
services and meetings, presentations of gifts, a Lambeth doctorate

of divinity to be conferred, an emotional farewell in the East End and finally a service in St. Paul's Cathedral on 18 September. The Dean of Chester (Michael Gibbs), who had been a distinguished Dean of Cape Town left de Blank in no doubt what was expected of him. 'To many African Christians he will symbolize in his own person the protective character of the Church; the Church which, in age long Christian tradition has espoused the cause of the poor and hungry; the Church which has put down the mighty from their seat, by attacking their privileges and exposing their selfishness, and has exalted those of low degree, by giving them a place in the Kingdom of God.

'But he will be looked to as a father-in-God by many Europeans too, in their sense of bewilderment; by many who have an uneasy conscience about the way things are going in their country. There is a considerable section of European people in Africa which will look to him to make articulate for them that sense of justice in human relations which they have never entirely lost, but which waits for the right lead at the right time to call it into being and give it definition.'

The clergy would look to de Blank for encouragement and his brother bishops for a fresh and detached outlook upon their problems.

The word on everyone's lips was 'expectancy'. Then no time to dream, no time to brood, hardly time for Matins and Evensong before he was on his way.

Meanwhile there were more press interviews but reporters had to be content with a few personal details such as he liked to work in an almost tropical temperature with windows tightly closed and several electric fires blazing away at once, at the same time drinking pints of strong, very sweet tea. Reference was made to his passion for spectacular American musicals, modern painting, foreign films, early Disneys, fast driving, food and wine. And there was emphasis of his Dutch background, the assumption being that as a result it might be easier for him to make contact with the Afrikaners than for somebody whose background was exclusively British. It was a bad mis-reading of history. The British were hated and despised as the victors of the South African war at the beginning of the century, which victory was more and more successfully undermined and negated by the activities of the Broederbond (a sinister Afrikaans secret society) and other nationalist institutions. As the twentieth century gathered pace,

Holland was scarcely less unpopular in South Africa than was Great Britain. A large section of the population would have nothing to do with the war against Germany, and there were many of the Dutch Reformed Churches whose doors were closed to serving men in uniform between 1939 and 1945, and they could not be married in church unless they were in 'civvies'.

Hitler's brutal invasion of Holland went by virtually uncondemned (a very different state of affairs from the time when Queen Wilhelmina of Holland sent a battleship to South Africa to rescue President Kruger from the danger of being captured by the British), and the fact that towards the end of the war Holland was liberated by the Canadians did nothing to add to Dutch popularity.

At the same time it should be noted that Holland had passed harsh sentence on apartheid, and the Reformed Churches of the Netherlands did all in their power to tell the world that there was no connection between their Churches and the Dutch Reformed Churches of South Africa.

On 29 September, de Blank left England with his eighty-six year old mother (in a wheelchair) and one of his sisters. First there had been a 'family service of hymns & prayers' at home. After a few days in Johannesburg and some good conversation with its bishop, (Ambrose Reeves, 'an impressive person') de Blank left by the Blue Train, South Africa's crack express, for Cape Town. At stations on the way, such as Kimberley, there were crowds on the platform to see and greet their new archbishop. This was heady treatment and there was more to come wih genuflecting dignitaries kissing the episcopal ring when the train arrived in Cape Town. A seething mass of people knelt to receive his blessing.

The Enthronement was not until 25 October. There was business requiring attention 'and I need to get myself spiritually ready' but settling into his new home, Bishopscourt, was important. de Blank the whirlwind traveller needed his home base. His home was and had to be a peaceful oasis. The house was built in 1780 and was in English Georgian style contrasting with many Cape houses which were erected in Dutch style with Dutch gables serving as the main exterior decoration. de Blank waxed lyrical on the grounds of sixteen acres 'three or four cultivated to make one of the loveliest gardens in the world, the rest, woodland or allowed to run wild, with the waters of the Liesbeek River, flowing straight down from Table Mountain, babbling its way through the middle of the garden. A tributary skirted the altogether fascinating water garden on four different levels [restored by Bartha] with a wonderful seat by the side of one of the pools ideal for meditation under some beautiful weeping willows'.

Of the household de Blank retained the services of his predecessor's chaplain, Roy Walter Frederick Cowdry, who was shortly to have another appointment. de Blank had brought with him his own chaplain, 'Peter' Priest, with the expectation that other priest friends from England would follow. There were a number of staff. 'It is quite a community. Nothing has been done in the past about their religion, and this we must see to.' (21 October 1957.)

As for the Enthronement on 25 October in St. George's Cathedral, 'words fail me'. And for the spectacular lavishness of the enthronement words failed the crowds. Here was a new archbishop in striking contrast to his predecessor. A priest who was there captures the dramatic change: 'Mere colonials were perhaps surprised to discover that their new Metropolitan was very much the "Prince Archbishop". His advent seemed orchestrated, almost choreographed. The Archiepiscopal Car now sported a pennant bearing the arms of the Diocese. By contrast with the crumpled appearance of his ungainly predecessor, in a cassock stained by food and cigarette ash, Joost was resplendent in a magenta cassock of corded silk, skull cap and buckled shoes. His personal friend and chaplain, 'Peter' Priest, fussed around, clearing the way for this tiny little man, who nevertheless had the bearing and in some respects the appearance of Napoleon. Joost loved it. But so did the members of his new flock, most of whom 'bowed down and worshipped'. Cape Town buzzed with rumours of his charm, his graciousness, his powers of conversation, his oratory in the pulpit or on public platform, his business acumen, the warmth of the welcome to all who called at Bishopscourt . . . '

For most of the congregation this was their first sight of de Blank. They listened with an intensity of interest and watched with the greatest of care. They saw the mobile lips of an eloquent speaker. A mannerism of his was to purse his lips as he paused before a flow of arguments. He had a rhythmic manner of quickening his words as he worked to a climax. He paused shortly. Then his voice started again on a slightly deeper tone. He had a conversational delivery and used careful expressive gestures. For a period his hands would be still. Then he would pound a palm

98

Enthronement at St. George's Cathedral, Cape Town, October 1957

with his fist or, with his elbow bent, make up-and-down gestures with his right fist as if hammering in his point. He had a habit of extending his right arm and slowly turning his hand outward, making an appealing gesture. And then he would make the same gesture with both arms.

Voice and gesture never detracted from but enhanced what he had to say. On this occasion his text was 1 John 4: 7 'Beloved, let us love one another, for love is of God.' If the congregation were expecting fireworks rocketing off against the Government they were disappointed. Yet all that was to come was in that sermon.

He had one criterion for all communities and that was the touchstone of love. This love embraced the whole world and no arbitrary limit could be placed on it. God's love in Christ extended to all without exception, thus making every individual a brother for whom Christ died.

'Policies come and policies go' (did he mean the apartheid policies of the Nationalist Government?) 'but of all that endures love is fundamental and love is the greatest'. There was a suggestion that the Government were in opposition to the divine will, for the one who sinned against love was sinning against God. But neither the Government nor its policies were referred to by name. Nevertheless de Blank warned of an impending conflict, for those who put love into action would meet with opposition from 'the world's greedy selfishness'. He then became more specific: 'Love asserts equality' — and added two warnings: 'First, we must beware of an attitude that betokens any sense of condescension or patronage. For patronage and love are not the same. Patronage implies superiority. Love asserts equality. Not equality of achievement but of value, of value to Almighty God.

'Secondly, if we are to live in love we must abide by the command to love our enemies and not only their victims. Without this active love towards those who are opposed to us, even to those who are to us misguided in their treatment of those weaker than themselves, we are failing in our basic obedience to God. We have to pray for them — to do good to them. Never are we to allow their evil to overwhelm us, but we are to overcome their evil with good.'

He also alluded to white South Africa's appeal to blood and birth: 'Remember that the only blood we dare to plead is the precious Blood of Christ, the only birth in which we place our trust is that rebirth by water and Spirit into the Kingdom of Heaven.'

He warned of the possibility of persecution but drew confidence from his sufficiency in the 'Catholic Faith first accepted and then dynamically enacted'.

Finally he asked a question 'Who knows what yet we may be called upon to bear and to do for the love of God?' Indeed! The rest of his life and of this biography is a descriptive answer to that question.

CHAPTER NINE

The Fight is On

de Blank had arrived in South Africa determined to listen and learn. His first weeks were passed quietly like Brer Rabbit "layin' low and sayin' nuffin'". That did not mean that nuffin' was happening. There was a climate of expectancy and exhilaration: the one created by promise, the other by performance. At a welcome meeting in the City Hall on the evening of his enthronement to which more thousands failed to get into than the two thousand who packed it, de Blank was deliberately mischievous and dramatic. 'Many people have a secret shortcoming of which they are somewhat ashamed and they do not like their friends to know about it. I have a shortcoming like that and I must tell you about it. I suffer from an incurable disease.' There was sufficient time in a moment's dramatic pause to sense the gasp which went shuddering through the audience before he continued 'I am colour blind'. Someone at the meeting later recalled that 'there was a sense of real exaltation amongst the people. I remember thinking that here was someone larger than life. I never forgot my first impression of him as someone with a tremendously powerful personality and the sort of aura that aspiring politicians dream of.'

These first weeks were ones when many individuals and groups were trying to influence the new archbishop or enlist him to their causes. In his autobiographical notes, written after he left Africa, he noted 'I do not think you have to go to South Africa before you know apartheid to be contrary to the command that we should love our neighbours as ourselves. But the South Africans claimed to be a religious and God-fearing people and I did my best to believe that what went under the name of apartheid could not be as bad as the evidence suggested.

'I remember soon after my arrival at Bishopscourt receiving a visit from the editor of *Die Burger*, the local Afrikaans and

101

nationalist newspaper. He went to great pains to point out to me that he personally represented the more liberal and tolerant wing of the Nationalist Party and that while accepting apartheid as the best solution to the country's racial problems it did not imply holding on to privileges by the whites to the detriment of those of other races. I almost fell for his line at first, as many other residents in South Africa have done, and only later did I begin to discover that this was a deliberate camouflage to lull me into a sense of friendship and understanding, while he did everything in his power to distil and misrepresent everything I said and every statement I made — this often at times when the more typical Government mouthpieces, like the Afrikaans newspapers of the Transvaal and the Free State, were reporting my activities much more honestly and objectively.'

de Blank accepted a dinner invitation from Professor N. Oliver now a Member of Parliament for the Progressive Federal Party, then of the South African Bureau of Racial Affairs (SABRA) whose officials were recruited almost exclusively from the Dons of Stellenbosch University. 'They could not have been more charming, and although I expected our conversation to concern itself with inter-race relationships I found in fact that the whole evening was spent in talking of the misunderstandings existing between the two sections of the white population ... and a perhaps legitimate anger that the British would not even want to learn Afrikaans — a language which to one with some knowledge of the Dutch language must be quite the most hideous in all the world.'

de Blank soon learned that this was a major pre-occupation stemming from the South African War, as they termed it, or Boer War as the English prefer to remember it. The peace may have been one of the most generous ever offered by the victors to a defeated foe, yet it was one of the main objects of the Afrikaner people in the end to win the final victory. Many thought that end had been achieved when South Africa left the Commonwealth and became a Republic. de Blank observed: 'The war is kept alive by many means, one of which is by the enthusiastic preservation of a war museum at Bloemfontein which enshrines a number of 'atrocities' committed by the British troops on the people kept in concentration camps. Until recently there used to be among the exhibits a glass jar of marmalade with a fish hook unhappily bottled inside it to reveal the nefarious plans of the British jailors.

Needless to say the jar had quite frequently to be renewed, and the fish hook inserted afresh. It appears that the absurdity of this has struck home even to the most bigoted minds and the marmalade jar has been removed. It seems a pity as it somehow served to indicate the level at which dislike of the British showed itself.'

There was another aspect of history too which should not be overlooked. When the British settled in the Cape Peninsular and inland with some of them going to the Eastern Province and to Natal, the Boers trekked northward and eastward. The British brought with them liberal ideas, and the Boers who had escaped the Enlightenment shunned contamination by these dangerous ideas either in political interpretation or in human relationships. They ran away, like the children of Israel out of Egypt, to settle in the promised land where no winds of corruption or change could blow. With great heroism they embarked upon the Great Trek to set up their paternalistic societies in towns and dorps or villages throughout the country, even setting up what could be called theocratic but not very viable republics along the way, until Pretoria was established as a kind of Afrikaner Mecca for the whole Afrikaans speaking country. Whenever de Blank looked at the Voortrekker Monument in Pretoria he felt it had more a pagan than a Christian feel about it — 'a harsh, square and solid erection where the altar is replaced by an ox-cart, and the sanctuary lamp by a hurricane lantern. Surrounding the monument is a wall with a frieze suggesting that all within are huddled within a laager (a defence square made up of the wagons) to keep at bay the savage hordes without.'

There was yet another aspect of the South African scene. The Afrikaans speaking and the English speaking South Africans were growing closer together. The Afrikaner was moving out of the farms away from the land into the towns and the world of industry. When the barriers crumbled what had they in common besides colour, or rather lack of it? It must be said that both liked the idea of white superiority and cheap labour. The Afrikaner may have expressed his preferences in legislation and statute; the Britisher as a less astute politician but with greater self-confidence, believed in his exalted status as being born the Lord of creation. In reality there was little to choose between the two. Many Africans even preferred to work for an Afrikaner because he knew exactly where he stood. He had his place in the hierarchical, patriarchal structure of the homestead even though his status may be only that of a 'hewer of wood and drawer of water'.

Was not the Anglican Church caught up in this? Was there not a feeling of superiority? Was pastoral care for the African regarded in a different light than work amongst the white population? There is nothing more unctuous than the self regarding liberal parading his conscience and good deeds. Helping and ministering to the African (now the word would be 'serving') for some was rather like doing a stint in the slums by day and returning to a comfortable home by night, if not exactly character-building at least enabling one to claim a nodding acquaintance with poverty and perhaps salving a bit of conscience?

The effects and absurdities of apartheid are known and caricatured to a point where the facts are ignored and forgotten. In a country of some three million whites three million of mixed descent and ten million blacks the motivating force for Government policies was fear. The twin architects of apartheid, Dr. W.W.M. Eiselen (once Professor of Social Anthropology and then Secretary for Native Affairs) and Dr. H.F. Verwoerd (one time Prime Minister) admitted as much. Writing in *Optima* (March 1959) a journal produced by the Oppenheimer Anglo-American Mining Group and circulating internationally among shareholders, Dr. Eiselen said: 'White South Africa is numerically not strong enough to absorb and can therefore only choose between being absorbed or surviving by maintenance of separate communities.' Dr. Verwoerd *(The Times,* 3 January 1963) said that the white people of South Africa 'refuse to commit national suicide — they are determined to survive and to rule this country'.

That determination led to many disabilities for the majority population, the African. No African enjoyed a vote of any kind anywhere in the Union or South-West Africa. They were not represented in Parliament, Provincial Councils or Municipal Councils. In the Cape there had been disfranchisement. A franchise open to Africans from 1854 to 1936 was first limited by putting Africans on a separate roll to vote for a limited number of European members (1936) and finally abolished altogether (1960).

In the African Reserves there was no right of public meeting. Meetings other than *bona fide* religious or sporting activities required the approval of the Bantu Affairs Commissioner of the District. The main political organisation of the Africans — the African National Congress was banned in 1960 after Sharpeville. No African, except the small number permanently domiciled in towns, could seek work in an urban area at will. Custom, and in some cases (for example gold mines, the building industries) law, closed the higher posts of industry to Africans. South Africa's mines and industries were based mainly on migrant labour which gave rise to very grave social problems and was an enemy to normal family life. It also, coupled with inadequate wage rates, had deleterious effects on the health of Africans. Striking examples were the introduction into the Reserves of venereal disease and tuberculosis by returning labourers.

By the time de Blank arrived, all education for Africans, from nursery schools to universities, was under the supreme control of the Minister of Bantu Education. It was a punishable offence to open or conduct a school or any classes for the education of Africans unless it was registered by the Minister, who could refuse registration without assigning any reason.

Africans had no property rights. Then adding to this list in 1957 were the new restrictions placed on the freedom of religion.

Restrictions on Indians and coloured people, though by no means so extensive as those on Africans, were nevertheless crippling to full civic participation in the community.

These restrictions did not apply to Europeans. Yet their liberty was imperilled by the Criminal Law Amendment Act of 1953, which imposed the severest penalties on 'any person who . . . uses any language or does any act or thing calculated to cause any person or persons in general to commit an offence by way of protest against a law or in support of any campaign for the repeal or modification of any law . . . ' An important comment was made on this by Brookes and Macaulay *(Civil Liberty in South Africa)*: 'these savage penalties have in fact silenced many people who would otherwise have taken action, not least because they realise that the Government, fearing to incur odium by imposing them on well-known and respected citizens, may easily select for arrest their less-known non-European colleagues, and that the penalties will fall on them.'

Throughout the Autumn of 1957, de Blank continued receiving a stream of callers asking him to take a lead in opposing apartheid. There were even some who hoped that he might unite a fragmented opposition into a concerted and organised opposing force. That was never a possibility. Although increasingly de Blank was in touch with many groups he had never the contacts amongst the more politically militant groups with which Ambrose Reeves consorted and in whom they had confidence.

It was December 1957 and still de Blank bided his time. He was even capable of appreciating the fears of the white South African who could see his identity disappearing in the southern tip of the African continent if the apartheid legislation were relaxed. There were voices close at hand at Bishopscourt which counselled caution. Although he was listening hard he had no close colleagues of sufficient weight to advise him or to enable him to keep a clear perspective on an issue too easily shrouded in mist. Furthermore, he had not had time to know his fellow bishops and the considerable distances which separated most of them meant that contact was occasional rather than regular. Following his first episcopal synod 14–21 November he recorded:

> The bishops very kind to me & I really like them all — I suppose the weakest among them is Natal [Inman] & Damaraland [Vincent] but the latter is probably a wonderful missionary in S.W. Africa. Reeves is extemely good — & so are Basutoland [Maund] and St. John's [Schuster]. Robert Selby Taylor [Pretoria] and Grahamstown [Cullen] are more synodically minded & like the formal resolution. Bloemfontein [Burnett — just consecrated] a very pleasant man came in half-way through.

The complexion of the bench of bishops changed very significantly during de Blank's time and relations with them will be considered later. But at the outset he had few episcopal friends with whom he could share his thoughts and plans. Yet as Metropolitan he was capturing the limelight and in the eyes of the country and the world, but not the Constitution of his Church, his pronouncements could appear to commit and thus embarrass all his colleagues to a stated case or unproven view.

A visit to a shanty town and a newspaper leader provided the justification for breaking his self-imposed silence earlier than he intended. The shanty town was Windermere which had developed in the Second World War through the influx of Africans into the Cape Peninsula in search of employment. In 1956 the labour force was being moved from shacks, called Pondokkies, to better housing. Within a year, twelve thousand African bachelors had been moved to a township called Langa, and intensive screening of the remaining inhabitants was taking place to determine who would be eligible for a house when African families were moved in accordance with Government policy. The Minister for Native Affairs had ordered that the Windermere slums should be demolished. It was the task of the Cape Town City Council to act on the order. de Blank visited Windermere on 22 December 1957:

> There has been a good deal of excitement about the evictions from
> Pondokkies at Windermere. So the Dean, Fr. Rumsey [Cowley
> Father] & I spent the afternoon looking round. We gathered that
> under the Urban Areas Act, Section 10, it is quite possible to retain
> the husband in the area while sending his wife & children back to
> the reserve. There is no doubt that some pondokkies have had to be
> pulled down in order to make room for a decent housing area —
> everyone wants to see the end of Windermere. But we are not
> happy with it.

The following day (23 December) a hastily convened meeting was
held attended by de Blank, the Dean and ministers of the
Methodist, Congregational, Presbyterian and Baptist Churches.

> All felt strongly so we made our way to the City Hall where we
> interviewed first Santilhano, Chairman of Native Affairs (quite
> prepared to resign over this issue), the Mayor (Co. J.W.O.
> Billingham) & Bakker (Chairman of Housing). Public opinion has
> been pretty well roused & the Mayor got on to the housing officer,
> Rogers (Manager of Native Affairs) who assured him on the
> telephone that only bachelors had been evicted from Windermere &
> then all had been rehoused in bachelor quarters at Langa. We went
> away with his assurance, agreeing to meet Bakker & Rogers at
> Windermere on Friday.

On Friday 27 December further assurance was given that no
officially recognised families had been broken up as a result of the
evictions.

> Some people attacked the Govt. legislation quite rightly — but this
> was neither the time nor the occasion — and we came away feeling
> that the City Council did everything possible in an impossible
> situation.

Instead of being the end of the matter, it was the beginning. The
diary entries mask the reality. Windermere had been referred to as
a 'festering sore on the body of Cape Town'. Fifteen thousand
people had lived in an eczema of shacks made from rusted tins,
boxes and newspapers without light or drainage, and with the
rubbish dump of the city rotting around it in the sunshine.
Stronger in the nostrils than the decay was the fear and the
waiting, the smell of people crouched in hiding with an ear to the
door. The fear was eviction. For a family, eviction meant
separation. A cruel riddle was 'when is a slum not a slum?' And

the answer — 'when it is a *home*.' For a man and his wife would far
sooner live in such a hopeless, down at heel district as
Windermere than live apart in hygienic, well-built quarters.

de Blank could see only too clearly that the whole system of
migratory labour had corrupted South Africa, and although it had
degraded the African it had degraded to a greater extent the
European who condoned and encouraged it. At the Meeting at
Windermere:

> The Government representative agreed that offering men accom-
> modation in Langa's 'bachelor' barracks and ordering the women
> and children back to the Reserve must lead to the destruction of
> family life. Whereupon I asked him what would happen if, rather
> than consent to this separation, the man travelled back to the
> Reserve with his wife and children; would there be work awaiting
> him there?
>
> I had to press the question home, but the decent and honest
> Government servant had to admit that the chances of a man finding
> work in a place where the family could live together was exceed-
> ingly thin. Almost certainly he would have to leave his family
> behind and he would have to earn a living for himself and his
> dependents as a migratory labourer. Thus there is no hope for him
> either in the Cape or elsewhere. His family is condemned and
> family life an impossibility.

Even yet de Blank had not exploded in public. A few diary entries
show what led him to do so.

31 December 1957

> Interesting that the London *Times* had a leader about South Africa at
> the end of last week & it mentioned the fact of the Most Revd. Joost
> de Blank's arrival & the uncertainty what action he would take. It
> had no doubts about my racial attitudes but was waiting to see
> where the battle would be joined. So am I. I am sure the main-
> tenance of the Buddha's 'noble silence' is a good idea as long as
> possible.

5 January 1958

> Managed to find time to write my *Good Hope* (monthly diocesan
> leaflet) article. Strangely enough I have raised the apartheid issue.
> In a sense I didn't mean to — but the Prime Minister's New Year
> broadcast in which he talked of inspired race relations was too much
> for me. But having written one article, I changed my mind &
> thought I wouldn't make much of the issue after all. Nevertheless,
> on re-writing it I found I had come back to it again tho' perhaps on

At Windermere, December 1957

a more domestic front saying that I would resist any attempt at apartheid in any of the churches in my jurisdiction. In a sense I realise I have bitten off more than I can chew — as I know of churches where apartheid doesn't exist but where, say, the choir is all white. But if I bring things to a head so much the better.

All this largely the result in *The Times* a week ago (sic).

11 January 1958.

It appears that I am being forced into action in relation to apartheid & all that. Not only my *Good Hope* article — but have had to do a foreword to a Treason Trial Fund Raising Auction catalogue. Ronald Segal, editor of *Africa South* has also been to see me again and I have promised to write some comments on the Windermere situation.

The February issue of *Good Hope* appeared towards the end of January and the article was carried in full in the *Cape Argus* (22 January). In it he referred to Windermere but the thrust of the article was condemning apartheid as a national policy, and warning Anglican congregations that he would withhold episcopal ministrations from any who practised apartheid. Misquoting Scripture he wrote: 'Let apartheid not be once named among you as becometh saints.'

He was prepared to admit that it might be possible to work out by mutual agreement a just system of territorial division, 'but I am quite certain as a Christian I shall never be able to discover any justification for *baaskap* in any form or guise. This is the point where the issue forces itself on the individual Christian conscience and on the life of the Church as a whole. European domination we utterly reject as inhuman and unchristian.'

de Blank drew attention to those who were denied basic human rights and privileges: 'If we do not see Christ in our neighbour whatever the colour of his skin, we have not begun to understand what Christianity is about. All the redeemed are partakers of the Divine Nature. We live blasphemously if by any action or disrespect we deny this potential divinity to any child of man.'

He had opened his letter by reminding his readers of Napoleon's maxim 'Defeat your enemy in detail' and added 'it is my earnest prayer that we may corporately and individually put the enemy of souls to flight in detail.'

He himself had combined a general condemnation of apartheid with some detail about Windermere. The fury of the Government came quickly. On 24 January there was an Opposition Motion of No Confidence in the House of Assembly. Government Ministers and others used the debate to attack de Blank and the leader of the United Party, Sir de Villiers Graaff. It was pointed out by Mr. Blaar Coetzee (North Rand) that de Blank was condemning 'not only the Nationalist policy of apartheid, but the United Party's policy of 'white supremacy' as well, as inhuman and un-Christian.' Perhaps there was a case for parties uniting against the common enemy.

110

The Minister of Justice (C.R. Swart) was clear that 'the sooner we, not only as political parties, but as leaders of the white community, repudiate him, the better. We repudiate him entirely. We say he has no right to describe our centuries-old way of life here as un-Christian.'

The Minister of External Affairs (Eric Louw) a particular antagonist of the Anglican Church, challenged de Blank to prove the sincerity of his remarks by admitting non-white pupils to Anglican Church Schools. de Blank put out a statement saying that if apartheid legislation were removed he would do all in his power to see that all children of all races were allowed entry.

1958 was an election year so there was much sensitivity by the United Party, which was supported by many Anglicans. de Villiers Graaff was embarrassed at being drawn into the crossfire between Government and Archbishop. He was a fence sitter and was elected as party leader in 1956 because, as one report put it, 'he would give offence to no one'. This is not quite fair, for after his election people were hugely excited by his charisma. In any case the United Party was liberal on race questions only in comparison with the Government. In his statement, de Villiers Graaff politely but firmly told de Blank to keep out of politics by resorting to the worn out argument: 'It is necessary for the Church to guard over the moral and spiritual life of the people just as the State should safeguard the national, political and social welfare.' But he was not allowed to slip off the hook about mixed schools and here he upheld the existing system. 'The United Party considers this practice should be continued and is against the establishment of mixed schools. Any attempt to ignore this practice must ignore the realities of the South African situation.' The Government smacked their lips with satisfaction.

There was no doubting de Blank's position. Suddenly he was on the world stage receiving an enormous fan and hate mail, the former outweighing the latter. The columns of the newspapers were full of letters and articles but written from prepared positions, no one leaving his or her corner to debate the issues. There was a flurry of activity. The Nationalist MP for Langlaagte (P.J. Coetzee) asked in the Assembly (4 February) whether the time had not come to deport de Blank. An invitation to preach in the Anglican Church at Simonstown dockyard was withdrawn. In the Senate, Senator J.J. Boshoff linked de Blank with Ambrose Reeves, Alan Paton (Chairman of the Liberal Party) and Patrick Duncan as being guilty of furthering the ends of extremists.

The Minister of the Interior (T.E. Donges) taunted de Blank in a speech to a Nationalist Party rally. He accused de Blank of hiding behind the law when it suited him. If he was determined to have mixed Anglican Church schools why did he not break the law of the land for he had hinted that he would do so if they clashed with his conscience. He was accused of 'spiritual superiority and self righteousness'.

There are some attacks that are best left well alone particularly if one has a sharp tongue. Donges' attack was one of them. de Blank could not resist. If anything he should have put out a press statement and left it at that. But not only did he decide to make a slashing attack on Donges but chose a most inappropriate place to make it, namely the annual speech day at St. Cyprian's School in Cape Town in Febrary 1958. He said that it was hardly surprising that the crime wave was assuming gigantic proportions when a Cabinet Minister jeered at those who respected the yearnings of an informed conscience and who believed in the necessity of obeying God's law: 'It is a well-known fact that distortion and misrepresentation are the stock-in-trade of cheap-jack politicians the world over, but it is seldom in civilised communities that a Cabinet Minister descends to deliberate distortion and malicious misrepresentation.' The reference was to Donges' use of a phrase attributed to de Blank — 'without hesitation' in connection with disobeying the law. de Blank had not uttered those precise words and for Donges to use them was 'a calumny that no decent man would either fabricate or utter. ... such conduct is a shameful attempt to mislead the people, and it is hard to see how anyone guilty of such practices can be entrusted with any responsible portfolio in national or public life.' It was more like election banter than a measured response and many at the Speech Day were disturbed that the occasion had been used for this level of attack.

In the March 1958 issue of *Good Hope* he criticised the failure of the Dutch Reformed Church to criticise the Government. He also turned the tables on the Government by stating that conflict arose when the politician stepped out of his well-defined limits into the theological arena. 'In a Christian society it is no part of his duty to be a law-giver. Principles governing man's relationship with his fellow men have been laid down in God's self-revelation. The politician's vocation is to work out these principles in practice. The moment he begins to question these principles, the moment he seeks to implement a policy which cannot be squared with these principles, he assails the Divine prerogative by acting as a law-giver instead of a law-maker. Though not deliberately, he is committing a blasphemy.'

de Blank albeit not deliberately was laying down a challenge for a debate with the Dutch Reformed Churches. He was shortly to leave for America and then England for the Lambeth Conference. Earlier he had promised an article for *Africa South*. It appeared in the April-June 1958 issue under the title *The Fight Is On*. It was a vitriolic attack on migratory labour and the effect it had on Africans. He described the policy as 'devilish' and 'damnable'. 'Christians must resist it by reason of their Christian faith. I speak for them. ... it is our avowed purpose to slay this ungainly Goliath of migratory labour that has encumbered our fair land far too long.'

The impact of de Blank was felt even more on church life in Cape Town. He usually worked on the basis of reorganising what he could not rejuvenate but there was resistance to much that he wanted to do. In the Church too, the fight was on.

CHAPTER TEN

Folie de Grandeur?

A biographer has to remove some of the drapes surrounding or covering his subject if a worthy and just portrait is to be drawn. As each drape covering de Blank is taken away one sees completely different men and images revealed or emerging. Remove one drape and there does not seem to be a man there at all — simply a caricature of a despotic ruler who, because he cannot afford familiarity between himself and his subject, has interposed a protective barrier of ceremonial and etiquette. Is that right, or have other people surrounding de Blank erected these barriers? And if so for whose benefit? Another drape is removed and one sees the introverted diarist: 'Lord I am not worthy ... give me both humility and strength.'

For interest, even edification, if not clarification, it is useful to look at a few pictures submitted by different people who portray de Blank the diocesan bishop in contrasting ways. Each captures only a glimpse of one or more aspects of an enigmatic person. Add them together and they do not give a complete picture. Only at the end, when all drapes this side of eternity are removed, is it possible to look Joost de Blank in the face and begin to know him. Those many people, the majority, who met or knew him only at different junctures of their lives and his, would hardly recognize *that* man!

For the moment it is Cape Town and clergy and laity are tremendously excited at the possibility of being led by a dynamo who exceeded 'sixty miles an hour'. Before the pictures it is well to record the publication of two books within the first six months of his time in South Africa. Although he said he was always grateful for his childhood conversion and conviction, the manner and expression of it had left pockets of unassuaged guilt remaining in many a recess of his mind. If the sensitive child had been brought

114

under the influence of a gentler and brighter version of Christianity the spiritual catastrophe of his last years might have been averted. There was a time that he would have had a one word answer to the question 'Are you saved?' By 1957 he was sceptical of pastors and evangelists whose sole stress was on the *act* of conversion as something final in itself although de Blank often made direct appeals for commitment. In *This is Conversion* (1957) he looked for a less superficial means of defining conversion and classifying the 'saved'. He examined the anomaly that 'it is not always those who in peaceful times cry 'Lord, Lord' most loudly, who in times of testing live up to their profession most faithfully,' and the problem of why people who had undergone spiritual conversion of an apparently sincere nature were able later to renounce the experience. He had learned that 'the act of conversion clicks home in Baptism and Church membership' and leads back into the world. The Christian in relation to the Church and the world must have an in and out rhythm to his life: in for worship, repentance and renewal; out for giving, fighting, serving.

The second book of the period *Uncomfortable Words* (1958) was the Bishop of London's Lent Book and as such, a parting gift from de Blank to 'the priests and people of North and East London.' Like the majority of his books it comprised short, sharp chapters and if reading this one did not quite realise the bed of nails for somnolent Christians that its title suggests, nevertheless it had some pointed things to say making it plain that man's salvation is in sacrifice and service.

In a chapter on *True Greatness* de Blank considers that 'the Church of England may well have lost something of incalculable value by omitting [the foot washing] from her rites and ceremonies. ... How much might the contamination by the world's ideas of rank and greatness have been avoided had the Church been as sedulous in maintaining the practice of washing one another's feet'.

How does a Christian live in a world whose standards he cannot reverse? How far is it legitimate for the Church to go in its approximation to the customs of the world? And what of bishops, of himself? He writes with more caution than conviction. 'It [the Church] has tried to find a solution by differentiating carefully between the man and his office. Not for nothing did some of the saintly medieval bishops wear a hair-shirt next to the skin. It was

115

At Bishopscourt

right that they should accept the dignity proper to their office, but they wanted to remind themselves that their dignity was that of their office alone. Apart from their episcopal status they were one with the humblest penitent seeking absolution — no, even less than the humblest, because from him to whom much had been given would much be required.'

This leads appropriately to the first picture, drawn by Canon

116

Folie de Grandeur?

Cecil Thomas Wood to whom the Church of the Province of South Africa owes much for his work as Provincial Archivist (1958-1979). He was much else besides, including Domestic Chaplain to Archbishop Phelps for five years, Director of the South African Church Institute and from 1958 de Blank's Archdeacon of Cape Town. He had an amusing but accurate way of drawing attention to people's foibles — and sometimes their gifts. Yet there is much to be learned from foibles particularly in the case of de Blank. A short time before he died in 1980, Wood wrote a pamphlet entitled *Random Recollections of some Archbishops*. He referred to five archbishops of Cape Town, thus: 'William Marlborough Carter (1909) Benign: Francis Robinson Phelps (1931) Grace abounding: John Russell Darbyshire (1938) Hypersensitive: Geoffrey Hare Clayton (1948) A lonely man: Joost de Blank (1957) *Folie de grandeur*. Of de Blank he continues: 'He tried to incorporate the trappings of an 18th century bishop into a 20th century setting and it did not work in South Africa. When 'Peter' Priest, who stage-managed his enthronement, asked me what I thought of it, I replied: "My dear Peter, it had Holiday on Ice (then showing in Cape Town) stone cold." He flew a diocesan flag on his car and I vividly recall an incident on his second arrival at the airport after a visit to America where he had been extremely outspoken. I heard that the Black Sash were going to greet him in force, and not wishing to be outmanœuvred I booked the V.I.P. room and notified the Chapter. He had just bought a new car with automatic, one pedal control, and this was the first time the chauffeur had driven it. I duly ushered him and his sister to the car, the Chapter grouped behind me and the Black Sash lining the route out. Slowly at first, but with increasing speed, the car moved backwards into the darkness. I never enquired how he reached Bishopscourt.

'His entourage which accompanied him everywhere were dressed like Indian headwaiters, we always had to wear cassocks and sash. It was extremely embarrassing to enter a hotel dining-room *en masse*. At one time he conceived the idea of the Diocesan entering the Cathedral surrounded and supported by his Chapter, as in London. We killed this at the very first attempt; one member strutted, another walked crab-wise, a third limped, a fourth shuffled, and I did the Foxley-Norris walk (heel, toe, wobble), all in copes.

'He had a fetish about punctuality in his own house. Many a

117

time he has asked people to drinks before lunch or dinner and left me standing with them while they finished their glass because the gong had gone. This once happened with the British Ambassador.

'He was inclined to take very immediate decisions and was very Press conscious, and only later would the Chapter learn to their astonishment that such decisions had their unanimous consent.

'By and large it was a colourful time.'

Another picture is of life at Bishopscourt, in the plush white suburbs some seven miles from the centre of Cape Town. The home is in the parish of St. Saviour, Claremont. Canon John W. Aubrey was rector during de Blank's time and for a short period in Clayton's. His memory of those years is vivid. 'Dr. Clayton had said to me, "I know I live in your parish. You may interfere with the religion of anyone in my household, but *not* with mine." The clergy had a profound admiration for Archbishop Clayton, but maintained their distance and went to Bishopscourt when invited. The new occupants of Bishopscourt longed for people to 'drop in' rather than 'call'. The problem was how to accept their very warm and loving hospitality without being 'smothered' or 'engulfed' in a sea of family affection.

'In the afternoons, old Mrs. de Blank, no longer mobile and looking for all the world like a very portly Queen Victoria towards the end of her reign, held court in the drawing room, seated in a wing-chair, usually playing dominoes. In spite of years spent in England, her English was almost non-existent. Guests in turn were seated next to 'Mama'. Conversation was impossible, since the guttural noises she emitted were only understood by members of the immediate family circle, but she was graciously content to have someone on whom to lavish her affection, while she herself picked up from the guest allocated a few crumbs of polite concern for her welfare. She was always delighted to see children. Simon, my son, was aged about five, a Nordic blond, a ball of fire and a real live wire. 'Mama' particularly loved him. The game of dominoes at a crucial stage was happily abandoned and together they would build walls of dominoes. They had no language problems.

'Everything stopped for tea. There was a fleet of servants. The Archbishop's sister, Bartha, did the house-keeping. She was a dear person, highly efficient but not really domesticated. The household bills must have been enormous, because for guests who had casually dropped in 'luxuries' were invariably produced,

118

many imported from Fortnum & Mason, and the left-overs were later consumed by the staff in the kitchen! The Archbishop was very attentive to his mother and the guests. Chaplains and secretaries flitted in and out, laughing, joking, all part of this very happy, extended family, but some guests sadly found the atmosphere somewhat overpowering, almost cloying. I could not help wondering how on earth the Archbishop could be so relaxed and give so much time to his guests and still get through his enormous work-load *and* be so disciplined about his daily offices and devotions in his private chapel. Sometimes after tea the Archbishop would take the children to play croquet on the lawn.

'Dinner parties were always generous. Charades were sometimes played afterwards. Caterers were brought in for Garden Parties and the larger cocktail parties. For minor conferences held at Bishopscourt Bartha used to call in her friends to help. The tendency was invariably to over-cater and 'the wives' sometimes wondered why, with all the servants available, their assistance should be required, but the answer was that Bartha needed their support. Bishopscourt parties produced a strange medley of guests in addition to the predictable ecclesiastical crowd. But any guests who failed to enjoy the Bishopscourt hospitality had only themselves to blame, because at all the de Blank parties incredible munificence was offered in a delightfully relaxed family atmosphere against an idyllic background of garden and Table Mountain. A new departure at the larger parties was the presence of Charles, the gardener, and his wife, Katie, the cook and other coloured members of the household staff. They tended to hover, uncomfortably, in a little huddle on the fringes, unnoticed by the milling throng of 'liberals' present. It was left to those of us who wondered about the advisability of inviting one's servants to be guests at parties to try and make them feel welcome and at home.'

Bishopscourt and its chief occupant could be intimidating too. Another picture comes from a priest who as a young man of twenty five years remembers, 'being summonsed to his presence a few months before ordination to the priesthood and being told that I would be required to spend a week with him at Bishopscourt to write several examinations and to discuss my spiritual life with him, before he could decide whether or not I was ready for ordination. He was the only one to decide that. I sometimes wonder if I would have made the grade had all the modern techniques been used — a Selection Board with a doctor, psychologist, several clergymen and a bishop. His word was final. He even told me when I could get married! He preferred his priests not to be married, at least not before the age of 30 years, so if one got married before that 'sacred' age, one would not be entitled to a marriage allowance! After serving my first three years in a parish in Stellenbosch, I received a letter from him informing me that I was to move in a month's time to a large city parish as the Senior Curate. There was no question of discussion with me about the move.

'Looking back over the years, my main impressions of him are of awe, fear, admiration — a real autocratic man. He had a great gift for preaching to the crowds, but often seemed to be a little awkward with individuals. If a person had a problem or a particular question to ask him one came away with a definite answer — there seemed to be no vagueness about his approach to what was right or wrong, or what the best thing to do in the circumstances would be.'

Are these pictures accurate? Do they capture at least some of the many facets of de Blank's character? Is the image portrayed the reality conveyed? A look at some of the issues facing de Blank in his first period as a diocesan bishop will provide clues towards answering the questions.

It is natural that a bishop and particularly an archbishop should like a number of trusted friends and counsellors around him. It is equally natural to want these counsellors to be people of similar outlook to oneself. At the same time it is sometimes tempting but always dangerous to have either echoes of oneself or lesser mortals in advisory positions. The protective servant may use his position as a guise for exercising power of his own.

de Blank was in a difficult position. He needed people near him at Bishopscourt whom he already knew. This meant they had to be imported from England. 'How soon can you pack?' was de Blank's first comment to 'Peter' Priest when they first met after the appointment to Cape Town was made. He had brought him from Dover to the Isle of Dogs and now he was to be his chaplain in Cape Town. There was to be a junior chaplain too, also from London's East End although this appointment did not materialise. The chaplain was to be a trusted member of the household, friend to Mama, part confidante, Ceremoniarius and jester to the archbishop. To some extent he controlled ecclesiastical access to the archbishop. Some senior clergy of the diocese found it extremely irritating to have to deal with the Bishopscourt coterie rather than with the Archbishop. They saw the succession of chaplains as a sycophantic group dancing attendance on His Grace the Lord Archbishop!

de Blank had a number of early opportunities to unite the diocese under his leadership but he failed to do so by miscalculation and errors of judgement. Bishop Sydney Lavis, once dubbed 'the best-loved man in Cape Town' retired in 1957. It was announced at the public meeting on the evening of de Blank's enthronement. de Blank made a diary note:

25 October 1957.

I thought it right to announce Bishop Lavis' retirement at the end of the year. He has been so wonderful & he of course said he is going then, but it was necessary to nail him down. Small wonder after 56 years in the diocese & 26 at Cape Town as Coadjutor Bishop he finds it hard finally to register his decision. So I had to do it for him.

When Lavis died in 1965 an obituary writer in *Good Hope* (September 1965) returned to the earlier phrase of 'best-loved'. 'But why? That was the puzzle. What could there have been in the prime of this kindly old man that I was privileged to meet, that could have made him the *best*-loved, not just the loved? The answer is now plain to me, having delved some little way into that prime and visited or corresponded with many who knew him in it. And it's an answer with a moral. That you don't just become 'best loved' for your kindly smile, your beautiful thought, your feelings of affection, or your handsome face (although all of these he had in full). No, the bed-rock foundation of the esteem in which Cape Town held him was his sheer unremitting, imaginative and dedicated *hard work* — as Parish Priest, Social Reformer and Public Figure.'

de Blank had the opportunity of making an imaginative appointment, of someone who would be primarily responsible for diocesan affairs yet with whom he could share episcope. Instead he appointed Roy Cowdry, Geoffrey Clayton's chaplain, who had stayed on in a state of suspended animation awaiting a nudge or a call elsewhere. Some clergy welcomed the appointment, heralding it as a brilliant move on the part of de Blank to provide continuity with the old and to use Cowdry's undoubted knowledge of the diocese. He was a generous, outgoing affectionate person but was

121

handicapped in a number of ways. Bishop Lavis retired from Office but not in person. He was the embodiment of the Church in so many eyes and these continued to look to him for guidance. Withdrawal did not come easily to him. Further, chaplains to bishops need an independent sphere of work after a chaplaincy to prove their pastoral worth and leadership potential before attaining high office. A domestic chaplaincy is not necessarily a good episcopal breeding ground. Again, Cowdry was to be handicapped by lack of cooperation from the Bishopscourt coterie. He never really became de Blank's right hand man. They did not really share episcope. de Blank would have liked Cowdry to be named Bishop of Simonstown but the Chancellor vetoed that. Instead he became Assistant Bishop of Cape Town. It was a strange appointment, one of impulse rather than conviction, for de Blank did not know Cowdry in any deep sense. Nonetheless, Cowdry had to carry heavy burdens during de Blank's visits abroad and in the Province and during times of illness.

Another early appointment was to the Deanery of Cape Town when Thomas Savage was elected Bishop of Zululand. de Blank's nomination had to be approved by the Cathedral Chapter. His first two choices were from England and included Michael Hodgins, Archdeacon of Hackney. They said 'No'. In January 1958 he turned to his own chaplain, 'Peter' Priest, and nominated him for the Deanery. The Cathedral Chapter rightly vetoed the appointment. Canon John Aubrey re-captures the atmosphere of the time. de Blank's silence on apartheid had been broken following his Windermere visit and subsequent letters in *Good Hope* and speeches. Conservative and moderate opinion in the diocese had been rocked. Where was the Archbishop leading them? 'Confidence had been further undermined by the Archbishop's nominations to the vacant offices of Assistant-bishop and Dean of Cape Town. Joost was a bachelor, who longed for affection as well as adulation. He had inherited Roy Cowdry who was immediately 'sucked in' by the tentacles of the 'Dear Octopus' which now reigned at Bishopscourt. 'Peter' Priest appeared to outsiders as an amusing and somewhat eccentric personality. There had quickly developed around the Archbishop what seemed to be an esoteric 'Bishopscourt set' (all bachelors), whose object was not just to be a mutual admiration society, but also to run the diocese. When Joost nominated Roy Cowdry, who had proved to be an admirable domestic chaplain to the previous Archbishop, but whose credentials on paper for elevation to the purple seemed somewhat slim, to be assistant-bishop of Cape Town, most people welcomed the appointment as inspired. The Archbishop was being wise and statesmanlike in choosing an *assistant*, who really *knew* the Diocese and Province and could provide the very necessary continuity. But when shortly afterwards the Archbishop nominated 'Peter' Priest to the Deanery, whose main qualifications seemed to be a flair for ceremonial and clerical adornment, suspicions darkened. What was going on?'

de Blank accepted the veto with anger and frustration. He then offered the Deanery to Edward Laurie King, thirty eight year old Rector of Stellenbosch, which he accepted and he still remains Dean in 1987. The appointment was a good one but it was not a post that attracted King. The Cathedral was rather too 'English' for King's more Catholic predilections. There had been an Oxbridge tradition but King was a young redbrick via Johannesburg and the University of Wales. He recalls that, 'Joost invited me to Bishopscourt to talk it over. I went with my wife determined to say 'No' and with an admirable list of reasons as to why I shouldn't take the job. After tea I was whisked to the study where he shot my reasons to pieces and, still against my better judgement, I left Bishopscourt as Dean-elect.

'He was, I think, the most persuasive person I have ever met — perhaps dangerously so? On many subsequent occasions I found him a person determined to have his way. He once invited me to go to America to do an exchange job. It wasn't convenient for me and I didn't really want to go — but I resisted his pressures to go only by a desperate rearguard action. I think that was about the only time I really got my own way!

'He had a restless and driving nature which drove himself very hard; he demanded results, action, decision and he saw most things as clear-cut issues.'

King has made the Cathedral not only a focal point for the Diocese of Cape Town but also a vigorous worshipping community. ('The Church is what you've got left when the building has burned down.') Little wonder that Albert van den Heuwel's (a Dutch theologian) words on *The Role of a Cathedral* are used in the guide book of the Cathedral Church of St. George the Martyr:

A *Sign* of pro-existence — visibly existing for the whole community.
A *Symbol* of diversity in unity.

A Pentecostal *Laboratory* — a place to experiment 'to let the Spirit in.'
A *Temple* of dialogue.
A *Theatre* of basic drama.
A *Clinic* for the exorcism of pessimism.
An *International Exchange*.
A *Broadcasting Station* for the voice of the poor.
A *Tower* of reconciliation.
A *Motel* for pilgrims.
The *House* of vicarious feasts — a place of celebration.
The *Hut* of the shepherd — where the Bishop and Christian leaders meet.

At his Enthronement de Blank was required to make solemn declaration that he would 'protect the rights and liberties' of the Cathedral and 'observe the customs ... that have been approved.' In the Diocese of Cape Town the Cathedral Chapter had its own Statutes setting out the authority of the Chapter and the work for which it existed. Chapter was the guardian of the spiritualities and may offer advice, counsel to the Archbishop when requested and also may offer advice, make suggestions, criticisms, freely of its own volition, individually or corporately. The Archbishop must consult the Chapter before making any pastoral appointments (incumbents, chaplains of institutions et cetera and Honorary Canons). He may make other appointments, for example, assistant curates, without consulting Chapter. The Cathedral Chapter consisted of the Archbishop, Assistant Bishop, Dean, Archdeacons and six Canons, three Canons being elected by the clergy of the diocese and three appointed by the Archbishop. This was not at all what de Blank expected. And the unexpected was disliked. Yet he wanted an advisory group.

13 December 1957

Chapter. Very anxious that Chapter should be my Cabinet but somehow don't think it's alive enough to be that. I tried to raise various issues today but didn't get much of a comeback.

Did de Blank understand the synodical processes of Cape Town — for that is what they were? He was irritated with the Chapter from the start. He had not expected that he would be circumscribed by rules and regulations. Surely as Archbishop he would have near limitless freedom to act and appoint as he wished? Had he not come to Cape Town with big plans and wide vision? Had he not heard the cheers from all quarters of the Anglican Communion?

124

Could he not at least expect loyalty from those who would not accept his views? Whatever the true position was, the impression of many members of the Chapter was of an Archbishop who wanted his own way and required obedience. In Chapter he treated criticism as disloyalty. There were many painful confrontations and repercussions by way of unhappy correspondence and threats of resignations. There was also much trivia being discussed, as Dean King recalls, 'I don't think he thought we were a very lively lot — on the other hand we were startled to find ourselves cast in unexpected roles ... We found ourselves discussing new apparel for Chapter (red piping on cassocks etc.) and also the Chapter dinner (à la St. Paul's Cathedral, London) — and I found myself assessing possible menus for the dinner, arranging the various speeches, and inviting the Cardinal, Admiral, Mayor and anything else going. All this was in amazing contrast to our erstwhile Archbishop, Geoffrey Clayton, to whom all this would have seemed quite extraordinary'.

It was indeed extraordinary that de Blank failed to realise that the Cathedral Chapter of Cape Town was not the Parochial Church Council of Harrow. They were not going to underpin and underwrite de Blank's ideas without query or investigation. And de Blank was determined not to have his ideas mutilated or die the death of a thousand qualifications. Moreover, there was much in the Diocese that needed an injection such as de Blank was resolved to give. Writing to the Diocesan Secretary (G.D. Abernethy), 16 November 1958 regarding official expenses, de Blank mentioned some of them: 'It may be that my predecessors never made any objection such as I have made above. But, without in any way wishing to detract from the value of the work they did, the fact remains that I have inherited a situation where, for example, with regard to ordination candidates has been quite shocking, and drastic action needed to be taken. Furthermore nothing has been done about the training of Catechist and Lay Ministers, nor is there any system of Diocesan inspection in being for our Schools. Our Settlement and Youth work are unco-ordinated and we are no further on the way to providing a Retreat and Conference centre for our people, and it takes little thought to add considerably to the list of urgent matters requiring attention'.

Relations with the Chapter were never satisfactorily resolved, and de Blank increasingly bypassed Chapter with unfortunate results.

Yet there is another view too. de Blank was not a scholar but the Chapter quickly realised he had a remarkably quick and agile mind and considerable business acumen. As a chairman he was able and the pervading atmosphere was relaxed. One chapter member writes: 'While discussion was taking place on a suggestion thrown out by Joost, ideas had quickly crystallised in his mind. The moment he spoke, he had a definite plan to propose. One learned to try and duck, because to implement his plans he had also made up his mind about those to do the work and one invariably found oneself landed with another new job'.

The thrust of this chapter is to give some different — even contradictory — impressions of initial difficulties in the Diocese, many of de Blank's own making. But the *impressions* are important for they have much substance in them. The questions continued to be asked: was de Blank a lonely and sensitive man who needed group support? Was there a real Joost de Blank behind all the projected images? There was de Blank who preached the Gospel of Hope with great power and moving simplicity; the de Blank who wrote personally to a bitterly disappointed priest with words of gentle encouragement which lifted an almost broken soul up again; there was also the de Blank who did not visit one of his senior priests when he was confined to bed for seven or eight weeks. But again, there was the caring father in God who knew when to help a busy priest by giving him a free holiday. There was also the Archbishop who knew the value of an unannounced informal visit to encourage a priest in his work.

A little later there were to be great efforts to challenge and renew the diocese. But it is well to register this early a number of different impressions of the new Archbishop. What is the sum of them?

It must be remembered that de Blank was a man of action. He was a master of telling, direct speech and provoked against himself the suspicion and dislike of some of the duller and perhaps less educated men who occupied the rectories and vicarages of Cape Town. They felt their inferiority in knowledge and ability and valued their assured superiority in preserving the status quo.

That de Blank needed people around him with independent minds and sound judgement is evident. That he did not have such people is equally evident! Those whom he might have consulted with confidence remained outside the coterie.

As for his love for publicity, it is important to realise that under the surface de Blank was a shy man. His assertive and almost pugnacious character was a natural reaction. He found ordinary social contacts a burden despite many appearances to the contrary. He may have entertained magnificently, almost lavishly, but on reflection people realised that he took very little part in the general conversation.

And *'folie de grandeur'*? de Blank could never separate the leadership and pastoral care of a diocese from the work of an archbishop. It was the Archbishop who prevailed and he appeared to see the role of a Metropolitan and Archbishop in princely terms. He arrived with a flamboyant style and seemed to represent a Catholic triumphalism that was dated and certainly inappropriate in a South African setting. If he went to the theatre he went dressed in a magnificent cassock, accompanied by three or four chaplains similarly attired. He believed it to be important that the Church (in its representative the Archbishop) should be visible and that even bad publicity was better than no publicity at all. A story is told of him making a somewhat dramatic entry at a Garden Party at Bishopscourt. He had awaited the arrival of most of his guests among whom was the Roman Catholic Archbishop or his representative. de Blank made a majestic 'entry' down the steps from the patio towards the terraced garden in a cream-coloured cassock and purple cummerbund and skull-cap, with two chaplains in attendance. His Roman Catholic guests were heard to mutter 'Il Papa'. There were occasional solemn evensongs in the Cathedral where de Blank would make a triumphal entrance in a red chimere with train plus train-bearers. It seemed a strange anachronism to onlookers. If his first chaplain was responsible for a good deal of the trappings they did not disappear when he left for a Cape Town parish. de Blank's 'dressing up' and his being surrounded by charming young chaplains led to jokes and tittle-tattle. These were the chaplains in purple cummerbands and purple pom-poms on their birettas who were greeted with the ribald description of 'archiepiscopal budgerigars'.

The problem was that de Blank arrived with his concept of the Metropolitan's role predetermined instead of working his way into it and understanding the Church to which he had been called. Nevertheless, the archiepiscopate developed on encouraging lines, putting de Blank on the world stage. New qualities emerged bringing him not only into the limelight but also into the first rank of Church leaders. This began when he left first for America and then for the Lambeth Conference in 1958.

CHAPTER ELEVEN

World Stage

27 May 1958

Left Cape Town for Jo'burg . . . besieged by reporters at Jan Smuts.
. . . Then by Pan Am en route to Leopoldsville. . . . Once again I'm
very impressed with Pan Am. We have lots of room and excellent
service and a wonderful dinner prepared by Maxim's of Paris!
Smoked salmon, roast duck and orange or fillet of steak and then
the normal sweets, dessert, cheese, coffee.

5 June

New York. Went to see Dr H.K. Sherrill, the Presiding Bishop [of
the Episcopal Church in America]. He was most kind and we had a
long talk. Although he comes from Virginia he is certain it was right
to push through desegregation in America. He wants every man
equal before the law. Civil rights matter more than social
integration. A very sound point.

6 June

Long Island. Reuters have rung up quoting reports of Dutch
Reformed Church resentment to my sermon in New York last
Sunday. They appear to object to my saying that the D.R.C.
supports apartheid. But doesn't it? Every other Calvinistic Church
rejects their theology in social matters. And my sermon only
mentioned D.R.C. *en passant* as believing in apartheid. Its main
burden was an appeal for sacramental (and therefore social) religion
& was a plea to Anglicans to be true to the Catholic Faith. I made a
point of saying that the D.R.C. gave more to Missions & Education
than all the other churches combined.

These three extracts are typical diary entries, reflecting de Blank's
interest in travel, meeting different people (not only distinguished) and recording notes of controversies which might be
required in the future. And there was a furore over the sermon

128

preached at the Church of the Heavenly Rest, New York, on 1 June 1958. Before leaving Jan Smuts airport in Johannesburg, de Blank had indicated that there would be 'no fireworks' on his American and European tour, but added ominously, 'All I attack is inhumanity wherever I find it'. If his critics had read *The Parish in · Action* they would have found a typically hard-biting and revealing sentence: 'A vigorous churchman in the prime of life, who is not politically, civically, or socially alert and therefore almost certainly involved, is a religious monstrosity.' In the same portion of the book they would have read that the faithful Christian, 'is bound to work for a better ordering of society. There must be something of the revolutionary about him, and revo-, lutionaries are uncomfortable to live with.'

Perhaps the critics would not have been so outraged or feigned surprise had they realised that de Blank did not enter the political arena in partisan terms. His concern for justice among men was more passionate than was to be found in those who did not see men as made in God's image. 'His activity in society is part of his Christian obedience and, as Christian obedience involves cross-bearing, he will be prepared to take costly decisions and to act sacrificially in a cause he accepts as part of his discipleship.'

What when the clash is not with secular authority but with another organised Church? In his New York sermon de Blank said, 'It is a sad commentary on the work of the Dutch Reformed Church in South Africa that it spends a good deal of its money on · missionary work, but believes in keeping its African and white congregations separate. It has a warped and inaccurate Calvinistic outlook ... The Anglican Church is trying to fight this · segregation.'

These remarks roused instant and widespread resentment throughout South Africa.

Press comment was critical. The Cape *Argus* (4 June 1958) accused de Blank of 'warped, inaccurate criticism' and thought it was regrettable that, 'the millions of heathen in South Africa should be offered the spectacle, bewildering to them, of one great missionary church attacking another.' The *Natal Daily News* (9 June 1958) advised de Blank to take care in what he said, 'when there is a small but perceptible change in thinking among the apartheid-supporting Afrikaner intellectuals', whilst the *Cape Times* (10 June 1958) criticised both content and venue 'in a distant country and before a congregation that knows little and probably cares less about the exact shades of South African truth'. Nationalist politicians were acutely angry. They were also head-strong following a triumphant election on 16 April when they had become electorally impregnable. The new parliament had 103 Nationalist members, nine more than in the previous House. The Labour Party had been slaughtered from five members to none although for some time it had survived by the grace of the United Party which did not contest its seats. The pusillanimous, white supremist United Party, which contained many Anglicans, had been reduced to fifty-three. de Blank considered he was the victim of, 'a deliberate and well-planned attack' (diary, 10 June 1958). After all, a few words plucked from one sermon was the cause of the eruption against him. He was annoyed at misrepresentation but not at the controversy itself. 'I'm all against polite dishonesty so that we may keep on speaking terms' (diary, 8 June 1958).

Above all, de Blank's views were attacked by the Dutch Reformed Church. The immediate practical consequence was a succession of people announcing that they were withdrawing from a proposed fraternal inter-Church conference in December. However, the Dutch Reformed Church did not speak with one voice. The Church in the Union was composed of various autonomous bodies. The Transvaal D.R.C. (Nederduitse Gereformeerde Kerk van Transvaal) was the largest and most powerful of the Dutch Reformed Churches and it, taken together with the Cape Dutch Reformed Church, really did represent the 'Dutch Reformed Church'. Representatives of the Moderatures of the Dutch Reformed Churches of the Cape, Transvaal, Free State and Natal made a united and immediate response to de Blank's New York sermon and wrote to the Diocesan Office in Cape Town (in de Blank's absence) on 4 June. They were particularly incensed at the remarks being made not to them but to a biased audience in a foreign country.

> ... The Dutch Reformed Churches do not know how that action can be reconciled (a) with the sisterly relations that have existed for many years between the Anglican and the Dutch Reformed Churches, as recently again demonstrated in the joint action of these Churches in the investigating commission of the World Council of Churches into the Christian responsibility in areas of rapid social change and in other similar matters; (b) in the light of the recent public pronouncement of the Archbishop himself that he was not attacking the Dutch Reformed Churches on apartheid as

such; (c) the undeniable fact that a certain measure of apartheid is practised by the Anglican Church in her institutions and that this Church is thus placed in a highly vulnerable position if she ` condemns apartheid in another Church.

But especially do the Dutch Reformed Churches regret that, if the Archbishop has objections to the practices of these Churches, he does not bring these objections to the attention of these Churches in ` a brotherly manner, rather than broadcast the matter before an overseas audience, and in so doing wittingly or unwittingly creating in a foreign land a spirit of animosity against another Christian Church.

We disapprove of this action, and its continuance by the Archbishop on his overseas lecture tour cannot but create an unhappy and strained relationship between the Churches concerned.

We would kindly ask you to bring this letter to the attention of His Grace, The Archbishop.

With regards.

During the summer, de Blank was at the Lambeth Conference and on his return to South Africa there were the annual meetings of the Episcopal Synod of the Church of the Province and massive arrears of routine work, so a considered reply was not sent to Ds C.B. Brink of Johannesburg, on behalf of the group, until 11 December 1958. Part of the reply is worth quoting, for although it sustains his attack yet it erects a bridge across which both Churches might cross. Reconciliation may not be a possibility but understanding was not impossible.

... I deny that I so singled out your Church; I accused all churches in South Africa — my own particularly — of their non- and sub-Christian conduct that had led to the present inter-racial *impasse* in South Africa. But I do not deny saying that only the group of churches under the general designation of 'Dutch Reformed' had managed to accept the policy of apartheid (in spite of manifest injustice and inhumanity) and that such an attitude was possible through a twisted Calvinism ...

I now realize that the official policy of the Dutch Reformed Churches in this country is not based on theology but on practical expediency. This idea raises many interesting problems and can prove a source of fruitful discussion; but it must be admitted that there has been every excuse for misunderstanding and confusion. For example I need refer you only to certain speeches made by D.R.C. leaders at the recent S.A.B.R.A. Conference in which (if I read rightly) in inter-racial matters certain theological principles and doctrines were invoked. It would be most helpful to all Christian bodies if the official policy could be more positively and strongly proclaimed and if the opinions of those who see theological implications in apartheid could be more positively and strongly disavowed.

I must repeat my astonishment at the rapidity with which your spokesmen seized on certain phrases in my American sermon without waiting for a complete transcript — particularly when your much greater experience of the State Information Service's news must have convinced you long ago that they are notorious more for their boosting of Government policy than for the impartial accuracy of their reporting. I am astonished too that you refused to accept the explanation I gave as soon as I heard of the storm that had been engendered.

Nevertheless, I am sincerely grieved that you remain convinced that the Dutch Reformed Churches were unfairly and unjustifiably attacked. That there are differences between your Churches and the other Churches in this country, the whole world knows; that no church works so hard or gives so generously in evangelistic enterprise as do your churches, I proclaimed wherever I went; and that I exonerated my Church at the expense of your Churches is palpably untrue.

It may be that if a small body of us could meet together in fraternal consultation, we might find far more to unite us than is obvious at first sight. We own a common Lord; all our hope is in His atoning death; we seek to live by His grace; and we pray daily for the coming of his Kingdom.

If I have sinned against the law of truth and love that should bind our churches together in honesty and goodwill, I am deeply penitent.

If you and your authorities consider that any profit can result from 'conversations' between two or three of your leaders and two or three of ours, I shall be happy to do all I can (from our side) to organize and take part in such conversations.

(There was a meeting in 1959 which will be considered in a later chapter.)

Meanwhile, de Blank had arrived in England for the Lambeth Conference. Three hundred and ten bishops from forty-six countries assembled under the Presidency of Geoffrey Fisher, Archbishop of Canterbury. There were committees on The Holy Bible: Its Authority and Message; Church Unity and the Church Universal; Progress in the Anglican Communion; The Family in

Contemporary Society and The Reconciling of Conflict between and within Nations. de Blank was Chairman of this latter committee: the Bishop of Southern Ohio (Henry W. Hobson), Vice Chairman, and the Bishop of Kurunagala (Lakdasa de Mel) Secretary. It was a difficult committee with the group's members holding such divergent views, and at times antagonistic, so that the unity of purpose and the ability to produce any report was threatened. The Bishop of Southern Ohio subsequently recorded his impressions:

> For days we debated what should be said about thermo-nuclear weapons; racial conflict in South Africa, the United States and Asia; the basic rights of men and nations; the sharing of material resources; the United Nations; the place and responsibilities of the Church in an industrial age; Israel and the Arab world; and the threat to peace which political conflicts in certain nations present. The fact that the differences in opinions held by members of the Committee were based upon deep and sincere convictions, and were born from beliefs which were founded upon the dictates of conscience, made it difficult and at times impossible for those holding opposing views to come to a common agreement.
> It was in the hard struggle to create reconciliation within the Committee that the members gained a clearer understanding both of the true nature of reconciliation, of how respect and understanding can be a basis for unity even among those who differ greatly in their convictions, and of what the Committee and Lambeth should say to the Church and society about how to deal with conflict between and within nations. It was no easy task. Mistrust, suspicion, misunderstanding, pride, hurt feelings, and even ill will were temptations which we on the Committee had to fight against before we achieved the respect, confidence, insight, humility and understanding which in the end bound us together in a close unity of spirit. Many of us saw in our differences the causes which create conflicts in society, and as we reconciled these differences (even without the ability to agree always) we caught a vision of the road which must be travelled by men who are in conflict in order to achieve understanding and peace instead of disunity and war.

The most difficult aspect of the Committee's work was concerned with 'modern warfare and Christian responsibility'. That sub-committee was chaired by Ambrose Reeves of Johannesburg, and William C. Campbell, Bishop of West Virginia, was Secretary. Although the committee was unanimous in re-affirming (from

Lambeth Conferences of 1930 and 1948) that 'war as a method of settling international disputes is incompatible with the teaching and example of our Lord Jesus Christ', it was divided over the issue of thermo-nuclear warfare. Some bishops 'convinced that the use of [nuclear] weapons is morally unjustifiable in any circumstances' advocated unilateral nuclear disarmament. Other bishops — the majority — considered 'that in the present uncertain situation, and until international agreement is reached, individual nations are justified in retaining these weapons as a lesser evil than surrendering them and increasing the possibility of an unscrupulous attack'.

Amongst its resolutions, the Lambeth Conference affirmed 'its belief in the natural dignity and value of every man, of whatever colour or race, as created in the image of God', and condemned, 'discrimination of any kind on the grounds of race or colour alone'.

Many bishops watched with interest, listened with care and contrasted Ambrose Reeves with de Blank. William J. Gordon Jnr., Bishop of Alaska, later wrote of Reeves and his sub-committee: 'I have the greatest respect and admiration for Bishop Reeves as a forthright, fearless, committed and dedicated follower of Jesus Christ. I found him to be a man of courage and without guile, but with the awesome gentleness that comes with true commitment. Like most totally committed people and those completely involved in a specific cause, he is inclined to be somewhat oblivious of the causes and opinions of others, and on several occasions his committee in Lambeth described it as being a chairman with a *minority* of 14 members!' But he could also say: 'The world needs far more men like Ambrose Reeves, totally committed, fearless, and dedicated, so much so that they probably have to be arbitrary. Like St. Paul, this may not have made Bishop Reeves always an easy man to live *with*, but he certainly has made his world a better place to live *in*'.

The controlled intelligence and prickly earnestness of Reeves was expected to be complemented by the charged dynamism and effortless flamboyance of de Blank. That is what was expected. Instead, we find Philip Carrington, Archbishop of Quebec, referring to de Blank's 'careful and balanced utterances'. de Blank perceived and developed the theme of reconciliation. It was the great word of the Conference. It was not deliberately planted, but group after group were driven to this word as the most living and pertinent expression of the Gospel for the second half of the twentieth century. Lecturing on this theme in 1961 (The Bohlen Lectures at Philadelphia) de Blank said: 'The idea of reconciliation has nothing in common with compromise. This is no attempt to find peace at the expense of truth. But in a recognition of our humanity, in an acknowledgement that all men share in our fallen human nature, arrogance and pride give place to humility and patience. Because no one is without sin, so no one dare cast the first stone; and in humbleness of mind we declare what we believe and are prepared to listen to what others believe, praying not that our views as against those of others shall prevail but that the Holy Spirit of God may lead us all to the truth as it is in Jesus. This is the dialectical process so consistently denied by those who are its most vociferous advocates'.

If Reconciliation was the major word of the Lambeth Conference it increasingly became the dominant theme of de Blank's preaching. In *Uncomfortable Words* he had taken the Sermon on the Mount, ('first be reconciled to thy brother, and then come and offer thy gift') and united reconciliation and forgiveness. People who do not suffer fools gladly or at all are often intolerant of weakness and insensitive to strength in others. How difficult it is for genuine reconciliation to take place. On forgiveness, de Blank asserted that it must, 'reach out to embrace the offender; we must convince him that the separating barrier has been broken down. Like the prodigal — who knew that his father's heart of love beat unceasingly for him, so must those who have wronged us know that we are not patronizingly demanding justice or satisfaction, not even apportioning blame, but that we are ready and eager to create an even richer communion than we experienced before'.

How difficult in practice! de Blank knew that, 'knowledge puffeth up, but love edifieth' yet the element of love, the considerateness of sympathy, the tender solicitude for the backward, and scrupulous and ignorant was frequently lacking. Pride of superior knowledge, pride of spiritual office, pride of ecclesiastical dominion, pride of self assertion — everywhere pride. He detested these blemishes in himself and again and again cringed before God's Judgement, for an aspect of his Calvanistic youth never completely left him. There was an inner anguish and it is significant that he took with him from Stepney to Cape Town a seventy-one year old priest, Fr. Thomas (Bernard Gilpin

135

Hepworth) who was his friend, confessor and spiritual adviser. de Blank wanted to pray more and deepen his spiritual life. He did not always find it easy to realise that Christian penitence is intended to be stimulating rather than depressing. It is a time to strengthen the good in us and not merely a bromide to quieten the evil. It hurts of course. Purgatorial pains are a reality in this world. But it is the bracing hurt of returning health, the growing pains of restored grace in the soul.

One wonders if the Lambeth Fathers might look at some of the particular temptations which are strewn along episcopal paths. And before clergy and laity unite to blame bishops for lack of, or too much, leadership, they should look to themselves and remember the inveterate duplicity of the human heart, and the strangely mingled character of human motives.

de Blank could not help but read the rumours surrounding his name at Lambeth. It was annoying but natural to read of speculations about 'Lambeth's incoming tenant?' It could not be long before Geoffrey Fisher retired as Archbishop of Canterbury. Who would succeed? The able and safe candidate apppeared to be Robert Wright Stopford, Bishop of Peterborough, Episcopal Secretary to the Lambeth Conference, who was subsequently translated to London in 1961 — by which time de Blank had wrecked his own chances of succeeding to that See. There was nothing 'safe' about de Blank but 'Joost Cantuar' did not appear an impossible dream to his supporters or an unmitigated nightmare to his critics. A 1958 report referred to him as 'a man entirely in command of himself, relaxed yet sombrely intense, courteous yet withdrawn. However outspoken his statements, it is always clear that they are considered and that he means what he says.'

It was natural that the dominating figure of the conference was the Archishop of Canterbury, but the theological heavyweight was Michael Ramsey, Archbishop of York, who chaired the Committee on the Bible, and it was he who would three years later succeed Geoffrey Fisher.

Lakdasa de Mel of Kurunagala was described thus: 'a profound realism and sense of urgency was compatible with a certain gaiety and sense of drama'. How like de Blank! And what did de Mel observe in de Blank during the meetings of the Committee on Reconciling of Conflicts Between and Within Nations? 'Joost at work gave clear guidance and got the work done. One admired him but there were one or two disturbing thoughts ... The brickbats of the South African racialists were countered by the undisguised admiration of most of us, but was there appearing at times the hint of a Prima Donna?'

An interesting All-Africa Bishops' Conference was held at St. Augustine's College, Canterbury, on 1 and 2 July 1958 and over forty out of a possible fifty bishops attended. In a group photograph it is interesting to see de Blank wearing apron and gaiters. One of those present, Lucian Usher-Wilson, Bishop on the Upper Nile, made the observation afterwards: 'Anyone who has worked in Africa during the last decade must be aware of the dawning consciousness of a sense of 'oneness' among the younger generations of Africans, hardly expressible, perhaps inexplicable in a continent so vast and varied, yet definitely felt'. Concern was expressed at the growing number of emotional ephemeral sects due to the lack of intensity and passion of witness to their Faith by Anglican leaders and members. 'One matter received considerable and even heated attention. It was discovered that whereas in West and East Africa there were now many African national Bishops, none has as yet been consecrated in South Africa. Eventually it was explained. African nationals have not yet been elected, not because of any constitutional or racial barrier (indeed in some dioceses in South Africa, African clergy outnumber Western clergy) but because it is realized that in the present difficult circumstances they would stand no chance of fulfilling their episcopal office adequately'.

A.W.F. Howells, Bishop of Lagos, himself an African national, thought they should show solidarity with their fellow Christians struggling for freedom in the South.

Following the All-Africa Bishops' Conference, de Blank's restless innovative mind was thinking of ways to formalise the links between bishops in Africa. Should not the Church be sensitive to the growth of Pan-Africanism? When the first conference of independent African States assembled in Africa in April 1958 there were eight independent African States. When de Blank left South Africa in 1963 there were three times that number. There was a rising militancy too. Kwame Nkrumah of Ghana, whom de Blank admired, told the Conference of African Freedom Fighters (4 June 1962): 'We must unify ourselves in policy and in action, both between all of us who are independent and between the independent states and the still unliberated millions on this continent ... But there still remains the gigantic task ahead of redeeming from the grinding heel of colonialist-imperialism the parts of Africa still under its yoke. Africa is for Africans and unless those within our gates can accept the rule of the majority, they must either pick themselves up and go, or be forced to surrender to our just demands.' And this came from the President of the Republic of Ghana in which the Anglican Diocese of Accra, whose majority of priests were African, had specifically asked for an Englishman as its new Bishop in 1956! He was Reginald Roseveare of the Society of the Sacred Mission (a Kelham Father) who at the time was Provincial of his Community in South Africa. He too had served on de Blank's committee at the Lambeth Conference. When he arrived in Ghana he was shocked to find how little was known there about South Africa or its Anglican Church. He too thought there was need for some common policies throughout the Continent.

What de Blank contemplated went further than this. Like Dr. Nkrumah he wanted to get a conception of Africa as a whole and wrote to the Archbishop of Canterbury in December 1958 proposing a name *The Episcopal Church of Africa*. This proposal received a cold douche of water when the Archbishop replied (1 January 1959): 'My mind always goes back to the New Testament, and there it was the Church in Jerusalem, the Church in Antioch, the Church in Alexandria, the Church in Corinth, and so on. That is to say, the unit was a place; well, we have to go wider than that now, but I am sure that the jump to a whole continent, such as Africa, would be misleading. For the divisions of Africa have their own special characteristics. The Church of South Africa exists in completely different circumstances from the Church in West Africa, while the Church of Central Africa has only just come into existence and there is not yet a Church in East Africa or a Church in Uganda. Since titles are for convenience, I should say that without any doubt that the convenient and suitable thing is still for a long time to talk about the Church of the various sections of Africa which present themselves politically and geographically and historically.'

These words did not deter de Blank. He advocated a meeting of the Archbishops of the African Provinces planned to coincide with the inauguration of a new Province of Uganda in 1961. Writing to the Archbishop of West Africa, James Lawrence Cecil Horstead (26 October 1960) de Blank wrote: 'I am quite certain that far and away the most important item on the agenda must be the possible formation of a single Church for the whole of Africa — or certainly for Africa south of the Sahara — grouped together in a series of Provinces, each under its own Metropolitan and with one of their number appointed or elected Primate of the whole Church. I believe such a course of action to be right from every point of view and to outweigh in importance any other matters we could consider together.'

de Blank wanted the archbishops to consider the meaning of 'pan-Africanism' or 'all-Africa outlook'. How could the Church regain initiative in Africa? Was it too much concerned to preserve the status quo? (He thought it was.) Or was it open to new ways of obedience to Christ in a rapidly-changing world? (He thought it should be.) How could the Anglican Communion, with its long experience of varied Church-State relationships, guide African rulers and people in the new relationships in which they found themselves? Was there not need for rapid acceleration of leadership-training for African Christians? Was the church in its ordained ministry producing men of the calibre and drive of such men as Nkruma? Julius Nyere? Tom Mboya? Kenneth Kaunda? The small number of graduate clergy was a real danger. de Blank saw these issues clearly, but could not quite so clearly appreciate the problems of marriage and polygamy, urbanisation (for essentially the Church in Africa is a rural Church and it is rural minded), and the expansion of Islam.

In his planning, on a rather grandiose scale, de Blank failed to face the very considerable weakness of the Anglican Church in Africa. Over against the main bulk of the population which was not Christian and over and against the Christians of other denominations the Anglicans made a poor showing. Indeed, there was a real danger that the number of Anglicans in Uganda and Nigeria would inflate the figures out of their real significance. Omit those who were in concentrated groups and the total was not impressive. The *prestige* value of Anglicanism was in de Blank's mind. But what would happen when finally the prestige value of having been the Established Church of the Imperial power vanished?

In his dream — and possibly personal desire — for a primate of All Africa, he was still thinking in paternalistic terms. The Primate would have to be financed and have his own office and officials. The number of advisers and officials would not be small if an inter-provincial, inter-Anglican 'strategy' were to be realised. Questions of race, language and tradition posed enormous challenges. And with every challenge there was a financial consequence. Who would pay? England? America? *South Africa*? These questions were asked and almost always the wrong answers were given. Rarely did the financial finger point at the Africans themselves who were lamentable givers, having for too long received bounty from other countries. Few bishops turned to their dioceses and said, for example, 'If you want a beautiful and imposing Cathedral pay for it!' Instead, they sought money abroad. How could a truly African Church emerge in such circumstances? That was 1960 when there were only four Provinces (South Africa 1853; West Africa 1951; Central Africa 1955; East Africa 1960) with Uganda, Rwanda and Burundi joining them in 1961. All had English archbishops. By 1986 East Africa had been divided into the Provinces of Kenya (1970) and Tanzania (1970). Uganda stood on its own and a new Province of Burundi, Rwanda and Zaire came into force in 1980. West Africa was divided in 1979 when Nigeria became a Province. Another, The Sudan, was formed in 1974. All archbishops are now nationals and in 1986 Cape Town elected its first black Archbishop, Desmond Tutu.

At the archbishops' meeting in Kampala in April 1961 those attending were Central Africa (William James Hughes); East Africa (Leonard James Beecher); the Bishop of Ibadan, (Solomon Oduaiya Odutola) representing the retiring Archbishop of West Africa; the Bishop of Namirembe (Leslie Wilfrid Brown) who was Archbishop elect of Uganda, Ruanda and Burundi, and de Blank. The Archbishop of Canterbury and Bishop Stephen Bayne (Executive Office of the Anglican Communion) who were in Kampala for the inauguration of the new Province were also in attendance. It was a good meeting. Views were exchanged regarding relationships between provinces and partnership among provinces. Four themes were on the agenda: The Unity of the Church and the Union of Churches; The Ministry of the Church; Evangelistic Problems; Pastoral Problems. de Blank's idea for an Anglican Church of Africa was received with interest rather than relish. Of greater concern were relations with other Churches. The rise of world denominations has in most places very seriously hindered the progress of movements for a local united church and back in South Africa de Blank had faced intractable problems with the Dutch Reformed Church, vitriolic clashes with the Government of South Africa and tensions within his own Church ever since his return from the Lambeth Conference in 1958.

CHAPTER TWELVE

Doing Battle

On 2 September 1958 Dr. Hendrik Frensch Verwoerd was elected Prime Minister to succeed Strijdom who had died on 25 August. In a national broadcast on the evening of his election he said, 'It must be stated at the outset that we, as believing rulers of a religious country, will seek our strength and guidance in the future, as in the past, from Him who controls the destinies of nations ... In accordance with His will it was determined who should assume the leadership of the Government in this new period of the life of the people of South Africa'.

Strijdom had quickened the tempo set by Malan by underlining the dogma of white domination. He maintained that all legislation must bear the *Baasskap* or boss-ship of the white man. What the Aryan was to Hitler's Germany, that the white man was to Strijdom's South Africa. In both, the anti-Christian idea of a 'herrenvolk' was proclaimed.

With the coming of Verwoerd a more fanatical period was likely. He wanted to organise the Union so that white and black never came into contact. His conviction at least credited him with facing the logical outcome of his political theories. His time at the Ministry for Native Affairs had been devoted to the idea of complete apartheid, of a geographical separation into two or more peoples.

The English-originating industrialists, who were wealth producers in the Union, shuddered. They were 'mugwumps' — wanting maximum social segregation but minimum African labour problems.

Verwoerd was an intelligent and complex person. It is difficult to know the exact source of his theories. Though like de Blank Dutch by birth, he had nothing in common with the majority of Dutchmen who in Indonesia and in their other overseas possessions had

141

had less of a colour bar than almost any other colonizing power. One would have thought that a Professor of Applied Psychology (the chair he held at the University of Stellenbosch) would have read enough of Jung and Adler, if not of Freud, to have shown him the folly of any arbitrary psychic differentiation based on cosmetic pigmentation alone. Whatever the origin of Verwoerd's ideology, no one could doubt the determination with which he held it and the energy with which he sought to implement it.

Under Verwoerd, South Africa was virtually a one man government. Within a year of his election many who previously professed liberal opinions sank into silence or servitude. The pusillanimity of the Opposition shocked and saddened its supporters and well-wishers.

The sickening sycophancy around Verwoerd touched idolatry. A verse (translated) printed in the 'informal' monthly journal *Bantu* (November 1959) where articles gave the Government's view on apartheid, is a case in point:

> Dr. Verwoerd, thou art the Shepherd of the Black races
> Thou art the defender of the Bantu, our rock, our mountain.
> . . .
> The Saviour who rescued us at the time of need.
> We the Bantu boast and say: 'Glory unto thee Dr. Verwoerd
> And to all who are the defenders of the Bantu':
> . . .
> Dr. Verwoerd, thou art with us; Glory unto thee our redeemer
> Praises be unto Dr. Verwoerd, the defender of the Bantu.

This may have been an extreme form of propaganda, self-gratification or self-delusion of the Government, but it carries the stench of a leader on a pedestal above ordinary mortals. How could one oppose or deal with such a man?

In his first Charge to the Cape Town Diocesan Synod given on 3 December 1958 de Blank referred to the past year's events: 'In all this controversy . . . one thing has surprised me, and that is the vociferous minority who believe that a concern for humanity and social justice is politics and not Christianity'. Such thinking reflected a lopsided view of the Incarnation. God became man in Christ Jesus, and so all life, including its political aspect, was the sphere of Christian obedience. Would Verwoerd quarrel with that? The gospel brings to everyone who receives it the conviction that social service is a religious duty. To withdraw selfishly from the tasks and risks of social life, whether in despair or in self-absorption is the repudiation of a divine commission. Again, would Verwoerd take issue with that? That was — and remains — a great difficulty in attacking or reproaching the policies of a Government which is not godless nor an oppressor of religion , but one which claims to be divinely inspired and controlled. But de Blank's interpretation of the incarnation went deeper. His words and actions were motivated less by hatred than by love. There was another dimension too. Like many Christians he felt a certain responsibility for the world's sin, and for the sorrows which at once reflected and avenged it. As a disciple of Christ he was commissioned and challenged: 'We must work the works of Him that sent me while it is day: the night cometh when no man can work'. The world is saved from acquiescing in its scandals by the divine indignation of individual Christians. And de Blank knew it was his duty to resist evil where it met him and to attack , abuses when they crossed his path. What he was doing was simply translating his creed into conduct, giving a social expression to discipleship and illustrating his religion. If often his words were harsh and expressed in provocative language it was because he was determined that he should be heard. Righteous anger may not be attractive but in South Africa de Blank deemed it necessary. Yet to those whose diet was not limited to the *hors d'oeuvres* of newspaper headlines or the desserts dished out by Government ministers, there was content and wholesomeness in the main meal. de Blank spoke from within a company of sinners, not a community of saints, who being aware of their sins and shortcomings asked God for grace to amend their lives, corporately and individually. This did not mean that they should keep their heads low, for as de Blank told the 1958 Synod, 'Our own failures, our own blemishes, our own weakness — none of these things invalidate the word of judgement that in the name of God the Church is called to utter as Christian obedience demands. For the word we speak we speak to ourselves as well as to the nation.'

de Blank's problems arose, as they do for any bishop, in reconciling the dual functions of being leader and reconciler — the focus ' of unity of the Church in a particular place. Was his own Church in the Diocese of Cape Town free from practising apartheid? ' . . . even the slightest smell of a *compulsory* apartheid must be removed . from our churches. Man cannot touch pitch without being defiled — and we are forbidden to have any fellowship with the unfruitful works of darkness. We dare not let ourselves be contaminated by such a social poison'.

How could de Blank be a focus of unity when at this early stage of his archiepiscopate, opposition within the diocese to his stand on apartheid was either muted or underground. There were occasional outbursts, as for example by a retired bishop living in the diocese, Basil William Peacey (Bishop of Lebombo 1929 — 1935). He asked for leave of absence from the 1958 Synod as his universal right of judgment was being called in question. He held that in matters concerning, 'the differential treatment of different ethnical cultures' the Church of the Province had allowed him to exercise his right of private loyalty to the Church. He believed that had changed under de Blank.

At the Synod a resolution, based on a proposal by de Blank, that the Church should establish a mixed school for coloured and white pupils, was passed.

There is no doubt that de Blank expected Synod to follow his lead. At the beginning of his Charge to the 1958 Synod he used a self-revealing and in some respects an unfortunate phrase. Referring to his own election he said, 'You called me to reign over you in the place of Geoffrey Clayton'. Is there not a whiff of triumphalism in the word 'reign' — of a monarch who expects loyalty and requires obedience?

A week after the Synod there was the Day of the Covenant (16 November), a public holiday especially sacred to the Afrikaner people. St. George's Cathedral, Cape Town, celebrated this by having a solemn Eucharist. It was not unusual for white, black and coloured to worship in the Cathedral where outside its main entrance the following words were displayed so bravely: 'This Church is open for all services to all people of all races'. But it was the first time in the Cathedral's history that an African priest, Stanley Dilika Qabazi (of Holy Cross, Nyanga) acted as deacon. A coloured priest, James Ho Kim (Rector of St. Philip, Cape Town) was sub-deacon, and another coloured priest, George Alfred Swartz (then of Saldanka Bay and now Bishop of Kimberley and Kuruman) became the second non-European to preach from the Cathedral pulpit. The Dean celebrated and de Blank presided. This kind of occasion and the publicity given to it strengthened de Blank's hand within the diocese and increased opposition from Government sources.

The friction accelerated when de Blank wrote in *Good Hope*

144

(January 1959): 'We have no complaints about [*Die*] *Burger's* news coverage. But to its leader writers we offer a gentle reminder of the old Latin tag about *suppressio veri et suggestio falsi.*' The Editor of *Die Burger* wrote to de Blank privately (10 January 1959) asking him to prove his allegations. de Blank replied: 'In your official capacity I would have you know that I see no purpose in doing as you ask me. You have had a long innings and your attacks upon me have been persistent. You now offer me a single short innings to reply — and then, no doubt, you will think it legitimate to return to the attack, and your readers will be assured that you have treated me fairly'. Then, tongue in cheek, he added: 'If for the next twelve months you were willing to let me have a weekly column in the *Burger* in which I could comment on news and views giving these my own interpretation and being free to state my own convictions such an offer I might consider'.

de Blank said he was prepared to have a tape-recorded conversation with the Editor.

The offers remained as ink on paper but, following challenge and counter-challenge, the correspondence was released. *Die Burger* was regarded as the most moderate of the daily newspapers printed in Afrikaans but from thence forward it was 'total war'. This was no surprise as de Blank's name was increasingly linked with all manner of organisations opposed to the Government and its policies. Leaders of opposing organisations began to make their approaches to de Blank. He was already associated with the Treason Trial Defence Fund.

On 1 April 1959 de Blank accepted the Presidency of the *Campaign Against Racial Discrimination in Sport* — a British based organisation. Three Members of Parliament were Vice Presidents — Ted Leather (Conservative), Fenner Brockway (Labour) and Donald Wade (Liberal). A.J. Ayer, then Professor of Philosophy at London University, was Chairman of the Committee. The Campaign was started in April 1958 to try to secure the participation of Non-European sportsmen from South Africa and Southern Rhodesia in the Empire Games at Cardiff. Considerable publicity was given to this endeavour and public and private support for the Campaign increased. Its aim was not to substitute one pernicious form of discrimination by another, whereby white South Africans would be excluded from international sport. They attempted the impossible, namely, persuading whites-only associations to amend their constitutions to admit people of all races. They were asking no more than that the Olympic Charter should be applied — 'No discrimination is allowed against any country or person on grounds of race, religion and politics'.

de Blank gave much time and attention to the Campaign and to the South African Sports Association which was formed in 1959 to serve the cause of non-white sportsmen in a non-racial manner. Sport is akin to religion amongst white South Africans and thus a high profile was given to de Blank's interventions. Yet progress was hindered by the rules of the South Africa Olympic and Commonwealth Games Association: hamstrung by apartheid legislation and hampered by silliness amongst those the Association and Campaign were trying to help. An example of this was an inter-racial cricket match organised by a group of journalists and sportsmen to protest against apartheid in sport, planned for 22 March 1959 at Newlands, Cape Town. Eleven leading white cricketers, including three Springboks, and eleven top coloured cricketers were to be divided into two mixed teams, one captained by ex-Springbok Owen Wynne and the other by the coloured player Basil d'Oliviera. The match was cancelled at the last moment incredibly because the officials of the Coloured Cricket Board would not allow their players to play in mixed teams. They feared a protest of the kind planned might jeopardise the imminent West Indian tour. For de Blank this illuminated the urgency of the situation 'and the increasing isolation of all races.'

de Blank had already been approached by the Archbishop of the West Indies (Alan J. Knight) on the question of the West Indies Cricket team visit to South Africa. The Archbishop had received letters from such people as Alan Paton (author and President of the South African Liberal Party) and Canon John Collins (of Christian Action) asking the Archbishop to use his influence with the West Indies Cricket Board of Control to decline the invitation.

de Blank wrote to the Archbishop (11 March 1959):

> ... I am in complete agreement with you that to confine their matches to Europeans only in this country would be most unfortunate and would certainly be accepting the present Government's policy of apartheid in the realms of sport. I should have thought that the refusal of the West Indies Cricket Team to tour on these terms would be a most effective protest against this policy of total apartheid and I am quite willing that you should use my name in stating this.

In South Africa de Blank's statements were usually bold, but sometimes cautious for he was aware of conflict of opinion among the coloured population and knew the South African Government and its supporters were expert at discovering the slightest chink in the armour of their opponents. de Blank was drawn into debate over the non selection of non-white sportsmen into the Olympic team in 1960. The authorities, albeit disingenuously, simply referred to the fact that individual non-white sporting associations had failed to affiliate to the recognised South African Governing Body of Sport. Trials were controlled and governed by that Body so it was unlikely that the *best* athletes, irrespective of colour, would have joined the Olympic team.

In most sporting spheres the difficulties were immense. Even within the Church many individuals were torn between their loyalty to the principles of the Church and their worship of sport, which was and is one of the ruling passions of the average South African. In his personal relations with individual campaigners, de Blank, unlike his episcopal colleague Ambrose Reeves, of Johannesburg, was cautious. Dennis Brutus, one time Hon-Secretary of the South African Sports Association and equally active against apartheid in education and in housing, records his admiration and appreciation of de Blank's stand against apartheid, though of personal contacts he writes: 'I was received with great courtesy and sympathy (but perhaps a little caution! — it is not easy to explain the kind of fear and suspicion which the awareness of Special Branch interest generates in South Africa) and he was I think diplomatic enough not to indicate to me the full extent of his commitment and involvement in the particular area — very likely because he was working closely with contacts in Britain.'

Could any real achievement accrue from progress by stealth? Was it worth discussing anything with the Dutch Reformed Church? Perhaps it was, particularly after an important meeting of The Reformed Ecumenical Synod which had met at Potchefstroom in August 1958. Representatives attended from the Nederduitse Gereformeerde Kerke of South Africa, Gereformeerde Kerke in South Africa, Christian Reformed Church of the U.S.A., Gereformeerde Kerke of the Netherlands, Free Church of Scotland, Orthodox Presbyterian Church of the U.S.A., the Irish Evangelical Church, the Presbyterian Church of Eastern Australia, the Church of England in South Africa (not to be confused with the Church of the Province) and the Union Nationale des Eglises Reformées Evangeliques Independentes de France. These Churches agreed an historic statement on race relations, including the following:

> No single race may deem itself entitled to a privileged position and consider itself superior to other races.

> If the members of the other race are likewise believers, they should be received as brethren and sisters in Jesus Christ.

> The foregoing neither denies nor ignores the fact of the multiplicity of nations, but in that multiplicity the unquestioned equality of all races, peoples and manifestations of the true Church must be recognised according to the Scripture.

> It is the duty of the Church to avoid even a semblance of an attitude which can engender estrangement between groups, and to make every effort to improve the already strained relations.

> In order to progress towards the unity of believers, the efforts of the younger Churches to achieve full ecclesiastical equality with older Churches should be encouraged.

> No direct scriptural evidence can be produced for or against the inter-mixture of races through marriage. The well-being of the Christian community and pastoral care of the Church necessitate, however, that due consideration be given to the legal, social and cultural factors which affect such marriages.

> The Church should critically examine in the light of God's Word such concepts as trusteeship, racial distinctiveness, etc., which are the stock-in-trade of discussions of racial matters, in order to purge such concepts of any ulterior motives which may be lurking therein.

The postponed informal fraternal conference between members of the Anglican Church and the Nederduitse Gereformeerde Kerk took place on 19 May 1959. The original initiative had come from Quintin Whyte, Director of the South African Institute for Race Relations. Arrangements for the Conference were conducted between de Blank and Domine C.B. Brink, Moderator of the N.G. Kerk. Strong contingents from both Churches attended the meeting held in the N.G. Kerk building in Bloemfontein. From the N.G. Kerk were the Revs. Dr. A.J. van der Merwe (Moderator of the Cape Synod); P.S.Z. Coetzee (Moderator of the Free State Synod); A.M. Meiring (Moderator of the Transvaal General Synod), H.J.C. Snyders (Moderator of the Natal Synod); W.A. Landman (secretary of the Cape Synod) and C.B. Brink. The Anglican Church was represented by Bishops Ambrose Reeves of Johannesburg and Bill Burnett of Bloemfontein; C.T. Wood (Archdeacon of Cape Town); E.L. King (Dean of Cape Town); A.H. Zulu, (of St. Faith's Mission, Durban) and de Blank.

The difficulties of arranging such a meeting were immense and the fact that it took place at all was a kind of milestone. There may have been last minute problems when de Blank informed Brink (14 April) that, 'one of the Anglican representatives (A.H. Zulu) will be an African clergyman' but after consulting his colleagues in the Transvaal, Brink replied (29 April), 'I have been authorised to state that we are not in a position and do not desire to dictate to the Church of the Province whom it should send to represent it at talks of this nature'. The malady of apartheid was illustrated on the Anglican side when de Blank wrote to the Bishop of Bloemfontein (31 March) asking him to arrange hospitality at the Maitland Hotel or elsewhere — 'Canon Zulu will have to be accommodated elsewhere'. Canon Zulu stayed at the Bishop's home.

It was neither planned nor expected that much would emerge from a single meeting. At least it might be possible for a few frank exchanges to be made. Ambrose Reeves wrote to de Blank of:

Thoughts that disturb me about the Dutch Reformed Church:
1   the allegation that the leadership of the Dutch Reformed Church in the Transvaal is deeply involved in the Broederbond. (e.g. assertion Moderator for years member of Executive of Broederbond).
2   silence of Dutch Reformed church —
    (a) when know leaders of other churches being unfairly attacked both inside and outside parliament:
    (b) when grave injustice is being inflicted on some people, e.g. Group Areas Act.
3   attitude of Dutch Reformed Church to Native Laws Amendment Act, and in particular to the Church clause.
4   the admission that the support of apartheid has no theological basis, but is only matter of practical expediency. This is claimed by some to be an advance from the time when many Dutch Reformed Church leaders believed that there was a theological foundation for apartheid. But to my mind the present position of the church is even more untenable than the former. Now there can no longer be any serious theological discussion between us, even though I believe that between Christians it is

at the deep theological level alone that any fruitful discussion on apartheid can take place.

5   the inconsistency of certain Dutch Reformed Churches being members of the World Council of Churches and yet steadily refusing to co-operate on the Christian Council of South Africa. This means that whenever there is to be any collaboration between the Dutch Reformed Church and other churches a special committee has to be set up to make it possible.

6   the impression that a great deal of the money that it is claimed is being used for missionary work in the Transvaal is in fact being used for proselytism. There is a certain amount of evidence that this is so, although at the moment it is not clear how far the leadership of the church is responsible and how far it is due either to specially favourable treatment of the church by the government or to the misplaced zeal of some of the rank and file of the church.

The meeting also took place with some language difficulties, with the English of some of the Moderators being poor and the Afrikaans of some of the Anglicans being poor or non-existent. Although it was not the intention to issue a statement after the meeting, there were certain expectations, anxieties and suspicions about the meeting so that it was thought wise to say something, and the following statement was adopted and issued:

A STATEMENT adopted by a meeting of leading representatives of the N.G. Kerk and representatives of the Church of the Province of South Africa chosen by the Archbishop of Cape Town, on Tuesday May 19, 1959, in Bloemfontein.

1   The N.G. Kerk has been given the assurance that the Archbishop of Cape Town did not intend to go beyond a mere statement of conditions as he understood them when he delivered his New York sermon.

2   The Church of the Province of South Africa has been given the assurance that the N.G.K. did not start any campaign to vilify Archbishop de Blank.

3   The Churches agree to give full recognition to each other and to admit each Church's autonomy and responsibility to speak and act as they believe they must. Fundamental differences between the Churches should be honestly acknowledged in all discussions of vital issues.

4   The Churches undertake to inform each other on the reasons governing their policy and activity and to do everything in their power to avoid ill-founded deductions which are detrimental to the interests of either Church.

5 The N.G.K. and the C.P.S.A. will seek to devise new ways and means of consultation at all levels and will encourage office bearers and members of both Churches to foster a spirit of goodwill.

6 The Churches disclaim political affiliation to any party or group and recognise the sincerity of the convictions and intentions of each Church to act in the light of God's Word and under the guidance of the Holy Spirit.

Writing to Brink (21 May 1959) de Blank regarded the encounter as being 'fruitful and friendly'. But was there a real meeting of minds, any real appreciation of the other's convictions? Canon Zulu (of the Royal House of Zulus, who in November 1961 became South Africa's first black bishop) remembers the meeting as being neither fruitful nor friendly. 'In [apartheid legislation] Joost saw a denial of the personality of the black man and a curtailment of his human freedom. He judged it to be contrary to Christian belief and said so ... The Dutch Reformed Church leaders said they supported apartheid legislation on grounds of expediency and not of Church doctrine. The meeting ended abruptly in confusion when there was no theological point to discuss or dispute.'

de Blank was probably not the best man to lead a party of explorers into an area matted with theological undergrowth and towering trees allowing little light to penetrate the earth's bed. Dean E.L. King makes a general comment: 'Joost had a restless and driving nature which drove him very hard; he demanded results, action, decision and he saw most things as clear-cut issues. And from this side to his nature there sprung his unrelenting and clear stand on the peculiar issues confronting South Africa. Whenever I think of him in these matters I remember a phrase he was fond of using, 'have no fellowship with the unfruitful works of darkness, but rather ever reprove them ...' (Eph.5:11). To him the issues of the very strange society which is South Africa were clear. Apartheid society was unchristian, and any Christians (such as members of the Dutch Reformed Church) who defended it were untrue to the Gospel of Christ. His white-hot zeal for righteousness did perhaps lead him to judgments liable to the accusation of being premature. Tactically, I believe, he made errors of judgment. He could have won more sympathy for his undoubtedly courageous judgments and utterances if he had spent more time early in his ministry here taking 'soundings',

151

listening quietly, meditating on the complexities of life in South Africa. But it was typical of the man that he was in a hurry. In a hurry to speak out, to proclaim God's word to a generation dull of hearing in matters of injustice.'

de Blank continued to receive sustenance from the applause of the crowd and encouragement from individuals in high places outside South Africa. On a brief visit to West Africa in June 1959 at a state banquet President Tubman of Liberia, in whose honour it was held, 'talked of how the whole continent of Africa was moving towards freedom and independence — except for one country but where, thank God, we too have our friends!' (Diary 16 June).The Governor of Sierra Leone spoke of de Blank as one, 'who is known to thousands among us as a doughty champion of African interests and whose courageous stand we follow with our admiration and our prayers.' (Diary 16 June).

In Accra Cathedral, Ghana, on 21 June, de Blank preached on the dual citizenship of Christians. 'They are part of an earthly community with their own national and racial loyalties and other concerns. They are also citizens of heaven. Their loyalty is to God's Kingdom and His righteousness and if they have to make a choice, they have to seek the Kingdom of God *first*, to obey God rather than men.' de Blank saw the corporate people of God, the Church, as the herald and the agent of the cosmic redemption. 'And more than this the Church is to be the witness of this final redemption here and now'. He continued by outlining the situation in which the Church found itself in South Africa: 'We have reached the point where the State or anyway some of its ministers use every opportunity to vilify the Church. They attack its leaders, they impugn their patriotism, and they accuse the Church of interfering in political matters that are not their concern.

'But the Church does not interfere in politics except when political action exceeds its proper bounds and trespasses on the preserves of God. The Church has no quarrel with — indeed gives all honour to — the State which concerns itself with the things of Caesar; it comes into conflict with the State only when Caesar claims for itself the things that are God's.

'The conflict between the Church and State in South Africa is at heart not a political one but a religious one, based not on political theory but on theological principle.'

These words, albeit obvious and innocuous in most countries, provoked Prime Minister Verwoerd to launch a verbal attack on de

Blank in the Senate (June 1959). After stating that no strong action (*aan die bors gegryp*) had been taken against members of the United Party who had attacked apartheid he considered that de Blank, 'who, here in this land, has said only impolite things about people who stand for apartheid' deserved action taken against him. 'But this would not be because he attacked apartheid — anyone is allowed to attack a policy — but when a person goes overseas and besmirches his country, or his adopted country, or a country which he has not yet adopted; seeks his platform to libel the country, based on things which are not true, it is "damnable" — and this comes from a "churchman"'.

This was grist for de Blank's mill. His sensitivity to sharp and continuous criticism was equalled by his eagerness to do battle wherever and whenever he was attacked. In *Good Hope* for August 1959, fifty one year old short thick and dark haired archbishop of Rotterdam origin made an offer to fifty eight year old tall (6ft 2in) silvery haired prime minister of Amsterdam origin: 'For the sake of South Africa . . . I am prepared to withdraw from the country as Archbishop and Metropolitan if Dr. Verwoerd will withdraw as Prime Minister and return to his native land. His native land, it may be recalled, is the same as mine. It breaks my heart to make this offer, but I am willing for such a sacrifice because I know if it were accepted it would hasten the country's return to decency and sanity.'

Naturally this invitation received world-wide publicity. Was that the intention? He cannot have seriously expected Verwoerd to have seriously considered this form of partial hari-kari. If he was in any sense serious then he overestimated his own political clout as well as that of the Anglican Church.

However, de Blank could not be ignored by the Government as they increasingly saw him as a rallying point for a number of groups and organisations. One organisation, the Black Sash, asked de Blank to invite representatives of all races to meet and see how apartheid could be brought to an end. The Black Sash, (Women's Defence of the Constitution League) was a women's organisation, founded in 1955, whose novel tactics irritated the Government. Their most characteristic and arresting method of protest was to stand in public places in silent vigil, wearing their black sashes. The irritation was increased because they were women. A political commentator of *Die Burger* wrote: 'Their method combines the highly unfeminine quality of silence with

153

the extremely feminine quality of nagging troublesomeness' (11 February 1956).

Prompted by Black Sash, although he hardly needed it, de Blank invited 'progressive organisations and individuals' to a Conference on 1 August 1959. His letter of invitation showed that he thought there was much to encourage the true patriot: people were 'rapidly awakening from the drugged sleep of an untenable ideology and . . . rediscovering the fundamental decencies of life and of human relationships'. The past weeks had witnessed, 'the appearance of a series of large and encouraging cracks in the facade put up so long by the upholders of white domination and total segregation'. It was time to strike. 'Strenuous and united opposition to current policies is therefore urgently called for, outside as well as within Parliament, from all who believe in human dignity and fair dealing. *Now* is the time for the moral forces of the country to combine to bring a new policy of justice and co-operation to birth. If we do not seize the opportunity *now* it may never recur.'

The letter was not made public but *Die Burger* obtained a copy and gave it front page treatment. Was the Archbishop proposing a new political party? de Blank had to publish a statement denying any such intention.

At the Conference many organisations were represented including the African National Congress, the South African Coloured People's Organisation and the Liberal Party. Leo Marquand, author and publisher, remembered the conference, always referred to as 'The Archbishop's Conference', 'as a rather heterogenous collection of people presided over [by de Blank] with distinction and ability'. More generally he remembered de Blank as, 'a redoubtable fighter who enjoyed the fight but never for a moment lost sight of the things he was fighting for. He came at a time when we all needed cheering up and bucking up, and he acted as a shot in the arm to the opponents of apartheid'.

There were three addresses at the conference. Dr. Oscar Wollheim (first National Chairman of the Liberal Party) outlined the extent, causes and effects of poverty in South Africa. Ex-Chief Justice A. van der Sandt Centlivres (who was also for a time Chancellor of the University of Cape Town) showed how civil liberty had been constantly infringed with the endless procession of new laws passed since Union. Donald Molteno Q.C. who was a distinguished lawyer and head of the South African Institute for

Race Relations and had also been in Parliament as Native Representative for Cape Western (1938-49), revealed the shortcomings of the South African Constitution which had been drawn up by a National Convention composed exclusively of white delegates and largely dominated by representatives from the Transvaal.

Instead of celebrating fifty years of Union on 31 May 1960, organisations and individuals present were asked to dedicate themselves to the task of achieving these objectives:

(a) the ridding of our land of the scourge of poverty and the achievement for all South Africans of a minimum living wage, social security, and equality of economic opportunity;

(b) the enjoyment by all South Africans of those civil liberties that, throughout the civilised world, are regarded as undeniable human rights;

(c) a reform of the South African Constitution, as agreed by a new National Convention, truly representative of all races of our people, which will guarantee to individuals the above-mentioned liberties and rights, will grant political representation to men and women irrespective of race and will protect each racial community from domination.

A continuation committee was appointed to make recommendations on how fifty years of Union should be observed and to organise a campaign for the achievement of specific objectives. de Blank had been loud in his vocal criticism of apartheid. *Now* (a favourite word of de Blank's) he was showing that he was prepared to back up his words with positive action, which took place in the future.

During the early autumn, 1959, de Blank was again abroad first in Southern Rhodesia leading a clergy retreat in Bulawayo and then on to England and the United States where he undertook another lecture tour. There was a major meeting and speech at Central Hall, Westminster, on 25 September 1959. de Blank was concerned for the soul of Africa. So were Secularism, Humanism, Heathenism ('with its strong nostalgic pull'), Marxism and Mohammedanism ('knows no colour bar and is the religion of all men irrespective of race'). He declared, 'the open sore of Africa in 1959 is a society based on colour privilege ... And to its eradication we are by our Chrisitian obedience pledged.' He admitted: 'When I first went to South Africa I thought there must be many sincere idealists among the protagonists of apartheid policy ... But such an idealism can be validated only if there is insistence on equality of opportunity, and on equality before the law. This is not what *apartheid* means. It means white comfort and African misery. It does not mean 'separate but equal'.' He did not confine himself to generalised rhetoric but gave examples of gross inequality and injustice to show that, 'apartheid as a sincere policy for separate development is a lie'.

Yet he picked out with his spotlight things that encouraged him, including the Potchefstroom Resolution of the Reformed Ecumenical Synod mentioned earlier in this chapter. 'I cannot exaggerate the importance of this statement' — but he did so!

Nevertheless, he was looking for ways of working out an exciting pattern of a multi-racial society in which whites and coloureds, Africans and Indians, could live in harmony and goodwill. There was a less strident note in the speech, perhaps even a hint of conciliation. That was in part due to 'the stirrings of conscience in the official Opposition Party'. Throughout 1959 a number of United Party M.P.s of liberal persuasion were increasingly dissatisfied with the Party. It was in young M.P.s such as Ray Swart, Zach de Beer, Jan Steytler, Helen Suzman and Townley Williams that de Blank saw 'stirrings of conscience' and in November 1959 a new political party, the Progressive Party, was formed. Its policies included the extension of the franchise. There would be a Bill of Rights, and economic policy turned essentially on free enterprise with a dash of Keynesian demand management. A high and stable level of employment would be maintained and living standards improved for all members of the population. Trade union rights would be extended to Africans, social security benefits increased. These were big steps forward, but they did not constitute enough of a step to bring them to an area from which they could easily bridge the gap dividing white from non-white. Still, the Progressives' chief task lay in influencing the white community rather than non-whites.

de Blank sounded a variety of private opinions whilst he was in England and America. He was convinced that the hostile attitude to South Africa would change if the Union Government took specific action along four lines:

(i) It should sign the Declaration on Human Rights (among the member nations of the United Nations, Russia and South Africa alone have refused to sign the Declaration).

(ii) It should withdraw the infamous Church Clause from the Statute Book (I need not add that this Clause is a direct attack upon the Church qua Church which Christians have resisted on fundamental theological grounds).

(iii) It should grant passports freely to all people of all races who wish to travel abroad — and particularly to students invited to continue their studies overseas.

(iv) It should abandon any attempt to force reference books (or passes) upon African women. (Untold misery has been caused to thousands of Africans by these pass-laws. They had led to the break-up of countless homes — and if passes were extended to the women this misery would be multiplied a hundredfold).

Back home in South Africa de Blank was disturbed by something new. He wrote of it in *Kaleidoscope* (February 1960): 'More sinister has been the formation of the South Africa Foundation, established by leading industrialists in this country with the avowed object of presenting a 'fairer' picture of South Africa to countries overseas. There was a strange naiveté in announcing the formation of the Foundation at a time when Field Marshal Montgomery had just been staying with one of its founders and while he was asserting that South Africa's Government had been sadly misjudged abroad.

'Poor Monty! It seems unbelievable that a man of sensibility dared to write articles about *apartheid* and South African affairs while openly admitting that he had met none of the non-white leaders in the country. But the South Africa Foundation has made itself equally ridiculous and irresponsible by including no non-whites among its trustees or on its executive body. Not until leaders of the non-white communities are represented on the Foundation will any people of common sense be prepared to take its utterances seriously.

'One is bitterly tempted to ask whether the establishment of the Foundation is not an attempt on the part of leading industrialists and commercial interests in their search for capital to commend South Africa as a sound country for substantial investment.

'This suspicion is strengthened by what appears to be a changed attitude on the part of a few of the leading British national newspapers. Suddenly, it looks as if criticism of South Africa is being silenced or stifled. Suddenly, in some quarters the sweet reasonableness of current policy is being stressed at the expense of

157

truth and certainly at the expense of the whole story.'

The Cape Town Diocesan Synod met in November 1959. In his Charge, de Blank returned to the battle field. He was looking to the future when he stressed the importance of training Africans for leadership. The time could come when the non-whites, because of 'the evils of apartheid', would have nothing more to do with the white man but would only acknowledge leaders from their own races.

He called the Mixed Marriages Act, 'a monstrous piece of legislation which must be wholly repugnant to the Christian conscience'. To prevent a union of two people on the basis of a difference of colour was 'near blasphemy'. He revealed that the bishops of the Province were considering whether it would not be advisable for the clergy to relinquish their licences as marriage officers. (A month later the Bishop of Kimberley and Kuruman, John Boys, urged his clergy to surrender their rights in this matter).

On education, he asked Anglican parents, 'to resist any attempt to make education subserve any ulterior purpose. We want freedom for our children, not slavery'.

A number of important resolutions were passed, including a request for de Blank to set up a body to study the payment of adequate wages. He was asked to appoint a deputation to meet leaders of the Dutch Reformed Churches, 'in order to stress the denial of fundamental Christian theological principles by the [Group Areas] Act'. A deputation should interview the Prime Minister on the same matter. Parishes were reminded that there should be no form of discrimination on the grounds of colour alone. The Synod declared itself unequivocally in favour of free and open universities ... And much else besides.

The action and activity seemed to be increasing. It must not be thought that he was carrying the whole diocese with him. The Diocesan Secretary, G.D. Abernethy, was one of many who felt, 'he was trying to push South Africa along the path of integration too quickly. I know that in theory he was right, but in practice, especially with the large Afrikaner majority, South Africa was not ready to be pushed and his effort was wasted. Unfortunately I don't think he really carried the Church as a whole with him. The Church seemed to favour a slower approach to racial difficulties.' There were others who recognised a leader they wanted to follow. Clergy came from overseas to serve under de Blank.

The activity may have been unceasing, but never at the expense of the liturgical rhythm of his life. Every day began and ended in his chapel. Meditating before daybreak, saying Matins, Evensong and later Compline, made up a pattern of disciplined devotion which anchored him to God and the Church and sustained him in his pursuits. Both Church and Archbishop were going to need every sustaining morsel during 1960.

Cartoon in the Cape Times, *23 July 1959*
'After you, Joost.' 'No, after you, Henk.'

CHAPTER THIRTEEN

1960

In the agony of South Africa it is the inevitability that is so frightening. Step by step the drama draws to its climax and its doom. Has it to be that way? Is it really too late? Cannot the script be altered? These questions have a frightening urgency in 1986. They seemed just as urgent and no less frightening in 1960.

de Blank opened 1960 with an understatement of forthcoming problems by warning the diocese that, 'the demands of Christian charity and obedience are so opposed to current legislation and its outworking in terms of human lives and families that a life of loyalty to Christ and His Church is bound to evoke hostility and misrepresentation'.

Meanwhile, the British Prime Minister, Harold Macmillan, was undertaking a tour of Africa which included South Africa. There he spoke to a number of people opposed to Government policy, including de Blank, who told him that he should never have accepted an invitation from Dr. Verwoerd to come to the Union without obtaining an undertaking in advance that he would be allowed to talk with non-White leaders. After his private meeting, de Blank told reporters that the British Prime Minister had seen his point, and added, 'I think he's going to make an interesting speech tomorrow.'

That speech is now part of history. Speaking to both Houses of Parliament (2 February 1960) he said that the wind of change was blowing in Africa. African national consciousness had to be accepted as a fact, if the precarious balance between East and West on which the peace of the world depended was not to be imperilled. Britain's response to the rise of nationalism in Asia and Africa had been to aim for the creation of a society, 'in which men are given the opportunity to grow to their full stature — and that must in our view include the opportunity to have an increasing

160

share in political power and responsibility — a society in which individual merit and individual merit alone is the criterion for a man's advancement, whether political or economic'. Turning to British policy towards countries inhabited by more than one race, he quoted his Foreign Secretary, Selwyn Lloyd: 'We reject the idea of any inherent superiority of one race over another. Our policy therefore is non-racial'.

This speech embodied much that de Blank had already said and he referred to it in *Good Hope* (March 1960), 'Without any tub-thumping, without any flights of eloquence or tricks of oratory, the British Prime Minister reiterated quietly but forcibly those fundamental truths that are axiomatic in Biblical theology, namely that all men are of equal value to Almighty God and that the rewards of this life must be based on individual merit and on nothing else. As South Africa claims to be a Christian country, this should be the touchstone of all legislation — and until it is, Church and State will be out of step'.

Macmillian's speech was a masterpiece. He combined boldness with charm and wanted to be frank without wounding. Yet it was not enough to penetrate Verwoerd's heart or infiltrate his mind. He expressed confidence that in fifty years these particular differences would be regarded as of historical interest only. It was as if he expected the law of *solvitur ambulando* to apply. It was a misjudgement, although it is difficult to see what Macmillan could have said or done to soften a heart of stone. He cannot have felt encouraged by a silent audience and muted applause. The world reacted differently and praised the speech. Speaking the day after, de Blank said, 'They [the South African Nationalists] know now that the opinion of the civilised world is against them. But they have what I call the Bunker Mentality — they would rather go down like Hitler in the ruin of their own creation than change . . . . That's what we have to face ...'.

It was not *they* who went down some six weeks later! During the first weeks of 1960 a wide range of Government critics expressed their opposition to the pass laws, one of the oldest forms of racial discrimination in South Africa. The African who generally is by nature a patient and long-suffering individual, had under the Nationalist régime and apartheid legislation been harried from pillar to post and his patience had expired. Moreover, the African National Congress, then regarded as moderate, was supplemented by a break-away group from this A.N.C., the Pan

Meeting with Prime Minister, Harold Macmillan, February 1960

African Congress (P.A.C.) with its campaign against the pass laws and for higher wages.

In February the A.N.C., supported by a number of whites led by Ambrose Reeves, staged a silent anti-pass demonstration. In March, Mrs. Margaret Ballinger, (still a Native Representative in Parliament) introduced a motion condemning the pass laws.

The P.A.C. planned a campaign and emphasised on every occasion that there was to be no violence, no retaliation, and only peaceful surrender for not carrying passes. The idea spread quickly and was accepted enthusiastically particularly in the Western Cape, the Transvaal and Natal.

The campaign was planned to begin on 21 March. Members of the P.A.C. were asked to leave their passes at home and surrender themselves at their local police station to be arrested for not being in possession of them. Africans turned out in their thousands — between fifteen and twenty thousand at Sharpeville near Vereeniging in the Transvaal. P.A.C. leaders asked followers to disperse in orderly fashion if ordered by the police to do so. The police were informed of this. Naturally pulses were raised and the atmosphere became tense. Then the events took place which left 21 March 1960 seared across the civilised consciousness of the world. The Africans ran and ran, but running was no escape. As they ran some stumbled and fell, vainly shielding themselves with their coats. Many died where they fell from the bullets of the police who were firing from armoured cars. Sixty-seven Africans were killed and a hundred and eighty-six wounded. On the same day at Langa, near Cape Town, and in other areas, more people were killed and wounded.

The Government declared a State of Emergency on 30 March, but 1200 people of all races had already been detained in pre-dawn arrests. By 6 May, 18,011 arrests had been made. The A.N.C. and P.A.C. had been banned under the Unlawful Organizations Bill (28 March).

de Blank was due to leave on an extensive tour of Britain, America and France, but he cancelled this in the wake of the slaughter of Sharpeville and Langa. When he visited America the following year he explained himself thus: 'A Bishop's duty is to his people. The violence and bloodshed that ushered in a state of emergency ... convinced me that I had, at that time, no right to leave my diocese or province — I had to keep myself available for my children in Christ'.

Following the 1960 state of emergency, events concerning de Blank moved fast. On 24 March he issued a statement welcoming the judicial enquiry which had been announced, but called upon the Churches, 'to hold their own enquiry in order that the responsibility for such wholesale slaughter may be placed where it belongs'.

He summoned the Consultative Body of Bishops to Bishopscourt on 4 April. The Bishops of Natal (Vernon Inman); Grahamstown (Robert Selby Taylor) and St. John's (James

Schuster) attended. It was decided to send Archdeacon Cecil Wood to England and Switzerland forthwith where he was to see a number of people and then fulfil some of de Blank's engagements in April and May in London and America. There was much cloak and dagger work as there was always the possibility that he would be prevented from leaving. It was not until he was in the air that de Blank made a statement. Writing to other bishops of the Province (9 April) de Blank noted: 'Now that Cecil Wood is safely in England I can write to tell you that his going was determined by the Episcopal Consultative Committee which met on Monday — April 4.

'It was agreed that, apart from his giving all possible information to the Churches in Britain and America he should also pay an early visit to the Headquarters of the World Council of Churches in Geneva. The burning of Churches in the recent disturbances indicates how precarious is the position of Christianity in this country, particularly among the Africans. The Committee was convinced that, while all Churches have sinned, the continuing support for apartheid by the Dutch Reformed Churches makes African hostility to the Christian Faith inevitable.

'The Committee was agreed that it is quite impossible to maintain fellowship with Churches that have not repudiated the policy of apartheid now that its brutal working out in practice has been so clearly manifested.

'The future of Christianity in this country demands our complete dissociation from the Dutch Reformed Church attitude. Cecil Wood is therefore authorized to tell the World Council of Churches that unless the Dutch Reformed Churches are prepared to forsake their support for apartheid and to condemn the Government for its ruthless action, we can no longer remain as fellow members of the World Council of Churches with them. Either they must be expelled or we shall be compelled to withdraw'.

Meanwhile, Bishop Ambrose Reeves had disappeared. On 1 April reliable African friends advised him he was on a Government list for immediate arrest. Two lawyers who had assisted him in getting affidavits from victims of the shootings had been arrested. Reeves had vital documents and information. He consulted his diocesan officials late that night and they advised him to leave forthwith which he did, travelling through the night to Mbabane in Swaziland.

On 9 April at the Rand Agricultural Show in Johannesburg

David Pratt, a wealthy white farmer (found later to be deranged), shot, and just failed to kill, Verwoerd. *Die Burger* commented, 'In this miraculous escape all the faithful will see the hand of God'. This referred to the man who at his accession had acknowledged, 'I do not ever have the nagging doubt of ever wondering whether, perhaps, I am wrong'. A macabre joke was quickly in circulation in spite of Verwoerd's serious condition. Verwoerd is supposed to have been asked what thought crossed his mind at the time of the shooting. He replied. 'I thought it was Joost de Blank' (pronounced 'Just a blank').

de Blank wrote to all Provinces of the Anglican Communion asking that 31 May should be a day of prayer for South Africa. The Union would be celebrating its Jubilee: the Church 'regards the Jubilee as an opportunity for penitence and dedication'. The Archbishop of Canterbury, Geoffrey Fisher thought this 'particularly helpful' compared with '[Trevor] Huddleston who has been badly damaging the right cause by his excess of moral indignation. I heard him on the wireless the other day in which he stated that his object was to turn out the present Government of South Africa. That is of course a purely political object'. (Letter to de Blank dated 28 March).

In South Africa the Dutch Reformed Church would not criticise the Government. A statement issued by nine leading ministers of the Nederduitse Gereformeerde Kerke after Sharpeville assured, 'people of all races affected by our deepest sympathy' but warned the 'outside world' against condemning what it did not understand. It also claimed that it could 'justify and approve of the policy of independent distinctive development, provided it is carried out in a just and honourable way without impairing or offending human dignity. The Church has also accepted that this policy, especially in its initial stages, would necessarily cause a certain amount of disruption and personal discomfort and hardship, for example in connection with the clearing of slums. The whole pass system should be seen in this light'.

This kind of statement defies reason, denies facts and deludes only its writers.

de Blank issued a press release on 11 April:

The events of March 21 have confronted the Church in South Africa with the gravest crisis in its history. On that day the Africans turned not only against those whom they considered to be their white

165

oppressors but also against the Christian Church as being identified with them. In the terrible happenings of the days that followed March 21, churches were burnt, ministers of religion were attacked, and Christian members of congregations were threatened and accused of betrayal. Among a large number of Africans, the Christian Church stands as much as the Government for white domination and racial discrimination.

The Church is now at the cross roads. Its future is precarious. Unless it openly and publicly repudiates the doctrine and practice of compulsory segregation, it is condemning itself to extermination — and the whole of Southern Africa will be wide open to secularism and other non-Christian creeds.

The Church throughout the world has uncompromisingly rejected racial discrimination in any form. This was clearly enunciated at the Evanston meeting of the World Council of Churches in 1954. It was equally clearly stated by the Lambeth Conference of the Anglican Communion in 1958, and in the same year the Potchefstroom Reformed Synod put out its famous twelve-point plan on race relations. The Roman Church has declared its position unequivocally in a series of pastoral letters; and the other Churches of South Africa association in the Christian Council have strongly condemned all forms of racial discrimination.

But pious protestations are one thing — effective action is another. If the Church is to have any chance of survival in this country, the Africans must be shown by constructive action, and not by words alone, that the Churches have turned their backs on compulsory apartheid once and for all.

After Sharpeville almost every Church issued a statement clearly condemning policies that could lead to such a shocking state of affairs and calling for active co-operation between the races. But until the Dutch Reformed Churches identify themselves with this repudiation, the Christian Faith is unable to make much progress and is in urgent danger of complete rejection by the African people.

Unless therefore the Dutch Reformed Churches take such action, it is essential that other Churches should no longer be associated with them in any Council or federation. For this reason the Archbishop of Cape Town has appealed to the World Council of Churches to send out a fact-finding team to South Africa to investigate the racial situation at first hand. Much will depend on the findings of this commission but he has stated further that the Church of the Province of South Africa can no longer be linked with the Dutch Reformed Churches in the World Council of Churches unless they now accept the Evanston Declaration of 1954 and openly repudiate the policy of apartheid and its tragic outworking in the disturbances of March and April.

To every African the Dutch Reformed Churches are known to be closely identified with the Government, and many ministers are known to be members of the Dutch Reformed Churches. It is for this reason that the future of the Christian Faith in South Africa is today so largely in their hands. Their identification with the rest of the Christian world at this moment could give hope for the coming days. Without such identification, the prospect is black indeed and the other Churches in South Africa in their proclamation of the Gospel to the African must make it clear that they have *no connexion whatsoever* with any so-called Christian body that advocates racial discrimination and the suppression of the legitimate aspirations of the weaker races.

The Bishops of the Province had this statement: so did Visser't Hooft, General Secretary of the World Council of Churches in Geneva.

Visser't Hooft viewed de Blank's ultimatum to the Dutch Reformed Church with alarm and annoyance and asked members of the Executive committee of the World Council of Churches for their reactions. One of them was de Blank's friend, Lakdasa de Mel of Kurunagala, who replied: 'The Archbishop of Cape Town and the Bishop of Johannesburg have won the admiration of Christendom by the stand they have taken, but we must gently reason with them that expulsion of the D.R.C. would be in effect a kind of ecclesiastical apartheid adding one more scandal to an already scandalous situation. We must keep our links with these people and in this way encourage the more enlightened amongst them to convert their own brethren'.

The Archbishop of Canterbury was more pointed in his reply to Visser't Hooft: 'It is a stupid remark: The Archbishop of York [Michael Ramsey] said to me you do not cure one form of apartheid by inventing another form. You can be assured, therefore, that the attitude of the Archbishop of Cape Town (and of Bishop Reeves if he said the same which rather surprises me) is not the attitude of the Church of England or of the Anglican Community as a whole: quite the contrary. If necessary I shall have to say this at [the British Council of Churches meeting at] Nottingham, but I hope to avoid saying it in public'.

Fisher had cabled de Blank to ascertain if the statement on the

Dutch Reformed Church was his own opinion or the official policy of the bishops in South Africa, to which de Blank replied: 'Agreed by emergency meeting Episcopal Standing Committee but first call for World Council fact finding commission public repudiation of compulsory apartheid in Church and State essential for continued co-operation'.

The World Council of Churches decided to send one of its associated general secretaries to South Africa to confer with leaders of the Council's eight member churches in that country. The man chosen was Dr. Robert S. Bilheimer, an ordained minister of the United Presbyterian Church in the U.S.A. The member churches were The Bantu Presbyterian Church of South Africa; The Church of the Province of South Africa (Anglican); the Congregational Union of South Africa: The Methodist Church of South Africa; Nederduitse Gereformeerde Kerke in Suid-Afrika; N.G.K. van Transvaal: Nederduitsch Hervormde Kerk van Afrika and The Presbyterian Church of Southern Africa.

But Bilheimer and others failed to understand de Blank's fundamental point which he made in a Memorandum:

> The over-riding factor is the future of the Christian Faith so far as the millions of Africans in this country are concerned. This is far more important than inter-Church politeness or formal relations. Everyone in close contact with the African knows that we have reached a parting of the ways: if he cannot now be convinced of the reality of Christianity he will turn against the Faith for good. Unfortunately he is at present quite certain that the Church stands for White domination and White superiority, and if there is to be any hope of regaining his confidence at all every Church must state categorically its repudiation of such an ideology.

> In the light of the events that took place on March 21 and subsequently, the disastrous effects of the logical outworking of an apartheid policy are now plain for all to see. Whereas in the past there might still have been some excuse for Christian bodies to cherish the hope that this was a workable proposition which could find expression in accord with Christian principles, the terrible happenings of the disturbances and the means of repressing them can leave no room for doubt in any Christian breast. To every Christian now compulsory apartheid should be clearly recognizable for the sin it is. It is as blatant, perhaps a more blatant, denial of the New Testament commandment to love one's neighbour as oneself as the sin of adultery. No Church could be expected to associate with another Church which officially approved or condoned adultery:

168

the situation is precisely the same with regard to compulsory apartheid. A public repudiation of apartheid should be made as soon as possible by all the member Churches of the Christian Council, in the fond hope that we may not be too late in convincing the African of our sincerity.

In London, Cecil Wood met the Archbishop of Canterbury on 10 April and, 'found him most co-operative' as he noted afterwards. 'He had remained silent because he did not wish to re-utter platitudes and had always been careful to let the Church on the spot handle their own affairs. He had not realized that we were virtually silenced under the Emergency Regulations. I found him very willing to listen. His mind was very analytical over all statements'.

Fisher was much helped by Wood, and on 13 April issued a much reported statement including a ringing indictment of repression in South Africa and asking for sympathetic Christian prayer for Africans, 'in their bewilderment and long suffering; for those both Afrikaner and British who understand God's will and work for deliverance from the evil; for the Churches as they strive to do their divine work of enduring healing and reconciling; and most of all perhaps for believers in apartheid in the nation and in the Dutch Reformed Church who have the hardest task of all — to be humble, to repent, to make a change of heart, to build new hope for themselves and for Africans on the ashes of the dreadful past. Where is reconciliation and reconstruction to begin? The Archbishop of Cape Town asks us to pray especially that the Government will begin to consult with leaders of all races who believe in reconciliation including such outstanding African Christian leaders as Chief Lithuli (with whom de Blank was in contact) and Dr. Z.K. Matthews. Such consultation made in a contrite spirit might by God's grace be the beginning of a new South Africa'.

Fisher wrote to de Blank (19 April) saying, 'There was of course very much more I could have said: but in view of forms of over-statement and over-excitement which were inviting criticisms and opposition here, I wanted to say something which was plainly confined to our Christian duty here in England in prayer and spiritual travail with you. You know how deeply we feel for you and the Anglican Churches in particular and how universal is the shame and sorrow felt throughout the country at what you are having to endure'.

In his reply of 26 April, de Blank tried to focus the Archbishop's attention on what more was needed:

> The real need at the moment is for a categorical repudiation of
> - apartheid by all churches in this country if we are ever to re-capture
> the confidence of the African. There is no doubt that during the
> recent disturbances there was a good deal of anti-church and anti-
> Christian action. The average African thinks of the church as being
> ˋ committed to the doctrine of white domination which has found
> expression in the Dutch Reformed Church and which they have
> never formally disavowed. Moreover the African knows well that
> most of the Ministers in the Government are members of the Dutch
> ˎ Reformed Church and they regard the Dutch Reformed Church
> much more as a political than a religious institution. It is therefore
> imperative that the Church be able to tell the African that any idea
> of racial discrimination is abhorrent to it not only in precept but in
> practice, and if the Church is to be listened to at all it cannot have
> official relations with any Church that has not similarly 'come
> clean'.

Continuing his mission on behalf of de Blank, Cecil Wood went to the headquarters of the World Council of Churches. On 13 April he met Dr. W.A. Visser't Hooft, the Revd. Francis House (an Associate General Secretary), Bilheimer and Dai Kitagawa (Secretary for inter-group relations). Wood records: 'found them rather intractable because of the Archbishop's statement to the Press, released after I had left, that unless the D.R.C. disavowed Compulsory Apartheid he would call on the W.C.C. to expel them from the Council. I find this kind of negotiation by Press state-ments rather difficult to cope with. In any case my instructions were that if the D.R.C. could not now fall into line with the state-ments of the W.C.C. the C.P.S.A. would withdraw and inform the other Provinces of the Anglican Communion of the reasons.

'I said my instructions were to reaffirm their Evanston Statement ('that any form of segregation based on race, colour, or ethnic origin is contrary to the gospel . . .') at the highest level and to send out a Fact-Finding Commission to investigate the basic causes of the present outbreak from a Christian standpoint. I found them still thinking in terms of ten years ago and hoping for a gradual change and clutching at every straw that might indicate that the D.R.C. was becoming less intractable.

'They said they had already decided to send Dr. Bilheimer out to consult with the heads of the various Churches. I asked them to emphasise that this was not the Commission the Archbishop asked for. They thought such a Commission should be multiracial; because of the feeling of the rest of Africa. They agreed to re-affirm the Evanston Resolution.

'It was obvious that they were weighted on the side of not giving offence to the D.R. Church, so the Archbishop's statement may help to bring matters to a head. I told them that in my opinion the D.R.C. still held the key to the situation and were the only body that could ease the tensions. I added that they should realize that a refusal of the D.R.C. to do this would have grave consquences and it seemed to me to be much the best if this were faced in a realistic way. I did not see in the Archbishop's statement a threat so much as a realistic appraisement of the situation.

'The line they were inclined to take was that once any Church was expelled all hope of influence was gone. They instanced their relations with Hungary and Cyprus. I replied that there did not seem to be an exact parallel there since in South Africa we had a strong Christian opinion working within the situation which had already repudiated on more than one occasion the apartheid legislation for the last 10 years with the utmost consistency.

'They put out a statement that same afternoon but still refrained from quoting the actual words of the Evanston resolution. Fortunately Reuter's representative came to my hotel that same evening so I was able to make a statement also and insisted that the relevant words of the resolution were quoted in full'.

This report, from one who generally saw things coolly and clearly, is fascinating for the light it throws on the W.C.C. attitude in 1960. The eleven page W.C.C. record of the conversations confirms Wood's view. A decade later or more the W.C.C. were suspected if not accused of following a very different line of support, subversion and attack.

Cecil Wood was at the British Council of Churches' half-yearly meeting at Nottingham in April, and was asked to address the formal meeting on 21 April. He and his speech were sympathetically received but his overriding impression was that on the whole, despite strong-sounding resolutions, the Council would contort itself to preserve the facade of a fellowship at whatever cost of principle. Again, if the D.R.C. remained in the W.C.C. it would be within their sphere of influence.

Bilheimer arrived in South Africa on 19 April and met leading representatives of the eight member churches of the W.C.C. He

171

recorded in his diary his meeting with de Blank:

> It was a rough conversation. de Blank started by saying that we have come to a parting of the ways. The future of Christianity in Africa is at stake. We must no longer associate with those who believe in apartheid. The conversation moved so fast that I could not keep notes. I took the initiative and should probably say that I became aggressive. Indeed, I don't remember ever having talked as hard to any human being in my life. Main points: To ask for the expulsion of the Dutch Reformed Church starts something which breaks up the ecumenical movement. de Blank was shaken when I asked him point blank what we should do with the Chinese Churches. Expulsion means the power and judgement of the super-church, which is a surprising suggestion to arise from such high quarters in the Anglican Church.

de Blank was not happy that the W.C.C. had sent one man rather than a fact-finding commission with two or three impartial observers.

D.R.C. leaders were determined that de Blank should publicly withdraw his call for the dismissal of the D.R.C. from the W.C.C. Beilheimer was sensible enough to realize this could not happen. After much intense discussion a suggestion arose that the W.C.C. initiate a small conference or consultation in South Africa during 1960. It should be a consultation among the member churches of South Africa and this would mean between white and non-white Church leaders. The W.C.C. would also be present themselves consulting with South African Churches. The leaders whom Bilheimer saw gave their assurances of agreement with the general idea.

What was the W.C.C., through Bilheimer, trying to achieve? Paper over cracks in an edifice long since decayed? Patch up a quarrel between two parties who had irreconcilable views? Keep the illusion of the effectiveness and importance of the W.C.C. intact? The D.R.C. was already considering withdrawing from the W.C.C. What loss would that be? Unfortunately Bilheimer's own lopsided credentials were revealed in a report he made on his visit: a variant on 'I've made up my mind: don't confuse me with facts'.

These are not the words of a committed neutral: 'The Anglican Church, to put it very bluntly, needs a big reform of attitude at the above point [apartheid issue], and in regard to their attitude to the D.R.C. They speak and act as *The* Church, not only on theological grounds, but on historical-cultural grounds. They do not try to consult with the D.R.C. and are too greatly isolated from them'.

Nevertheless, it is a view that was held by countless people, in particular with regard to de Blank. Bill Burnett, a South African then Bishop of Bloemfontein and later Archbishop of Cape Town, writes trenchantly! — and perceptively? 'When he visited Bishop's Lodge in Bloemfontein we found him the easiest possible guest although it must be said that he could not bring himself to be warm towards some of the Afrikaans-speaking guests we invited to meet him in what is a predominantly Afrikaans-speaking part of our country. It is difficult not to see our political issues in terms of angels and devils and the response of the Government Press to Joost's sharp and indeed courageous attacks on apartheid policies led him, I think, to fall into the trap of not only hating the policies of the Government but also the men who were responsible for them.

'Joost was not afraid to lead from the front . . . . There is no doubt that this angered many white Anglicans, but led him to be loved and appreciated by many black ones. When I went to Cape Town as Archbishop (13 years after de Blank had left the country) there were still many black people who remembered his championing of their cause with deep gratitude.

' . . . I think part of his problem was that he failed to understand that in South Africa the Anglican Church is not an established Church with a kind of built-in political rôle . . . I think Joost overestimated the political clout of the Church.

' . . . Joost failed almost completely to understand the Afrikaner people and could not find a place in his heart to love them. It is not enough to be an apostle of unity and reconciliation in word only. It needs to be expressed in terms of relationships and attitudes. The Church to which I belong and to which Joost belonged in South Africa was a champion of unity and reconciliation in its struggle against apartheid. We have unfortunately more often than not been ourselves part of the disease against which we have striven.'

In these post-Sharpeville days de Blank was like a tree in a desert to Africans. Amongst his own church members there was both admiration and anxiety. At a lunch-time Service in St. George's Cathedral (11 April) two thousand people filled the building to capacity and overflowed into the streets outside where the Service was relayed by loudspeakers. In his short address de Blank emphasised the note of penitence for it was only through penitence that reconciliation would be achieved: 'In this penitence not one of us is excluded, to this reconciliation each one of us is called'. It was the Monday in Holy Week and the shadow of the Cross lay heavily on South Africa. But still Christians must never lose their grip on invincible hope that leads them always to greet one another with the age-old Easter salutation, 'Christ is Risen'.

There was a warm ovation for de Blank by part of the crowd as he left the Cathedral.

The initial reception was not as warm at a meeting of the clergy which de Blank had arranged for 21 April. There was much division in the Diocese of Cape Town. The lust for justice against the Government, its policies and the Dutch Reformed Churches was not always tempered with mercy, and rarely motivated by love. There was much talk of love, but it seemed to be directed exclusively towards the non-white peoples.

After Eucharist in the Cathedral, the brethren retired to the Cathedral Hall there to 'pray and discuss' — euphemistic words for what took place. Clergy were incredibly frank in their criticism of their Archbishop but there was no display of uncontrolled temper or rancid bitterness. de Blank, like St. Sebastian, bravely stood up to all the arrows aimed at him, warding off some and trying to turn others aside but looking not like the saint but more like a hare surrounded by beagles closing in for the kill. Much that was said was unwarranted and due to complete misunderstanding. Canon John Aubrey recalls: 'The more thinking at the meeting, who had come to criticize, quickly found themselves newly cast in the rôle of sympathisers and possible supporters. Mistaken (by South African standards) the Archbishop may have been in some of his pronouncements and actions, but there was no doubting his altruism or his sincerity. While the debate continued I struggled to find a formula which might be put forward formally as a motion and hopefully resolve the tension. This was found'.

Bishop Roy Cowdry, who had, 'feared a great furore' was glad, 'some got a good deal off their chests'; (but not, it might be added, from their minds) and noted in a letter to Cecil Wood written the day after the meeting, 'We have declared our complete confidence in the ABp and have set up a body which is to meet fortnightly while the state of emergency continues to exist — the Chapter plus eight other priests.' People returned to their parishes, their fears partially allayed. But there were those *then* in positions of leadership, mostly anti-apartheid but anxious about just how fast the Church and the country could proceed towards complete integration; not racist, but conscious of the social problems separating ' privileged and underprivileged people. Coloured and black rank and file however were already convinced that in de Blank a prophet and leader had been sent amongst them and they went , their ways rejoicing in the champion they had found.

de Blank himself considered it, 'a very wonderful day' when writing to express his happiness to John Aubrey for, 'the nature of your proposal and the fact that it originated with you'.

A parallel anguish consumed de Blank. Bishop Reeves had been 'lyin' low' but not silent in Swaziland. He was receiving a great · deal of conflicting evidence as to what he should do. People such as Oliver Tambo and Alan Paton thought he should proceed to London in order to speak the truth about South Africa freely. Others, Alex Hepple (Leader of the South African Labour Party) and Fr. A.G. Sidebotham CR (his Vicar General) advised a return to Johannesburg. A crucial and influential letter (16 April) came to de Blank from a man he trusted, Tom Savage, Bishop of Zululand, who wrote:

> Only yesterday the paper gave the news that the Bishop of Johannesburg had gone off and was in Salisbury, so now I feel I must write to you.
>
> When, on 2nd April, I heard that Ambrose had arrived in Mbabane, Monica and I went up there at once to see what help and assistance we could give him. I cancelled various engagements and stayed with him until Palm Sunday, when Fr. Sidebotham C.R., the Vicar-General, came to take over.
>
> I was never in agreement with the original decision to leave Johannesburg, but that was none of my business and he left on the advice of the Vicar-General, Dean, and senior Archdeacon.
>
> During the time Ambrose was in Swaziland awaiting a clarification of his position from the High Commissioner, he saw a deputation from Johannesburg (his treason trial and Sharpeville solicitor etc.) urging him to return. They doubted the likelihood of his arrest and wanted him back to rally those who had looked to him. I agreed with them but said little as we were waiting to hear from the High Commissioner and Ambrose needed companionship as much as anything. Though physically in good health, the strain and tension , of these last weeks in Johannesburg had taken their toll of both Ambrose and Margaret Reeves, and made an objective consideration of the situation difficult for him and impossible for her (she

came down at the begining and again at the end of his stay in Mbabane).

On Palm Sunday Fr. Sidebotham returned to Mbabane with Mrs. Reeves, and Monica and I packed to return here. That day at lunch time I received a telephone call from Ambrose's barrister and from Anthony Sampson who was with him, urging a return to Johannesburg, while Margaret Reeves had come down specifically to see that he did *not* return.

This seemed the moment when I had to make my position clear and state that I was in favour of his returning to his diocese. I based my decision on the following four points:-

1 *The Church.* People will say, 'They speak so bravely but in the end they run'. This will detract from the weight given to the words and actions of the Bishop's successor in Johannesburg and of *all* the Bishops of the C.P.S.A.

2 *Those working for the defence and aid of Africans.* These people have assured us that the Bishop's immediate departure will damage the cause and this assurance cannot be lightly brushed aside.

3 *The Bishop and his family.* They naturally have a desire that the Bishop should go off immediately particularly in view of the heavy mental and nervous strain of these last weeks, but will it ultimately be in his own best interests to have declined to take the most courageous course?

4 *Overseas Support.* To what extent would this be damaged by a week's delay? And if the Bishop were arrested would it not add to the strength of the appeal?

I realised that there was *some* danger of his being arrested and therefore said that I refused to *urge* him, since one man could scarcely urge another to put his head in a lion's mouth while one didn't have to do so oneself.

I fear that my coming down on that side of the fence was very unacceptable, and I haven't heard from Ambrose since, although he promised to wire me his decision.

Meanwhile we are thinking and praying for you very much in your difficult task of leadership at this time, and I am certainly grateful to know that you have cancelled your trip overseas. This makes me think there may still be an opportunity for all the bishops to meet. I am still unhappy that there has not been a chance of consultation between us all, especially as telephone calls and letters have to be so guarded. Perhaps I feel specially cut off in this backwater where only censored press news penetrates.

I am sending this for security reasons via the Weatherston menage.

As the letter shows, Reeves decided to proceed to England going via Lourenço Marques and Salisbury, Rhodesia, to arrive in London on 21 April. At his London press conference and meetings during May, Reeves was able to say little about why he had left and what he had taken with him. Opinion against his having left South Africa hardened as he could say nothing whilst his *Memorandum* was before the Commission and the matter therefore sub judice. It was later admirably documented in his book *Shooting at Sharpeville: The Agony of South Africa* (Gollancz 1960). At the Judicial Commission which followed Sharpeville the Commissioner, Mr. Justice P.J. Wessels, acknowledged that without Reeves' assistance his task would have been exceedingly difficult if not impossible, as he would have had only the police version in front of him. This was a vindication of Reeves' earlier assertions about the importance of the evidence which he had collected. Indeed, the world no less than the Church owes him a debt.

But, now in England, should Reeves return to South Africa? Archbishop Fisher thought, 'one should not refrain from offering [him] work here'. (Letter to de Blank 3 May). de Blank agreed when replying (10 May): 'I believe a change would be for the best'.

de Blank was kept informed of developments in London by Cecil Wood and was still not satisfied that Fisher, the World Council of Churches or the British Council of Churches appreciated the real agony of the South African nightmare. He wrote again (21 May) to Fisher and this time more fully as the letter was going by hand. In it he refers to the Christian Council of South Africa with which de Blank had much contact:

> ... the general feeling of the Christian Council of South Africa has been one of dissatisfaction with the World Council's attitude towards the Dutch Reformed Church. This may be due in part to Visser't Hooft's own D.R.C. background, though the D.R.C. in the Netherlands has made it abundantly clear on several occasions that it has no use at all for South African racial policies. The fact remains that whenever a World Council officer arrives in the Union he is inclined to by-pass the Christian Council (which the D.R.C. left in a huff in the nineteen thirties), to underestimate the difficulties that separate us, and to allow himself to be managed by the D.R.C. authorities at the expense of spending sufficient time with the other

177

churches in the country. Even Bilheimer's recent visit suffered from this — and his views are no doubt reflected in the very wordy letters from Geneva. The World Council officers who come here almost always give the impression that our difficulties are really insignificant, and that a little goodwill on both sides would put everything right.

Nothing could be further from the truth. It is quite useless to think of the D.R.C. as a church like any other church. That may be true in other countries, but it is not so in South Africa. Quite frankly it is much more a political party than a church. Professor Pistorius in his famous book, *No Further Trek*, stated categorically that 86% of the D.R.C. ministers belonged to *Die Broederbond*, which is a secret political organization pledged to Afrikaner domination of South Africa. The moment we think of the D.R.C. as a church and nothing else we are in danger of falling into sentimentalism. This note could be heard in the meetings of the British Council of Churches and also in some of the statements accompanying the most courageous resolutions passed by both Convocations.

For those outside this country, it is probably impossible to realize the machinations in which the D.R.C. engages. In general education, in more specific Bantu education, in the chaplaincy work in prisons, in the establishment of the new University Colleges, the D.R.C. has been playing its own political game for its own partisan ends. It infiltrates everywhere, manages to squeeze out the other churches and claims increasing privileges for itself. One of the latest and most bitter of their efforts is their concentrated assault upon the Diocese of St. John's. In the past no new school could be established within five miles of any other school. This regulation has now been lifted to enable the D.R.C. to push into Anglican and Methodist strongholds and they are spending much money and sending many men into the area.

I could go on with this at length — but the point I wish to make is that the D.R.C. cannot be considered merely as one of the Christian Churches in the country with which we ought to be in friendly relations. They are clever. They use a few men like Brink and Landman to go overseas and present a friendly and co-operative facade to the world — but their statements overseas bear no resemblance to their attitude and behaviour in South Africa. The most obvious example of this is their refusal to be in the Christian Council of South Africa while enjoying membership of the World Council. It is a bit too easy to love the World Council that they have not seen while having nothing to do with the Christian Council that they have seen.

178

Meanwhile, the misery here continues and still the D.R.C. has done nothing to repudiate the evils of apartheid or to plead for compassion for the detainees. The estrangement of the Africans from the Church continues and we have no hope of regaining their confidence *until the Churches break with apartheid in a manner that is public and irrevocable.* This is the real crisis of the Church in South Africa — and peace between the Churches cannot be secured at the expense of African confidence.

Whilst part of South Africa was celebrating the Jubilee of the Union with festivities, de Blank let off some fireworks in his Jubilee sermon preached in St. George's Cathedral on 29 May: 'What in heaven's name (and I use that expression in all serious-ness) are we in this country supposed to be celebrating? Instead of proclaiming liberty, we maintain a State of Emergency. Instead of returning every man to his possession, we know of at least sixteen hundred people who are detained in prison apart from the refugees who have fled abroad for sanctuary.

'. . . We ought not to be rollicking at this time in Bloemfontein but beating our breasts in Sharpeville. We ought not to be roystering in Pretoria but lamenting in Langa. And I dare to say in the name of the Lord that to indulge in officially-sponsored jollifi-cation at such a time as this is both immoral and indecent.

'No doubt there are those who will say that all this is yet another example of the Church indulging in politics. I would to God that these uninformed and stupid people would learn what Christian-ity is about; I would to God they would go home and read their Bibles — and they could do a lot worse than begin with the story of the Feast of Jubilee in the twenty-fifth chapter of Leviticus. (Which also says, "Ye shall therefore not oppress one another").'

In mentioning the Good Samaritan, he noted: 'It was the Jew who was rescued by the Samaritan, and not the other way around. And quite likely this country will yet be redeemed by the patience, good humour, the charity, the forgiveness, of our own twelve-million Samaritans with black and brown skins.'

The Government made one concession to celebrate the Jubilee by releasing two hundred and fifty prisoners in an amnesty.

On Union Day itself, 31 May, there were two starkly contrasting occasions. At Bloemfontein, Prime Minister Verwoerd made his first public speech since the attempt on his life, to over one hundred thousand people. He appealed for support for a republic based on white government and co-operation with the United

179

Kingdom and the rest of the Commonwealth. He painted a future of, 'one united white nation with the heritage of white South Africa solving problems totally different from problems anywhere in the world'. He released a dove, 'as a symbol of peace' and stressed, 'that the only solution to our racial problem is to live as good neighbours'. But the biggest cheers greeted his declaration that, 'whites must rule South Africa'.

The scene was different in Cape Town at an event organized by the Archbishop's Conference Committee. Here there was no frenzied applause, no sycophantic ogling of a white man, but a multi-racial crowd estimated at ten thousand marching in silence to the Drill Hall adjoining the City Hall. The march was led by de Blank, A. van der Sandt Centlivres (the former Chief Justice), Leo Marquand and Alan Paton of the Liberal Party, Donald Milteno of the Progressive Party and Patrick Duncan. (Sir Villiers de Graf of the United Party was speaking at the Bloemfontein festivity). In English, Afrikaans and Xhosa (the African language) they dedicated themselves to 'ridding the country of the scourge of poverty and achieving inter-racial justice on the basis of Government by consent'. There were brief speeches by Centlivres, Joseph Nkatlo and the Rev. R. Joorst.

The silence and sobriety at Cape Town had its own majesty in contrast to the flag-waving and bunting bouncing jingoism at Bloemfontein. It was a memorable event. But still no meeting of hearts or minds.

Following de Blank's Jubilee sermon, the Minister of External Affairs, Eric Louw, said de Blank had 'been abusing the hospitality which he, a stranger, enjoys in our country'. These were mild words for what he and Afrikaners, in a crescendo of criticism, were feeling towards de Blank. *Die Kerkbode* articulated these feelings more accurately:

> The Archbishop's latest utterances on the subject of the Union Jubilee convince us that he should no longer be regarded as a responsible Church leader. With him, arrogance takes the place of sober judgement. So blind is he in his racial and colour prejudice — a sin of which he accuses the Afrikaner people and the D.R.C. — that the latter can do nothing which he does not feel called upon to condemn.
>
> What has he to gain by representing all non-Europeans as martyrs? What is his object in labelling the twelve million non-Europeans as Good Samaritans? We would not dare to assert our own position,

but there would be good grounds for assigning the rôles of Samaritan and Jew in the opposite way to that proposed by Dr. de Blank. To this our extensive mission work and service of the non-Europeans bear witness. He certainly is not the only champion working on behalf of the non-Europeans. If Dr. de Blank were not distressingly colour conscious (a sin of which he accuses us!) he would not have dared to give such an outrageous exegesis and application of the Scriptures.

...has he any genuine desire to meet the Afrikaans Churches in conference when any prospect of better understanding and co-operation is being endangered in advance? We do not expect Dr. de Blank to be in complete agreement with us, but it would now appear that he wants to rally all the non-Europeans — regardless of whether they are Christians or not — against Churches which confess the same Christ he confesses and which therefore are much closer to him than his chosen allies.

de Blank was not surprised by this editorial vitriol. It underlined what he had been asserting about the Dutch Reformed Church. He wrote immediately to Visser't Hooft and to the Archbishop of Canterbury indicating that any possibility of conversations with the D.R.C. had been sabotaged by the editorial. To Fisher he wrote on 6 June: 'It is clearer and clearer every day that the D.R.C. is just playing a hypocritical game with us. Their latest is an attack in their official magazine *Die Kerkbode*. I have from time to time assailed their approval of apartheid, but I have never attacked any of their leaders by name. ... There is no hope of any consultation between the C.P.S.A. and the D.R.C. till this latest attack is repudiated. I am certain it would be healthier all round if things were brought to a head. Until there is a change of heart in the D.R.C. the C.P.S.A. cannot be associated with them; I see no hope of our remaining within the W.C.C. on the present terms. We have a Provincial Synod later this year and already resolutions are being prepared calling upon the Church of the Province to withdraw from the World Council'.

Fisher and the W.C.C. were not going to allow plans for an inter-church consultation to fall because of a brick thrown by *Die Kerkbode*. It had already been decided that Bishop Stephen Bayne, the Anglican Executive Officer, should attend a meeting of the South African Bishops on 20 June. There had been some discussion at Lambeth Palace attended by Fisher, Reeves, Bayne, Wood and Bilheimer. To Wood, Fisher outlined the immediate tasks (6 June): '(a) to pacify the conflict between the Archbishop [de Blank] and the W.C.C. and restore trust, and (b) to secure between the Archbishop and the D.R.C. such a relation as will make it possible for them to sit in on a General Conference in some degree of mutual respect'.

At the bishops' meeting in June, de Blank was persuaded not to jettison the proposed consultation and he wrote on behalf of the Province to the W.C.C. accepting participation in a 'fact finding conference' proposing that the agenda should include consideration of the responsibility for the Christian to witness within the life of the Church as well as within society; the obligation of the Church to the State; and the areas and nature of the missionary duty. Fisher was well pleased when he wrote to de Blank (29 June):

> Bishop Bayne's report on his return and your message filled me with thankfulness and rejoicing. Dangers which I was afraid of have been removed and we can all walk together, whether in Geneva or in Cape Town or here at Lambeth, with complete confidence that whatever stresses and tribulation of soul there may be there will be an agreement at heart and in public relations.

Yet a hint of how de Blank had niggled him, as did anyone else who 'rocked the boat' or rather 'his boat', is contained in another paragraph.

> You think that I have not yet seen that apartheid as practised in South Africa is anti-Christian. But I have always seen that and have been always convinced that it is diabolically anti-Christian. In almost my first public utterance years ago I denounced apartheid as slavery; but there are actions, even political actions, of the Church of Rome as practised in some parts of the world, which also seem to me anti-Christian and diabolically anti-Christian. Please do not think that because I do not often refer in public to these practical aspects of evil that I am not aware of them, and do not deeply sympathise with all who have to suffer from them.

The Cottesloe Consultation (as it became known) was planned from 7 to 14 December at Cottesloe, Johannesburg. If the traumatic interventions of previous months were thought to be over, the position of Ambrose Reeves (himself a member of the Central Committee of the W.C.C.) had been overlooked. He was still Bishop of Johannesburg even if staying in England where he had been due for a long leave in any event. de Blank was not alone in his view about the position:

(Letter to Cecil Wood — 21 June)

> It is desperately important that Ambrose should *not* come back.
> Reports from Johannesburg make this quite clear. Let him be given
> a job of comparable status soon — and let his resignation be
> announced. Then they can start looking for a new Bishop. Do
> inform Geoffrey (Fisher) with the urgency of this and perhaps it will
> be worth your while to see the P.M.'s Ecclesiastical Secretary.

Reeves was receiving different advice from Johannesburg. As a
result of such advice he decided to return to South Africa. He
informed Stephen Bayne by telephone on 16 August who wrote to
de Blank on the same day:

> I truly think that the years ahead for him in Johannesburg cannot be
> very productive, but God may have quite other plans; certainly
> there was no indication that he was called to stay here; and knowing
> Ambrose I am sure that his choice is an exteremly obedient and
> costly one.

de Blank, who was 'praying hard for Ambrose' thought he had
'chosen a very tough course and we must bear him up as best we
can'.

Reeves arrived at Jan Smuts Airport, Johannesburg on 10 September and went to Rosettenville to stay with Fr. Sidebotham of
the Community of the Resurrection who had been acting as Vicar-
General. Two days later Reeves was at the airport again, this time
in the company of Security Branch detectives who whisked him
onto a plane. He had been deported. Stephen Bayne who met
Reeves on his arrival in England wrote to de Blank, 'the line to take
is the strong one, that this is an attack on Christian witness and on
the life of the Church'. de Blank did not need informing of this. He
was on an official visit to the Diocese of Natal and was due to
preach at a service in the City Hall, Durban, on 13 September. de
Blank changed the theme and text of the sermon he preached
before four thousand people. He told his flock that they had
nothing to fear. They may be distressed at recent events
culminating in the deportation of one of the bishops but they must
not despair. 'It is an old saying, none the less true for being often
repeated, that the blood of the martyrs is the seed of the Church.
Whether martyrdom be to death or to exile, or to obliquy or to
unpopularity, is no matter. Whenever a Christian suffers for what
he believes to be right, the whole Church suffers with him'.

It was a rallying call to follow the Church's leadership. It was also a call to faith and discipleship. 'Are we daily in our private and our public life seeking to live faithfully as His disciples? Do we see the shadow of His Cross fall on all our daily plans, on our relationships, our pass-books, on every room in our homes? Does every Church service that we attend make others take knowledge of us, that we have been with Jesus?' With renewed commitment they could pray in all confidence and vigour: 'Let God arise, and let His enemies be scattered'.

Following the deportation, the Church of the Province took the position that either the Consultation should not be held because one of the delegates could not attend, or that it should be held outside the Union of South Africa so that full attendance would be possible. The Executive Committee (consisting of an Anglican, a Dutch Reformed and a Methodist representative) of the Planning Committee, however, sent a delegation (Revs. C.F.B. Naude and Dr. F.E.O'B. Geldenhuys of the N.G. Kerk Transvaal) to the Government asking that a re-entry permit be granted to Reeves to enable him to attend the Consultation. The Minister of the Interior, J.F. Naude, stated that although he personally regretted that the deportation had been considered necessary it was absolutely impossible for the Government to give Reeves a safe conduct to the Consultation. Questioned about the deportation he said it was and never had been the policy of the Government to give reasons for the deportation of any person.

The fact that this meeting had taken place demonstrated the solidarity of the churches on the issue. Diplomatically it was an ingenious device but there had been much scurrying hither and thither by W.C.C. officials and some unfortunate deviousness. The Dutch Reformed Churches were tiring of the 'Reeves factor' and some members thought that de Blank was using the new difficulty as a stick to beat the Government or to bolster his periodic bouts of scepticism about the Consultation. The exasperated W.C.C. even contemplated a Consultation without Reeves. Then de Blank announced that the Anglicans could not attend a conference in Johannesburg (Cottesloe) without the permission of Reeves. (By then it had been generally agreed that a Consultation outside the Union would not be worthwhile). Reeves sent a cable to de Blank (26 October): 'Agree to invite upon condition all member churches publicly denounce banishment'.

The cable came at a time when the Synodal Commission of the Transvaal Dutch Reformed Church was meeting and gave the

Moderator the authority to proceed with the arrangements. The cable had been suppressed. Had they known about it there is little doubt that there would have been no Consultation. The pressures on de Blank from other Anglicans were immense and there was clearly a change of mind by him, for the next that was heard was that the Church of the Province, with Reeves' consent, agreed to participate on schedule and in South Africa.

The approach to the Consultation was set against a continuing background of uncontrollable uncertainty and apprehensive anticipation. Verwoerd's referendum on the issue of a republic was held on 5 October. de Blank was one with the Progressive Party hoping that voters would register an overall repulsion of the Government's arbitrary and draconian rule by saying 'No' to a republic. A negative vote would have made no difference for Verwoerd said, 'If we do not succeed (vote by majority verdict, even if only a majority of one) next time we will adopt the method of allowing [the] decision to be taken by the majority in a Parliament elected for that purpose'. He had nothing to fear for the vote revealed that in all provinces but Natal a majority of whites favoured the change to a Republic although not by a large margin. By a majority of 74,000 or four per cent, the white electorate voted for a Republic. The thirteen million non-whites were not consulted. Fisher wrote to de Blank (19 October): 'The faint hope that the referendum might go the right way came to nothing, which means, I suppose, that the present tyranny will get no better for a long time to come'.

In the Referendum month a book entitled *Delayed Action* was published whose authors called for a new approach to the colour problem of the country. Nothing unusual about that! What made this book sensational was that it came from the hands of eleven leading theologians and ministers of South Africa's three Dutch Reformed Churches. Dr. B.B. Keet, a former Professor of Theology at Stellenbosch, wrote frankly that the fruits of apartheid, 'internally and externally have shown clearly that there is no hope for South Africa if black nationalism has to be fought by force . . . It is my conviction that the time has come for our Afrikaans-speaking churches to notify the state that they no longer see their way clear to supporting the apartheid policy'. Dr. Ben Marais, Professor of the History of Christianity at Pretoria University asserted: 'The Church must guard against being or becoming purely a champion . . . of the interests of the present white governing groups'.

The publication of this book also coincided with the issuing of a series of instructions by the hierarchy of the Roman Catholic Church in South Africa, stressing that nobody must be shunned socially because of different race or colour and that non-whites must be allowed to evolve gradually to full partnership in the life of the country. de Blank's relations with the Roman Catholic Archbishop (McCann) were cordial and would have been very warm had the Roman-Anglican thaw reached the pace of the next decade.

The week-long Cottesloe Consultation began on 7 December. The Chairman was Dr. Franklin Clark Fry who was also Chairman of the Central Committee of the World Council of Churches. In his opening statement he appealed for clear and candid speech based on conviction. The outcome of the Consultation should not, he said — and in this case could not — be predicted in advance.

Although the public presentation of the Consultation had been like flashing traffic lights minus the amber, the private progress had been substantial. Each Church had written a ten thousand word memorandum dealing with the attitude of that Church to the topics of the Consultation. In addition there was material from the W.C.C., the South African Bureau of Race Relations and the South African Institute of Race Relations. The Anglican memorandum was prepared after a series of important contributions had been requested on each of the topics. Its authors were:-

I   The Factual Situation in South Africa: Edgar Brookes, Professor of History, University of Natal

II   The Christian Understanding of the Gospel: *For Relationships among Races* Alan Paton, Author

III   An Understanding of Contemporary History from a Christian Standpoint: Monica Wilson, Professor of Social Anthropology, University of Cape Town

IV   The Meaning of the Current Emergency in South Africa: Walter Stanford

V   The Witness of the Church with regard to Justice, Mission and Co-operation: Bill Burnett, Bishop of Bloemfontein

The programme for the Consultation was very good. It consisted of worship, Bible study and discussion. Morning worship of forty-five minutes was led by Visser't Hooft and was followed by an hour of Bible study, conducted by persons drawn from the church delegations. Discussion took place in four groups each of which represented a cross section of the meeting, and each of which discussed all five agenda topics. There was discussion in plenary meetings to which group reports were presented and by the Consultation as a whole.

Each Church delegation consisted of ten people and there was one observer from the Christian Council of South Africa. The W.C.C. delegation, led by Franklin Clark Fry, included Visser't Hooft, Robert Bilheimer who, despite spasms of obtuseness and obstinacy, had persevered so hard to bring the Consultation to birth, Charles Coolidge Parlin, a Methodist from the U.S.A., Wilhelm Nielsel of the Reformed Church, Germany, and Lakdasa de Mel from Ceylon. Sir Francis Ibiam, a Presbyterian from Nigeria, was prevented from attending at the last moment on his election as Governor-General of the Eastern Province of Nigeria.

The Anglican Delegation was led by de Blank. Others were the Bishop of Natal (Vernon Inman), Bloemfontein (Bill Burnett), Bishop A.H. Zulu, Assistant Bishop of St. John's, the Archdeacon of Cape Town (Cecil Wood) in place of Ambrose Reeves, Fr. George Sidebotham CR, Professor Monica Wilson, E.H. Brookes and Z.K. Matthews, Attorney at Law, Professor-Emeritus of the University College of Fort Hare, and Alan Paton.

All but two delegations were inter-racial, and non-white people comprised about twenty-five per cent of the meeting. Living arrangements were fully inter-racial.

By deliberate intention the meeting was closed with a hungry press kept completely away. Any final statement had to carry an eighty per cent majority. The vigorous nature of the discussions never disguised the cleft-ridden differences between some of the delegations. From the start the Nederduitsche Hervormde Kerk delegation stood apart. A.J.G. Oosthuizen, Chairman of the Synod, stated his objection to integration on any grounds. T.F.J. Dreyer, Secretary of the Synod, saw apartheid as having different areas with a fence through which white and black may go from time to time for special purposes. Under the ideal of apartheid, there would be parallel development — namely two separate parts of the country in which the populations would each be fully developed.

This placed the delegations of the Nederduitse Gereformeerde Kerke of the Cape and Transvaal in a dilemma which they could only solve by themselves making a statement. They confirmed that they stood by their assertion that a policy of differentiation could be defended from the Christian point of view and provided the only realistic solution to the problems of race relations. As for participation in Government: 'in the case of White areas the statement refers to the Africans who are domiciled in the declared White areas in the sense that they have no other homeland'.

The Cottesloe statement which was issued was tame by Western and liberal standards but radically enlightened and daring by South African standards. This involved an expression of support for coloured franchise and direct representation, 'within the foreseeable future'; a clear statement that ownership of property and the franchise must be available to the Africans, or at any rate those who lived permanently in urban areas; a statement that there was nothing in the Holy Scriptures to forbid mixed marriages; a plea for higher wages and for the ending of migrant labour, and a statement that the Indians must be regarded as a permanent part of the South Africa population. These are only a few points from the statement, the cumulative effect of which amounted to a repudiation of the extremes and rigidity of the policies of the Government.

The most remarkable thing of all was that the Consultation was held. There were many moments when it appeared it would break down but it kept together for the seven days. People there experienced a togetherness and voted for a more representative ecumenical agency in South Africa. There was division but not derision, directness outlawed misunderstanding and disagreement was better than amiable, meaningless resolutions. In a way it was unity. It came from the worship. It grew in Bible study. It was forged in debate. It was a gift — at least for a time.

de Blank wrote some personal impressions of Cottesloe. He praised the World Council Delegation, not least Visser't Hooft and Bilheimer who, 'in the kindest but most incisive way ... exposed the follies and wickedness of racial discrimination, and — of equal importance — they condemned the official definitions of Communism and Communist activity so far as South Africa is concerned'. He continued:

> The delegates of the N.G.K. of both Transvaal and the Cape could not, for the most part, have been more helpful or more eager to find common ground with us. I think it would be fair to say that they divided themselves into three groups; the younger and more liberal of them, impatient of their own racial policies, keen to move

forward, but conscious of the opposition in the rank and file of their members; the older and more intransigent — some of whom were still advancing Scriptural arguments for segregation and differentiation, and strangely enough, included in this group were professors from Stellenbosch; the ecclesiastical politicians — playing a very careful game vis-à-vis both the Government and their own Church membership. But all these groups warmed towards the end and, as the findings show, significant progress was made.

The Hervormde Kerk delegation were impossible. Some were tied directly to the Government (an M.P. among them) and they refused at any time to allow any criticism of the Government or its legislation. This was Erastianism to the nth degree. Among them were individuals both friendly and forthcoming, but their official attitude was one of non-co-operation and non-accommodation. It is hard to understand why they belong to the World Council and why they wish to share in any future attempt to get together.

For many delegates the most dramatic moment came at the end of the Consultation when de Blank made a costly personal statement. It was a moment of humility and greatness. The potent passages are:

In our conviction that acquiescence in a policy of discriminatory segregation gravely jeopardizes the future of the Christian Faith in South Africa, we believed — and still believe — that it was right to speak urgently, clearly and uncompromisingly. But in the light of what we have learnt here and the information now put at our disposal, we confess with regret that in the heat of the moment we have at times spoken heatedly and, through ignorance (for which ignorance we cannot be altogether held responsible), have cast doubt on the sincerity of those who did not accept the wisdom of such public action.

Nevertheless the delegates of the N.G.K. have met with us in the fullest fellowship and we have been deeply moved by this spirit of brotherly goodwill. Where, in the past, we have at any time unnecessarily wounded our brethren, we now ask their forgiveness in Christ.

After Cottesloe it seemed inevitable that the Hervormde Kerk would leave the World Council of Churches. They did, but more surprisingly so did the N.G. Kerk van Transvaal, whose Synods could not swallow Cottesloe. Each Church withdrew from the W.C.C. in April 1961. Adherents of the Hervormde Kerk were 147,871 and the N.G. Kerk van Transvaal 606,436. Of those

Churches at Cottesloe the Church of the Province had the largest number of members at 1,230,509, followed by the Methodist Church at 1,146,479. (Figures at December 1960).

1960 also enveloped personal grief and abundant joy for de Blank. On 22 September he was visiting the Diocese of Lebombo in Portuguese East Africa and whilst staying at the mission station of Msumba on the shores of Lake Nyasa news reached him of the death of his mother a few months before her ninetieth birthday. He was fifty or more miles away from the nearest telephone. However, with the generous help of the Portuguese authorities he managed to get back to Cape Town for a requiem and the funeral which was like a triumphant thanksgiving for her life. She had been ill during 1960 and suffered an internal haemorrhage. Bartha wrote, 'Mother feared death itself though she was prepared for it. It was a sad homecoming for Joost for he and Mother had been very close and dearly loved each other. Nevertheless I often think it was a good thing that he was spared the agony of being at her deathbed'. She was right. de Blank was never at his priestly best with the dying. It would have been intolerable for him with his own mother. He was uneasy because he was unsure. The inner anguish surfaced when he faced death himself.

The Provincial Synod also met in 1960 when some important resolutions concerned with the prevailing racial policy of the country were passed. Taking advantage of the Synod, a historic service for the consecration of three bishops was held in St. George's Cathedral. Never had the Cathedral seen such splendour and joy. South Africa's first black African bishop was one of the three and he from the royal Zulu house — Alphaeus Hamilton Zulu as assistant Bishop of St. John's. Another one was an Englishman — Harold Beardmore for St. Helena and one was American — Robert Mize for Damaraland. The cathedral was packed with people of all races and a special choir from Langa township sang two Communion hymns in Xhosa. The epistle was read in Afrikaans.

de Blank's last and painful action of the year was to write to Ambrose Reeves (30 December) suggesting that the time had come for Reeves to consider resignation.

1960 had been a year when de Blank's name whistled round the world. By his authority, his refusal to compromise on principle, his demonstration of Christianity in action, he had immeasurably strengthened the Church in South Africa and elsewhere. He was

Consecration of Bishops at St. George's Cathedral, Cape Town, November 1960. In centre, left to right: Alphaeus Zulu, Assistant Bishop of St. John's; Harold Beardmore, Bishop of St. Helen; de Blank; Robert Mize, Bishop of Damaraland.

a leader. Within a month of the year ending he was one of the few names mentioned as a successor to Geoffrey Fisher as Archbishop · of Canterbury.

CHAPTER FOURTEEN

Restless and Rootless

On 22 November 1960 Geoffrey Fisher began a pilgrimage to the Holy Land. On the way back he called at Istanbul to visit Athenagoras I, Oecumenical Patriarch of the Orthodox Church, and thence to Rome where he spent a few days in the course of which he paid a visit of courtesy to Pope John XXIII. The last visit constituted a momentous slab of history upon which a sound edifice of Anglican-Roman relations has been built.

On 17 January 1961 Fisher announced his resignation to an unprepared Church and a surprised public. The following day he wrote to each of the Metropolitans in the Anglican Communion explaining his reasons beyond the important one that he was becoming conscious of the burden of his work. Of his visits to Jerusalem, Istanbul and Rome, he commented:

> It was a thing done once for all: and though I had decided on resignation quite apart from it, I was certain that if I tried to follow up the consequences of my visit I should spoil them. Others must do that.

There were exciting developments in the Church of England and the Anglican Communion:

> All of them are at a point from which there can be no return but must be a new and enterprising advance. This is the moment to hand over to the future and to one who can look forward to the future of his own responsibility.

Further, an interesting observation reflecting how he saw and tackled his work:

> I am not good at looking backwards, since my whole life has taught or indeed compelled me always to be looking at today's evil and forward without over anxiety to the excitement of seeing where God will lead us tomorrow.

And the Protestant work ethic was deeply embedded in Fisher to the extent that he could say, 'only work brings joy'.

After the resignation announcement there was speculation as to who would succeed him. However, the announcement of his successor came two days later. No time to pray, hardly time to wonder! The English Bench of Bishops was not strong. Arthur Michael Ramsey, Archbishop of York, was the theological heavyweight but not every pew-dweller's cope and mitre. It was thought that Frederick Donald Coggan, Bishop of Bradford, would have been Fisher's selection. A few other 'possibles' were named, but newspaper reports, including *The Times*, *Daily Telegraph*, *Spectator* and *The Economist* mentioned the fifty-two year old de Blank. He was at the height of his powers. It would have been a daring appointment, but whether good for de Blank or for the Church is doubtful and can be no more than pious conjecture. In the event, Ramsey moved to Canterbury and Coggan to York.

It would have been novel to find an Archbishop of *Canterbury* writing to *The Times* describing apartheid in this language: 'I believe it to be morally corroding, economically suicidal, politically senile and theologically indefensible'. That language is of course de Blank's in a letter to *The Times* on 1 March 1961 where he pleaded for the retention of South Africa within the Commonwealth. Not only non-whites would feel deserted, but also whites, who were working for a multi-racial society would find their task more difficult. 'Impatience, execration, shame and disapproval may be legitimate emotional states to assist in coming to a decision on so important a matter, but they must not govern the final issue'. He continued: 'Moral is a commendable quality, but let it be allied with sound reason. At this time there is every reason for keeping South Africa within the Commonwealth, none at all for excluding her'. And ended: 'I appeal to all who believe in social and racial justice to behave with dignity and restraint, particularly for the period of the Prime Ministers' Conference. More will be accomplished by sound argument and example than by a senseless parade of passion. Let us fight for our principles; let us not flaunt our prejudices'.

By this strange mixture of emotive language and statesmanship, de Blank allied himself with some Commonwealth leaders who were reluctant to see a break of ties with South Africa. At the meeting of Commonwealth Prime Ministers in London in March 1961 Verwoerd formally applied for continued membership of the

Commonwealth for South Africa as a republic. He explained his policy of separate development (or 'co-existence' as he called it) but the issue aroused such strong passion among the African and Asian Premiers that Macmillan had to devise a plan which led to Verwoerd withdrawing his application. The alternative was a tense, even a dissolved, Commonwealth. On hearing the news of South Africa's departure de Blank saw it as, 'a challenge to the Church of the Province to increase indigenous ministry and self-help'.

The unremitting pace of events in South Africa and de Blank's provocative responses to them form a series of snapshots taken from one position. There was another view. Everyday life continued. The white man rested upon his privileged position in his gracious house with an abundance of servants. The black man, his temporary protest having been ruthlessly suppressed, went about his labours with that incurable cheerfulness that was his characteristic. The deep undercurrent of frustration and resentment had once again been driven underground; this time even deeper into subterranean channels. But on the surface, life went on in a spirit of almost unbelievable complacency. They ate, they drank, they bought, they sold, they planted, they built.

And life continued in the Church too — although never in danger of becoming complacent under de Blank's bracing leadership.

From the moment he had arrived in Cape Town he was breathless with ideas. He was knocked breathless too by the size of the task confronting him. There was a shortage of money and of priests. One country area, covering some twenty thousand square miles, was worked by two priests who between them held services in twenty-three different centres, quite apart from the ad hoc services held in village stores or in barns on farms. de Blank soon had a vision of something like the Bush Brotherhood in Australia. 'It would be quite wonderful if a group of some six young priests would volunteer for a five-year period', he wrote to his Commissaries in England and America (5 January 1959). In the same letter he mentioned that he had formed a Fellowship of Vocation and needed many more priests for work in the parishes, particularly in the coloured areas: 'The people have a great love for their church, but I have to admit that their lives and morals are not always all they ought to be'.

In his visits to England and America, de Blank was always seeking and finding priests who were prepared to serve in South

Africa. It was also part of his entrepreneurial touch that he could prise large sums of money out of the most tight-fisted churchgoers in England and prey on the expansiveness of American generosity. However, many clergy were recruited from overseas and he realised that one of the most urgent needs of the Church was for more indigenous clergy. With his usual enthusiasm he started the Bishop Gray Theological College. He was anxious to foster vocations and he wanted to ensure that so far as possible ordinands of all races took the same course and wrote the same examinations. Bishop Gray College was non-racial, with African, coloured and white students all living and studying together. This was contrary to Government regulations, but, contrary to de Blank's usual attitude, he did not draw attention to what was happening and consequently did not provoke the authorities. Bishop Gray was closed when the Federal Seminary, Alice, which was also non-racial, opened.

African and coloured clergy were inspired by de Blank's leadership. They regarded him truly as their, 'Father in God'. When he went to African locations de Blank had tea with the local priest. Kaya Mandi, near Stellenbosch, was a favourite place and Stanley Qabazi a much loved priest who named his son Joost after de Blank. He was also able to meet African leaders informally. de Blank was first and foremost a churchman leading the fight against evil. The intricacies of political involvement in the rising Nationalism was not important for him as it was for Ambrose Reeves. In that sense he was a little apart — not aloof — from the Congresses and other secular movements seeking radical change if not revolution.

We have already seen how some of his own white clergy gave him less than muted support. There was even an unofficial 'movement' of some influential clergy who wanted de Blank to leave South Africa. His presence was uncomfortable for them. This 'movement' was called 'Joost must go' and letters passed with JMG marked on the envelopes. These priests and some senior laymen of the diocese held that they adhered to the principle that discrimination on the grounds of colour alone was contrary to the will of God but ... but ...! Corporate political action must be eschewed. The sufferers must be taught to endure patiently, returning injustice with love. The Church must wait in faith upon God's time. Be patient with the Government and its Ministers; understand their views; speak to them in love. Why

195

does not the Church of the Province enjoin upon the non-white peoples the duties of love, justice and patience: stop meddling in politics and preach the Gospel. These were the kind of views peddled by those who in secret used the initials JMG. Some of these people held high office in the diocese. When he was criticized for opening his mouth too often and too wide de Blank liked to tell the story of a condemned prisoner on his way to the gallows who proffered a ten pound note to the hangman. 'What's that for?' the hangman asked. 'To keep your trap shut', the prisoner replied.

de Blank created many pastoral opportunities in the diocese. As at Stepney he introduced a Lent Progress. When he visited a parish he shared in the ordinary life and worship of the parish for a few days, visiting the out-stations, getting to know the parishioners and encouraging the faithful people who kept the Anglican flag flying all over the diocese. In Lent 1962 he visited ten parishes and afterwards wrote: 'I believe in every instance, virtually all the centres of worship were visited, all the schools and all other local Anglican agencies. At a rough tally I reckon that I spoke at one hundred different centres, whether schools or churches or private houses where the congregations had gathered, and I celebrated the Holy Mysteries or presided at them in about twenty-five different places. Wherever we went there was much to encourage us . . .' And de Blank did much to encourage them. He gave them an experience of belonging to a worldwide Church and a feeling of pride to be a member of it.

de Blank always tried to make each act of worship a memorable act. He brought to the notice of his clergy in Cape Town the liturgical experiments which were becoming commonplace in England. Confirmation services caused him some difficulty in part because he did not find them easy. He wanted the service to be really remembered by each candidate as the day they entered into the full life of the Church. Confirmation hymns depressed him so he decided to write one which he believed, 'does express the mystery and wonder of the Sacrament'. It runs like this:

> Now is the moment of my great surrender;
> Now is the time when at Thy feet I fall.
> Now, O my Saviour, as Thy praise I render
> I bring to Thee my sins, my life, my all.

Now is the moment for Thy costly cleansing;
  Now is the time when for Thyself I plead;
Now by Thy Cross my total being cleansing
  I claim from Thee the powerful Grace I need.

Now is the moment of Thy Spirit's coming
  Through laying on of Apostolic hands;
Now by Thine own indwelling Grace becoming
  All that Thy love desires, Thy law commands.

From this day forth I shall approach Thine altar,
  Humble yet glad, in shame yet unafraid,
There to receive Thy gifts from off that altar —
  Thy strengthening Blood, Thy Body in the Bread.

Now and henceforth I am Thy willing servant;
  Now and henceforth I pledge myself to Thee —
Yet by Thy boundless love more friend than servant,
  For Thou art come ever to dwell in me.

Ever to dwell in me, and in Thy likeness
  Daily to fashion me according to Thy will
Until that day I see Thy glorious likeness,
  And one with Thee am freed from every ill.

Regarding the tune, he added, 'One or two tunes have been written, and these can be obtained from Bishopscourt, but if you would like to try it to a fairly familiar tune you may care to use the tune to "O Strength and Stay Upholding All Creation" or "O Perfect Love, all human thought transcending". It also goes to the tune of the Londonderry Air'.

'There was never a dull moment with Joost de Blank at the helm', was a remark heard from clergy and laity alike. As in Stepney de Blank felt the need for a spectacular development. Accordingly, at the Diocesan Synod in 1961 it was announced that there would be a Church Congress in November 1962. The title, theme and content was pure de Blank. The title was *Rise Up and Build* and the aim, 'to show every one of us that the Church is very much alive: to re-awaken many inside the Church to the wonder of their inheritance and to startle into attending many of those outside'. There would be rallies, speeches, dramas, films, music, massed choirs, lunch-hour activities, a display of Church treasures. First, there must be Congress Heralds — 'Soldiers aren't enrolled and sent straight away to the front line'. The Heralds were trained in the three Ps — Pray, Ponder, Prepare.

After training they were commissioned and let loose on the parishes. A parish priest recalls the momentum: 'My staff and I found ourselves engaged in writing Biblical and historical notes for parish study groups and organizing training sessions for clergy and laity all over the diocese . . . Halls were booked, programmes were printed, appeals were sent out. Intercession leaflets were compiled and circulated, revue sketches were conceived and written. Buttonhole badges were designed and manufactured. Anglicans all over the diocese, even the most conservative and staid, wore the badges proclaiming their allegiance to Christ (in the words of Nehemiah — 'Rise up and Build', printed on the badges) dedicated themselves to the extension of Christ's Kingdom and the outward manifestation of that Kingdom in bricks and mortar'. This latter comment refers to the launching of the Ten Churches Appeal Fund. There was urgent need for new churches — *now!* de Blank often quoted Cecil Rhodes' supposed last words, taken from Tennyson's *In Memoriam:* 'So much to do, so little done', as if to rebuke himself. Yet he never flinched or quailed at the enormity of the task. He leapt at each task with complete abandon. Of the preparations for the Congress a priest writes: 'Joost was everywhere, encouraging, inspiring, consoling, driving — keeping his foot on the accelerator, as it were to make us all do 60 m.p.h. or more, nothing less. But it was exhilarating, exciting and enormous fun. The whole diocese caught on fire and we experienced a New Pentecost before we'd even heard of the Charismatic Movement. ''Rise Up and Build'' was translated from a pious hope into hard fact in terms of bricks and mortar, thanks to Joost's inspiration and leadership'.

In July 1962 de Blank celebrated the tenth anniversary of his consecration as bishop, and there were a number of celebrations. On 24 July there was a packed-to-overflowing 'Meet the Bishop' meeting at the City Hall, addressed by Eric Trapp (Secretary of the Society for the Propagation of the Gospel, and a former Bishop of Zululand), Philip Wheeldon (Bishop of Kimberley and Kuruman) and de Blank. Included in the programme was an item, 'The Seven Ages of an Archbishop' or 'The Apocryphal Acts of Joost de Blank'. This was a much appreciated satire on de Blank's life, ending with de Blank going on stage, the curtains opening to reveal a cake and ten candle-bearers. One of the organ pieces was the Merchant Taylors' School Song. This was no surprise for he heard it quite often. The organist at St. Saviour's, Claremont, was

Style and Speed. June 1960.

Walter Swanson, a well-known South African musician who had been educated at Merchant Taylors'. The first time de Blank had appeared at St. Saviour's Swanson played the school song on the organ as de Blank entered in procession. He was delighted and it became customary to play 'Joost's signature tune' whenever he attended the church.

On the anniversary day itself, 25 July, de Blank celebrated Holy Communion in the Cathedral early in the morning. Later, at ten o'clock, there was a Solemn Eucharist in the presence of nine bishops of the Province. Afterwards de Blank wrote (in *Good Hope* September 1962):

199

I still cannot get over the wonder that some 350 people came to their communion in the Cathedral. ... At 6 o'clock in the morning (Wednesday) the weather could hardly have been worse but I know of people well on in years who walked nearly three miles and back again in order to be present and to share in the sacrament with me.

To mark the anniversary Mr. Deane Anderson of the Architectural Faculty of the University of Cape Town designed a beautiful travelling Primatial Cross and a Pastoral Staff.

For the November Church Congress itself de Blank had invited a number of people from overseas to speak and preach during the Congress. These included Austin Pardue (Bishop of Pittsburgh), John J. Weaver (Dean of Detroit), Stephan Hopkinson (General Director of the Industrial Christian Fellowship), A.W. Eaton (Rector of Kitwe, Northern Rhodesia), A.F. Hood (Chancellor of St. Paul's Cathedral, London) and C. Edward Crowther (Chaplain to the University of California). Subsequently de Blank persuaded Philip Wheeldon, Bishop of Kimberley and Kuruman, to appoint Crowther as Dean. Later Crowther succeeded Wheeldon as Bishop when he resigned because of ill health. In a very unusual development Wheeldon was re-elected to Kimberley when Crowther was deported from South Africa in 1968.

Between the anniversary celebrations and the Congress de Blank suffered a cerebral thrombosis and went to England for treatment. The specialist would not let him return for the Congress but his spirit was in all the acts — in the large multi-racial procession where old people and children walked side by side, where young people helped the blind and cripples who walked with crutches. The standard of innovative excellence pervaded the magnificient exhibition which was opened by Sir John Maud, the British Ambassador. His enthusing freshness was in 'The Get With It' show, presented by young people — a show which swung from laughter to seriousness with music from many lands, hymns in modern dress, ballet, drama and acrobatics. Above all his encouragement was felt in the big public meetings, in the musical performance of Haydn's 'The Creation' and the plays 'Boy with a Cart' by Christopher Fry; 'Go Down Moses' by Philip Lamb and 'The Vigil' by Ladislas Foder.

de Blank's intention was that through the Congress, people would catch a new vision of what Christ's Church really was — in its divine splendour and strength. They did — and something more! For de Blank never forgot the evangelical mission of the Church. In the *Congress Herald* newspaper he wrote:

There was an Old Testament writer who said: 'Where there is no vision the people perish'. And the opposite is also true: 'Where there is vision, the people are saved'. In other words, I believe the Congress will so set us on fire with love for Christ and His Church that we shall all be eager to go out to bring a lost world to His feet.

He led his diocese from the front, and would have liked to have led the Province in a similar way. However, as Archbishop among the other bishops he was no more than *primus inter pares*. His aim was to visit two dioceses each year. These visits were of great importance to the individual dioceses and to himself. He wanted not only the co-operation of his fellow bishops but also their friendship. Bishop Philip Wheeldon writes sensitively about this and of de Blank's visits to Kimberley:

When I was elected to the Diocese of Kimberley and Kuruman in 1961 I could not think why I received a letter from Joost in terms which suggested that we had been friends for many years. So far as I could remember we had met only once and this had been for a fleeting moment during the 1939 war when our paths had crossed in London while we were Army Chaplains. But I was soon to learn that this kind of thing was in character with Joost. He needed friendship. I believe he depended very much upon friendship, and I gained the impression that he would go a long way to try and establish this kind of relationship particularly with those alongside whom he worked. Not that there was anything forced about it. It seemed perfectly natural to him. So when I arrived in South Africa he greeted me like a long lost friend and I soon realised that this was the way in which he wanted his brother bishops to work with him. This was an approach which perhaps everyone did not understand. I myself had been brought up in a different school. I had been domestic chaplain and then suffragan bishop to Archbishop Garbett of York. My former chief had used Christian names only on rare occasions even among those with whom he had worked for many years. Here was something different. Joost wanted Christian names from the word go. From time to time I slipped into saying 'Sir' or 'Your Grace' when talking with him, but my Archbishop did not want that. I remember no occasion when he wrote to me as 'My dear bishop' except when he was sending a directive to all his bishops on formal occasions. It is my opinion that there is something very significant about this. Joost liked to have those who worked with him really with him. His efforts to establish close friendship with them might be regarded as part of his policy. There was something wrong for him if this kind of partnership was not established.

201

To my mind, no attempt to understand Joost as a man or as an Archbishop and leader could be fully carried through without bearing this characteristic in mind. I am sure he would have wished to have as friends many who disagreed with his views and his statements on matters of policy both in the close life and work of the Church as well as in other fields including politics. He would not have wished to clash personally with those who could not accept his opinions. As time went on, however, it became clear that his outspoken and determined efforts to express what he believed to be right, particularly in the field of human relationships in the South African situation, were going to stand in the way of friendly relationships with those who opposed him. A point of no return was reached and I am of the opinion that it was a very great hurt to him that the friendship he so desired could not be fully established and maintained. This hurt went very deep and only his own self discipline saved him from being broken by it. It also meant that as time went on he depended more and more upon those who were ready to extend the hand of friendship to him.

On the occasion of the Golden Jubilee of the Diocese of Kimberley and Kuruman in 1961 Joost visited the Diocese for a period of two weeks. He covered the greater part of the Diocese by air and road. He undertook the heavy programme with enthusiasm and enjoyment. When the rest of us hoped for a few minutes with our feet up between engagements he would prefer to make an informal and unplanned visit to someone. A social occasion was refreshment to him and he loved a party. After travelling hundreds of miles in the heat and dust, having addressed large audiences and shaken hands all round, he would say 'What are we going to do now?' We soon learned that to answer 'nothing' would not be very popular! So we found ourselves arranging on the spur of the moment one engagement after another until my Chaplain — almost in desperation — asked, 'Does he ever stop?'

Perhaps it was on this visit that we in the Diocese saw something of the real Joost. This revealed itself when we saw him as someone who came down from the 'pedestal' of an official Archbishop. Three things stand out. His love of God, his compassionate concern for people as the children of God, and his joy and sense of fun. The first two of these was evident in the way he led us in prayer and worship and in his sermons and addresses on some of the great themes of the faith. In simple terms he spoke of the love of God, of the meaning of faith, and of the importance of fearless witness for the cause of Christ. And he made a special point of stressing the value of hope as a Christian virtue. During the whole of this official visit

I remember no occasion when he made direct reference to anything specifically political. In view of the opinion expressed by some that politics was his main theme here was an occasion which was quite the reverse. Then there was his joy and sense of fun. There was plenty of evidence to make us feel that he thoroughly enjoyed himself. A concentrated tour of a Diocese like this can be a gruelling occasion. But Joost did not allow it to become that. At the end of a long programme we found ourselves one evening at a meeting where one long speech followed another. It was the fifth engagement of the day with many miles between each of them. A catechist welcomed us with the words, 'It is good to have our Lord and your Grace with us'. Joost turned to me with a twinkle in his eye, saying, 'Pretty quick promotion for you Philip!' Nor was I the only one who heard him say it. It was the kind of opportunity he would never miss and he loved it as much as we did. At the end of the fortnight we were approaching the last place on our schedule after a journey by road of several hundred miles. Joost always liked to be put in the picture beforehand so that he would know something of the local situation on his arrival. In the course of what I had to tell him on this occasion I warned him that the priest did not like being called Father. 'I understand', said Joost, 'Thus far and no Father!'

When his official tour of the Diocese ... was ending Joost made a comment about the Diocese which was certainly something we had not expected. 'I don't think I have ever spent so long travelling over nothing!' It was the kind of relief we needed, the kind of thing which helped us to laugh at ourselves and not become too 'heavy' about our many problems and difficulties. It was probably just what we needed and we have never forgotten it.

de Blank's visits to dioceses gave much encouragement. He also used them to learn as much as he could about the effect of Government policies on Church life. His first visit to another diocese, that of Lebombo, in December 1957, was not an easy one. Its Bishop, Humphrey Beevor, had resigned and returned to England. The Diocese was in some chaos and there were financial problems. Many mission stations had not seen their bishop for several years. If they were not to collapse episcopal encouragement was needed. It was a difficult diocese, set in Portuguese East Africa. Not all of Mozambique was in the Lebombo Diocese. The Archdeaconry of Msumba fell within the terrority of Mozambique but came ecclesiastically within the Diocese of Nyasaland whose bishop, Frank Thorne, was determined it should stay there.

de Blank had gone to Lourenço Marques at the request of the

Episcopal Synod to put before the clergy and the laity of the diocese certain recommendations regarding its future. Stanley George Pickard, Archdeacon of Msumba, had been nominated bishop, but as yet this had not been made public. The soil was still wet on de Blank's African shoes so it was unfortunate that he had to undertake this particular journey at this particular time. He considered the Episcopal Synod had acted hastily, that Lebombo's Archdeacon, John Alexander King, should be nominated bishop and work slowly towards amalgamation at some propitious time in the future. In the event Pickard and not King became bishop in 1958, and by 1960 the new diocese was authorised and formed. Once the decision was made, de Blank put his force behind the new bishop's plans and their execution. Stanley Pickard was consecrated by de Blank in Grahamstown Cathedral on 23 November 1958. de Blank made a number of visits to the diocese as Bishop Pickard recalls:

> He always enjoyed them whether it was saying Mass and preaching in a small 'mud hut' of a church or attending a sophisticated party in Lourenço Marques (Maputo). He was interested in everying that was going on which was most gratifying for 'insignificant' Lebombo, especially since his predecessor (Geoffrey Clayton) had shown little or no interest.

> On the whole I got on very well with Joost and certainly enjoyed his visits. He was not, however, an easy man to get on with. He was inclined, or rather appeared to be aloof and sometimes rather superior making the other men feel inferior; he certainly did not suffer fools gladly.

> He was very conscious of his office as Archbishop and was almost fanatically devoted to ceremonial and to what might be called 'archiepiscopal protocol'. He was always very punctual although sometimes this punctuality was carried a little too far, with resulting self righteousness and a little self glorification. On one occasion we were due to leave the Head Station (Maciene) at 5 p.m. I was just going out to the car when something of a minor crisis cropped up which needed my urgent attention. I went and told Joost that I would be delayed by about 10 or 15 minutes. He ignored me and went and sat in the car and complained about not keeping to the scheduled times. Peter Priest, his Chaplain, dealt with this and told Joost that he was not the only 'pebble on the beach', and there were others who needed consideration. Only Peter Priest could have dealt with Joost in such a way in such circumstances. However, Joost did not relent quickly and during the journey of 150 miles he hardly spoke a word.

Whatever some people thought of him there is no doubt that he made a contribution to the life of the Church in South Africa. In some spheres he sowed seeds which did not bear fruit in his time but they did later. One such example was help to the poorer dioceses of the Province. He often expressed the wish to help and ease the financial situation of Lebombo but he could not see a way unless the other dioceses took on the responsibility — this they did later in the time of his successor. He was, however, responsible for getting a certain amount of financial support from the Episcopal Church of America.

Another early visit was to the diocese of Basutoland. Each time de Blank crossed from the Orange Free State into Basutoland he filled his lungs with the freer air. In his unpublished autobiographical notes he wrote: 'The racial atmosphere of South Africa obstructed your breathing and corrupted the soul, and when I crossed the border into Basutoland and saw the Union Jack flying cheerfully and the African officials happy and full of confidence, if I did not want actually to roll on Basutoland grass I certainly wanted to kneel down and give God thanks. For all its past mistakes, there was an attempt to work out co-operation between people of varying races on the basis of human worth and service and not on the altogether unreliable standards of pigmentation'.

He liked the proud mountain people and Government officals he met. From the latter he heard nothing but 'contempt and usually downright hatred for Union Nationalist policy and legislation. And what is particularly interesting is that a large majority of men in the Government service are themselves South Africans who cannot abide their own country's policies.' (Diary, 23 March 1958)

When de Blank went to *encourage* the Church he meant the Anglican Church. Sometimes he looked with malice and envy at other Churches. 'The Romans are here (in Basutoland) in great strength and the Roman Mission is in the hands of French Canadians. Co-operation is difficult. They are quite unscrupulous — but they have fine buildings, eight times as many priests as we have and large numbers of religious. Canada finds a minimum of £100,000 per annum for Basutoland. I think the Romans have about 250,000 members'. The population was 630,000. Anglicans numbered between 60,000 to 70,000. The other major Church was the Paris Evangelistic Mission, dwindling, though still with 120,000 members, and co-operation with the Anglicans was good.

In Basutoland, de Blank learned of the power and influence of local chiefs. Witch doctors also exercised power and medicine murder was still comparatively frequent. 'He "puts the finger" on someone to be the victim (usually someone old, infirm or weak) and also on someone to be the murderer. I heard of one poor man who was told that he could choose to be either the victim or the murderer! What a dilemma. . . . A sad story one D.C. tells is of a chief who was hanged for medicine murder in 1949. He had been converted to Rome and when they went through his house they found a framed Indulgence absolving him not only from all sins he had committed in the past but from all sins that he would commit in the future! This is monstrous!'

de Blank wondered how local customs — not medicine murder! — could be harnessed in the service of the Church. Often the Christian Africans themselves despised them as a reminder of the time when they were heathens. Yet if Christianity was not to be regarded as a Western importation there must be effective indigenisation of the faith. In July 1959 de Blank visited Zululand in company with Walter H. Gray, Bishop of Connecticut. Here he learned about the influx and increase of sects which were making converts because they were entirely pro-African and anti-white and approved of polygamy. He discussed the challenge of these sects in a friendly meeting with the Roman Catholic Bishop (an Austrian), the heads of the Norwegian Mission and of the Methodist Church. The general policy was that on conversion the man should choose one wife but make free provision for the others. 'They all agree that this is a tremendous demand on the man — and hard on the women — but it nevertheless seems the only worthwhile policy. If a wife gets converted she has to go with her husband (unless he too becomes a Christian) because she has no right to break away. However, economic factors are entering in — a wife is so expensive (11 oxen or so) that only 20% of the Zulus now have more than one wife. Of course, once you have got her she is an economic asset'. (Diary 11 July 1959).

de Blank met Paramount Chiefs, each accompanied by a 'Praiser who sang the praises of his master going back generation upon generation'. One man de Blank met in Zululand who he regarded as 'an outstanding African leader!' was Chief Buthelezi who was also, 'unpopular with the Government and a keen Christian. He has been elected a delegate to Provincial Synod . . . The Chief lives in a small but pleasant European house. All the Zulus who come in never stand upright in the presence of a member of the royal house. They go about bowed with their hands placed just above their knees'.

Unlike many Africans, the Zulus are not by nature a peaceful people and disputes were still settled by the knobkerry, a rather dangerous cudgel. There was a happy moment when an African approached Bishop Walter Gray and asked shyly, 'Are there any Africans like us in America?' to which the Bishop replied with pride, 'Yes, about 20 million of them'.

As de Blank proceeded on his strenuous tours he began to wonder how far Prayer Book English in translated form was right for the Church in places like Zululand and Basutoland.

A year later, in July 1960, de Blank visited the Transkei — the Diocese of St. John's, whose Bishop, James Schuster, recalls:

> For just under three weeks he toured the parishes and missions of the Transkei; and I calculated that during those days he preached or gave other forms of public addresses on over fifty occasions. Nothing seemed to tire him, and he was always ready to fall in with the demands made upon him. Wherever he went, great crowds attended to see him. I have no doubt that the sight of him (for he was then at the height of his reputation) and his words brought encouragement and fresh strength to large numbers. He was particularly good when speaking to the small European congregations who gathered in the villages. His favourite text was, 'Fear not, little flock'; and he tried to hold before them a vision of the larger Church to which they belonged.

> He was always magnificent in his public appearances; but sometimes he disappointed his hosts, particularly among the Africans, on the social level. Maybe he was tired after the day's work, and had no further energy to engage in the social chat of the evening. I can recall several houses where we took him for a night's lodging where he sat virtually silent during the evening's entertainment ... To some it gave the impression that he was more interested in humanity in the abstract than in particular human beings. I am sure that this is an unfair judgement; nevertheless his silences, whatever their cause, were open to misunderstanding.

> Perhaps the climax of his visit was to an outstation in the Nqamakwe area. It was estimated that at least 1000 people were in the church — we communicated over 800 — and another 3000 outside. One hymn, sung to the tune of, 'What a friend we have in Jesus', so moved him that, when we were assembled outside for the speeches, he asked that it be sung again. I can well remember the

207

thrill of hearing 4000 voices lifted in song, with a thousand or more girls weaving in and out of the tune with their running harmonies. The whole situation was a landmark in diocesan history, and is still talked about.

There were many other diocesan visits, each in their own way memorable. There was never any doubt that de Blank had a presence which belied his physical stature.

At the meetings of bishops he was regarded a very good chairman. In debate he allowed neither himself nor his colleagues to flee from the subject under discussion. He watched closely for the reactions of bishops to his proposals. If he thought someone was not attending he would say 'Well Bishop N . . . What do you think?'

In Provincial Synod, de Blank could be cross if thwarted. At the 1960 Synod he was somewhat irascible especially with two of his fellow bishops. Kenneth C. Oram, then of the Kimberley Diocese and now Bishop of Grahamstown, writes:

He could be prickly if criticized but it was soon over and good humour restored. This was noticeable at the Provincial Synod at which he presided. His chaplain, C.T. Wood, excluded Bettie Cowdry from the press table because she worked for the *Burger*. (She was Bettie Peacey at the time). John Hunter, Bishop of George, asked on what authority she had been moved to the perimeter of the hall. Joost immediately took umbrage. 'I am amazed that so senior a bishop as the Bishop of George should make allegations without first ascertaining the facts. I will ask my chaplain to explain them'. The Bishop of George however rightly persisted that it was only Synod itself which could determine who should be present and where people should sit. Joost was soon smiling again. The Cape Times supported the Bishop of George and *Die Burger* and Bettie took up her place at the press table.

Later in that session of Synod Joost ruled Bishop Burnett out of order and made him sit down because he had expressed fear that a new proposal of an executive would mean a small coterie of leaders who lived near Cape Town would run the Province. 'Nothing is said in the motion about Cape Town' retorted Joost sharply. Later in the day Fr Hemsley SSM made a placatory speech reminding Joost of similar fears which Bishop Hensley Henson had had when Bishop of Durham. Joost responded smilingly and humbly. His quick temper did not last long.

Fellow bishops were often placed in an embarrassing position. Not all of them were prepared to go as far as de Blank in their revulsion for apartheid. They felt that he created an atmosphere of hostility, in which it was not possible to have any dialogue with either the Government or the Dutch Reformed Church, in which the word reconciliation had been discarded. It was thought also that he made pronouncements in the name of the Church which the Church itself, had it been consulted, would not have endorsed. He was perhaps not sufficiently sensitive to the views of his colleagues to be able to say what they would have wished him to say. More than one bishop was a little frightened of de Blank. It was fear of the image, for the man was largely unknown. Bishop Ambrose Reeves thought, 'Joost had built up a certain image of what an Archbishop should be like and I had the feeling sometimes particularly in the church that he had to fulfil this image, but it did not mean very much to him person to person; he was a humble person'.

In 1961, 1962 and 1963 there were more trips abroad, including a visit to Rome and a private audience with Pope John XXIII in June 1962. de Blank found the Pope, 'immensely interested in and disturbed by the racial problems of South Africa and eager to learn of the Church's witness, both non-Roman and Roman'.

There were also unpublicised private meetings of another kind. de Blank was determined to preserve and develop the friendships made at Cottesloe with some of the leaders of the Dutch Reformed Churches. de Blank held a number of private lunches and dinner parties at Bishopscourt. Most of these were held in strict secrecy and a good deal of subterfuge took place in the planning of them. After one meeting a Dutch Reformed minister wrote, 'I cannot find words to express my gratitude for the privilege of thinking and discussing together the problems of His Church and of our witnessing to His honour and glory in this country. I do believe it is an answer to prayer'. Unfortunately, those people could not carry their Churches with them, and de Blank was unable to build on meetings that were strictly private and unofficial.

In August 1963 he was at The Anglican Congress in Toronto. As Bishop of Stepney he had attended the first Anglican Congress in Minneapolis. This time he preached at the Closing Service. The Congress had taken to heart a warning given by the Archbishop of Canterbury (Michael Ramsey), 'The Church that lives by itself will die by itself'. It affected the delegates. A document entitled *Mutual Responsibility and Interdependence in the Body of Christ* was to ensure that the Anglican Communion would not be allowed to turn in upon itself. The ten days of the Congress showed that though it may be the destiny of Anglicanism eventually to melt into oblivion in an onrushing torrent of global evangelism, how vividly would it colour any stream into which it melted. More than twenty years on Anglicanism shows no sign of melting. In his closing address de Blank did not refer to the racial policies of South Africa but stressed the role of the Church in contemporary society:

> The Church has to be actively engaged in those places and among those people where power is exercised and where today sovereignty and authority are to be found. At the heart of the modern world must be the Church, offering Christ to all men, revealing Himself in terms that have meaning for them, suffering with them, giving Himself to them and for them'.

Friends at Toronto who had not seen de Blank for a little time saw a change in him. The anecdotes and laughter gave a sparkle, and yet they were conscious of the enemy that threatened his body from within. 'Let me burn out for God', was the aspiration of Henry Martyn in India. The same seemed to be true of de Blank.

Few people knew of the constant and often excruciating headaches he had suffered since his wartime injury. Everyone knew of the cerebral thrombosis he suffered in August 1962. Some friends had noticed a slight slurring of speech earlier in the summer. To an American priest, Courtney Carpenter, whom de Blank wanted to entice to work with him, he wrote:

> ... Come sooner rather than later. I am getting older and I'm honestly not clear how long I can do this job. I have actually been far from well for the last two or three weeks and really for the first time since being in this country, I have had to call for medical help. My head wound does seem to cause rather high blood pressure and the doctor suggested easing up. But I told him this job was all or nothing. I cannot do it at half speed. If I cannot do it properly I'd rather not do it at all. I don't think there's any likelihood of this in the near future — but it's a straw in the wind! So come soon — while I'm still here and able to do my job.

de Blank went to England and saw a number of specialists including Lord Brain whom he thought a 'wet fish' and whose impersonal approach he did not like. He also saw the Queen's doctor, Sir Horace Evans. The specialists hoped that he would be able to resume work given a long rest. That is what he did not want to do. He was a restless and bad patient. He wanted people round him and regular telephone calls. When he had wanted to return for the Congress in the autumn Bishop Roy Cowdry wrote to him on 27 September 1962: ' . . . The Holy Spirit did not guide your election for nothing. Your work is not nearly done here and I do not believe that you should prejudice its continuance by jeopardising your health'.

After pleading with de Blank to accept the advice of his medics, he ended his letter, 'Don't be impatient. After all, time doesn't matter very much. Eternity is our business'. Alas, time always mattered to this man of action, this man in a hurry.

de Blank returned to South Africa on 22 November and resumed his work steadily. In his heart he knew this chapter of his life was over as he wrote to Courtney Carpenter on 21 December 1962:

> I fear I cannot say yet what the future holds for me, but indications are mounting that I should probably return to England. This is very private news yet so please mark all letters 'confidential' and they won't be opened by anybody but myself. Health is the main reason, but I rather feel my work here is finished and that the Church ought to be led by a South African, born and bred, like the Bishop of Bloemfontein. Of course if I resign I have no guarantee that they would elect him but I feel I ought to make room for him. Of course I have absolutely no idea how long a scheme like this might take to work out and the chances are I shall be here for many months yet. We must just wait and see.

1963 was a very difficult year. He opened a new book, *Notes of Church Visits from 1963* in which he recorded his impressions of visits to churches in the diocese. Nearly everywhere he was encouraged by the size and spirit of the congregations. His notes are those of a Father-in-God caring for his diocesan family.

On the other hand, he was noting in his *Prayer Request* (16 January 1963):

The Future

Clear that I should go ahead in England. That God will guide preferably soon — when and where to go.

Money

Short of cash at present. If I could get as much as £8,000 problems of removal and travel would be solved. May God supply all my needs.

There was no new work offered at this stage or resignation put in hand. It was many months before the Answers to these Requests were recorded.

He was agonising over his future for most of the year and there was a good deal of self-approach and a little self-pity. Two diary entries are interesting:

2 August 1963

It is time Africa got somebody better — who loves everybody as I do not love everybody — who prays hard as I do not pray — who inspires loyalty as I do not inspire loyalty — who serves as I do not serve — who forgets himself as I do not forget myself.

22 August 1963

Lord make me patient about the future. I have, I'm sure, made a mess of things but I honestly want to do only Thy will and so I pray that Thou wilt over-rule everything to Thy will and Thy Glory.

On his way to and from the Anglican Congress in Toronto, de Blank saw specialists in London and though generally satisfied that he was making progress from the thrombosis they were firm in their advice that he should resign. He agreed and on 1 October notice of his resignation appeared in the press. The following day his appointment as a Canon of Westminster was announced in place of Canon Adam Fox, aged 80. So a man of fify-four was giving up his archbishopric at an age when many men are just entering high office. He noted his *Prayer Answer*, 'To be Canon of Westminster' on 9 September 1963. As for his finances, he had a *Prayer Request* (13 November 1963): 'Please make it clear whether I should take up ... offer or not'. *Prayer Answer* (December) 'Yes, quite clear'.

Despite ostentatious appearances and lavish hospitality, de Blank rarely had any money and spent little on himself just as he ate and drank little at the Bishopscourt parties. He had no private means of his own. He tried to live on what he had earned, at the same time doing his best to keep open house at Bishopscourt. He was financially helped by wealthy well wishers in the United States. Then there was another kind of help, the massive personal contribution of his sister Bartha. She saw to his needs, was sensitive to them to a degree and in large measure released him for much of the work he was able to do by her loving care and thought for him at every turn.

The Government were pleased at de Blank's departure and wished some other bishops would follow him. The previous year the Minister of Transport, B.J. Schoeman hoped de Blank would stay in England ('We are tired of these political bishops in our country') and this when de Blank was recovering from a thrombosis. de Blank was quick to remind the Minister that when Verwoerd was shot he had sent a message of good wishes for his speedy recovery.

In *Good Hope* (November 1963) he gave another warning about apartheid, reminding his readers that he had sought only to proclaim the Gospel to the individual and its outreach into the social life of South Africa. . . . 'Like St. Paul I have not ceased to warn you, not without tears — and I warn you again. *Now* is the accepted time; *now* is the day of salvation. Tomorrow may well be too late. Our feet are on the Gadarene slope. But there may be just time to turn back'.

That was to the Diocese of Cape Town. To the Province he returned to words he had used at the beginning of his archiepiscopate. Writing in the Provincial newspaper *Seek* (November 1963) he said:

I do not pretend that my record as Metropolitan has been without blemish. I am sure mistakes have been made, and errors perpetrated. But never deliberately. The Toronto message to the whole Anglican world in August labelled racial discrimination as sin, plain and unadorned. This confirms my own conviction that such discrimination is a form of blasphemy, and that those who condone it or allow it without protest place their own souls in eternal peril. It is a major tragedy that some who claim to be Christians still espouse gradualism and a step by step amelioration in inter-race relations. As if any minister of religion could say, 'I should like you not to commit adultery as enthusiastically or as promiscuously this year as last'. Such an attitude *will not do.*

Sin is sin, and has to be repented of and forsaken completely *here and now*. We cannot ourselves prevent some of the racial legislation that bedevils South Africa today; but we can see to it that we do not camouflage it by such high sounding names as *Separate Development* or *Territorial Homelands*. Some people hinted that I have tried to go too far and too fast. But how far and how fast are you supposed to go when you are running away from sin and seeking to do God's will?'

December was a month of farewells culminating in a meeting and presentation in a crowded City Hall on 30 December. de Blank had already preached his final sermon in St. George's Cathedral when he reminded the congregation that they were living in an irreligious age when even intelligent people, 'relegate Christianity

213

to an obscure corner of life where you speak the language of Canaan, sing the Songs of Zion and worry about irrelevant details of Sabbath observance'. The promised land of the future belonged to all people in South Africa. Knowing that there would be difficulties ahead he called upon his people, not for the first time, 'to be strong and of good courage'.

If part of White South Africa aligned itself with *Die Burger* in not mourning his departure, 'Black Africa can never forget our wonderful shepherd' cabled Chief Buthelezi. Messages of love and gratitude poured in from black and coloured South Africans and from a host of white people too who had recognised and responded to a leader in their midst.

On 31 December 1963 the archiepiscopate was over. The glory was departing. He gave his Office Book of services to a priest in the diocese, inscribing it: 'In love and gratitude for more than six matchless years'. They were 'matchless' for Church and Archbishop alike. And they were 'six'. de Blank's life, ministry and episcopate can be divided into equal periods of five or six years. Into each period he flung his all, but each period was limited in time. Westminster was to be no exception.

During the 1958 Lambeth Conference, de Blank had given a party for the bishops of the Province and some of his London friends. It was a very good party, which ended at about midnight with a tour round St. Paul's Cathedral. It was altogether a memorable occasion. During the course of the evening de Blank, in conversation with one of those present, mapped out his career and said Cape Town was only a passing phase. This was the other side of glory — tragedy. This restless man never really put down any roots in South Africa because he never had a sense of permanence.

CHAPTER FIFTEEN

Before the Ending of the Day

de Blank was not leaping in the air with excitement at the prospect of a Westminster canonry, although a lovely house in Little Cloister went with it. At least it would be a base for operations, there would be a pulpit from which he could preach and an altar where he could continue celebrating the Holy Mysteries.

Yet Westminster Abbey was not the place where de Blank really wanted to be. He had hoped that appointment to an English Diocese would have been possible and he confided to friends that he would have been pleased if Ely, which was vacant, had come his way.

The strong team at Westminster were not wildly joyful either at having de Blank in their midst. It was a star-studded cast, with Eric Abbott as Dean and Canons Max Warren (Sub-Dean), Edward Carpenter (Archdeacon) and Michael Stancliffe. There were three Minor Canons — Rennie Simpson, Gordon Dunstan — and Christopher Hildyard. Would de Blank accept his different status? He had written a strange letter asking what he should wear at the Abbey which caused more than one canon's temperature to rise. How could a world figure such as de Blank be concerned about such trivia. Could he adapt to Abbey life? Alternatively would the Abbey's history first enfold him — and then entomb him? That is always the teasing danger facing a canon of an ancient foundation. Not at Westminster under that powerful régime — and not de Blank.

For his part de Blank was conscious of the nineteen sixties, a time of questioning faith and changing standards. Surely the Abbey's endeavour should be to interpret Christianity in intelligible, pertinent and applicable terms. It should want no part of a segregated ivory-tower religion: an anachronism jutting out harmlessly into the mainstream of life. Eric Abbott knew that the

215

Abbey was not de Blank's chosen milieu and that he might feel frustrated. Could this eager, inventive, original and restless spirit be content in a seemingly quiet place? He stressed that if de Blank was physically well he could still be at the disposal of the whole Church. It is surprising how quickly de Blank adapted to Abbey life and in some ways transformed it. He continued to wear purple cassock and mitre when officiating outside the Abbey but at the Abbey he wore a red cassock like the other canons and only his pectoral cross and episcopal ring distinguished him from his colleagues. It was immediately obvious that he was not a spent force and he preached often brilliantly and always directly. His diary quickly filled with engagements all over the country. His health seemed to improve.

At the Abbey his concern was always for the visitor, the person who 'dropped in', the tourist who might never have been to a service before and if the Abbey failed him or her would never go again. The pulpit gave him an opportunity for evangelism. He managed to prod the Chapter into a few innovations, for example a hymn was sung after Evensong on Saturday. Let the people sing when the people come in their hundreds on Saturday afternoons. There were many frustrations in Chapter meetings for like many Chapters, its movement was geared to the slowest vessel in the convoy. As elsewhere in his life de Blank's approach was intuitive in the sense that if he made a judgement he would feel that the intuition could constrain the mechanics towards its realisation.

de Blank established a rapport with Eric Abbott who was immediately struck by the way in which he celebrated the Eucharist. He did it not only with unhurried dignity and an aura of timelessness, but also encased it in prayer. de Blank needed the quiet time of preparation and a moment of private thanksgiving at the end. The Eucharist remained at the hub of his life. Here all barriers are down, all boundaries crossed.

One canon who was surprised by de Blank was Edward Carpenter, historian, writer and much else besides. (He later succeeded Eric Abbott as Dean.) There was something larger than life about de Blank, who dressed extravagantly in Harris tweeds and wore large cufflinks and a large hat. He brought a touch of champagne into the life of the Abbey. There was actual champagne at his parties but he brought sparkle into the atmosphere of the 'Abbey family'. The workmen were fond of him and so were many of the staff. He was humble as a man and genuine as a priest. The 'bishop' was not in evidence. Carpenter warmed to this man who had mental energy and innovative ideas and liked the touch of professionalism which he gave to various undertakings. Let the Church use the best that is available instead of relying on amateur and well meaning endeavour. This was particularly the case with publicity and business methods. de Blank ' knew the best person for advice and action.

The 900th Anniversary of Westminster Abbey fell during de Blank's time as Canon. The theme *One People* was chosen by the Dean and Chapter to give unity, structure and coherence to the events of a year of celebrations beginning on 28 December 1965 in a beautifully restored and enchanced Abbey. The theme of the year included services and events connected with the Abbey Community, the Wider Community, Church and State, The Two Cultures, One World and the Kingdom of God. Was this enough? de Blank later wrote *(Westminster Abbey Occasional Paper,* Winter 1966)

> ... there were those who stated their fears that the events planned for 1966 might be too exclusively high-brow and *recherche.* Obviously the music to be offered in the Abbey would be the best and purest Church music possible. Obviously, the poetry readings would appeal to a limited though an extremely appreciative audience. Obviously, the special services would speak to those for whom they were planned and designed. But what about the ordinary people? What about those who preferred the Light to the Third programme? What about those who would sooner read Ogden Nash than Robert Browning? What about those who thought the Abbey was still a bit stuffy and the heart of the 'Establishment'? Were these ordinary folk to be forgotten in our year of celebration?

So the Market and Fair was conceived largely by de Blank. In one word de Blank wanted a whoopee! And he got it for a week in July 1966 in Dean's Yard where sixty thousand people enjoyed themselves. It had all the ingredients of a medieval fair with twentieth century trimmings.

It was no surprise to find invitations to write, speak, preach, preside, etc. falling on de Blank's doormat. Organisations wanted his name to adorn their notepaper. It was no surprise to find de Blank accepting most of them. Naturally many were connected with the racial conflicts of South Africa and human rights. The British Government was not blind to the position, but not with the urgency — and clarity, de Blank would say — that was required. Yet the Prime Minister, Sir Alec Douglas-Home, said at Southampton on 24 April 1964 that 'the greatest danger in the world today — as deadly in its way as the atomic bomb — is the threat of racialism'.

On 27 March 1964 in South Africa death sentences were passed on certain leaders of the African National Congress and other trials, many held *in camera,* were in progress. Banning orders were issued by the ream in an attempt to paralyse the organisations opposed to apartheid. Gag or banish the leaders and the opposition will melt away! That did not happen, though most of the leadership of the Liberal Party had been restricted by banning orders thus joining the leaders of such organisations as the African National Congress and the Pan-African Congress. In June 1964 de Blank visited the United Nations and took with him a Petition that had been prepared by the World Campaign for the release of South African Political Prisoners bearing signatures from twenty eight different countries and representing 258 million people. The Petition asked for the release of political prisoners in South Africa among whom was Nelson Mandela who, twenty two years on, remains in captivity. When he had received the Petition outside the House of Commons he reminded people that, 'It is of the essence of Christianity to stand up for the under-privileged and to work for social justice. In this present racial conflict, the Church stands in the forefront of the struggle for the recognition that all men are made in God's image and that all men are brothers'. He had conversation with U Thant in New York and was one of many petitioners who appeared before the *Special Committee on the Policies of Apartheid of the Government of the Republic of South Africa* at the United Nations. Other petitioners included people de Blank knew in or in association with South Africa including Oliver Tambo who was then Deputy President of the African National Congress, Ronald Segal, Convenor of the International Conference on Economic Sanctions against South Africa and a former Editor of *Africa South,* Ruth First a South African journalist; Barney Desai, President of the South African Coloured People's Congress, formerly Cape Town City Councillor and Dr. Yousuf M. Dadoo of the South African Indian Congress.

Back in England de Blank was invited to give the tenth Robert Waley Cohen Memorial Lecture on *Inter-Race Relations* in the University of London on 8 December 1964 under the auspices of

218

the Council of Christians and Jews. He had long had an association with the Council and he had many Jewish friends. He would agree with some words of J.B. Priestley placed in the mouth of a character in one of his novels *Saturn Over the Water* (1961) '[Jews], I like them. They don't as so many of the English do, quietly die while still moving around and talking. Jewish zombies are hard to find. While they're living, they're alive. I don't mind people being tough and aggressive, if at the same time they're intelligent and warmhearted'.

In the lecture de Blank was able to show how much basic common faith Jews and Christians shared — 'God made man in His image' and from that premise man's relationship to his fellow-man is established. It is interesting to find him mentioning the policy of the Arabs towards Israel: 'The Koran's proper emphasis on the oneness of mankind is seen to be utterly hypocritical unless and until this hostility is resolved. In fact, it may be argued whether there can be any true brotherhood of man where there is no belief in the universal Fatherhood of God'.

After the lecture the Rev. Dr. Aubrey Vine seconded the vote of thanks and said, 'If you have ever been in a power house and seen a switch thrown that is to connect with thousands of volts, there may be sparks and splutter as the switch connects. When it is well in, however, there is quietness — but you know the power is going unimpeded through that switch and I feel that is so with everything that Bishop de Blank says. Here is conviction that has gone right home. He is telling us of those things which have become a very part of his being and that, to me, anyhow, is something that goes right into me, almost like a cold douche — the first effect is shock, the second effect is tingle, but the third effect is bracing'.

Bracing is an apt word to use when thinking of de Blank even in these latter but not yet muted days at Westminster.

Aspects of his lecture reflected a new passion for universalism — in the unity of all mankind. This was reflected in other ways including his Presidency of the reconstituted Social Morality Council, an exciting positive new Council of Christians, Jews and Humanists that had arisen out of the negative Public Morality Council which was thought to have sex on the mind and nowhere else! The new Council was concerned with such questions as disarmament and overseas aid.

de Blank's literary output was regular, with articles and reviews for newspaper and magazines. In 1964 *Out of Africa* was published which was a collection of lectures, sermons and addresses delivered when he was Archbiship of Cape Town. There was a pamphlet *The Life of Jesus* (1965) based on a broadcast series of talks.

He was in touch with radical thought in the Churches and joined the Editorial Council of *New Christian* but he was ever critical of those who decried the Church and destroyed the faith. When he had come back to England he was shocked at the complacent dullness of Church life compared to what he had often witnessed in Africa.

> I am constantly exasperated by the Church and its unchristian self-concern. I am convinced that the Church needs to reform its whole institutional life so that it can really cope with the pressures of life in the 1960's but I am equally convinced that a Churchless Christianity is a meaningless phrase, is in fact a dangerous misunderstanding and that it weakens the faith at its heart.

> I certainly want to see the formalism and stuffiness knocked out of our English congregations. I am quite ready to see an entirely new approach to the kind of working plant the Church needs in the years towards the end of our century. I want to see the Church through its members penetrating every aspect of social, industrial, political, national and international life.

> But I have absolutely no use — and little patience — for those who bemoan the Church's weakness and yet who do nothing to build up the body of the faithful so that it may stand up an exceeding great army, inspired and led by the Holy Spirit of God.

His diary was full, yet he was restless. Then, something like a little miracle occurred as it seemed to de Blank. During November 1965 he received a letter from the Diocese of Hong Kong and Macao asking him if he would allow his name to be put forward as the sole nominee to follow Ronald Owen Hall as Bishop in 1966. The Chairman of the Nominating Committee, Lam Chik Ho, said they had decided on a candidate from overseas but:

> There is some feeling in the diocese that we should have a bishop of Chinese race: one of the Chinese clergy, proposed by nine parishes, would probably be elected if proposed. But we are quite sure he lacks the drive and powers of decision necessary in this diocese at this time. Bishop Hall has done a marvellous job, but there are a fair number of loose ends to be tidied up; these will require decision as

well as tact and diplomacy! We have also considered nominating Roland Koh, who has just moved from Kuala Lumpur to Jesselton (as bishop): but (as has been said) 'has a traditional Chinese reluctance to grasp nettles' and we feel he is not our man, just now.

We have come to the conclusion, in Committee, that Synod might be satisfied if a man of Chinese race became assistant bishop: we feel that the diocese needs two bishops now: we think that a Chinese assistant would be invaluable in coping with Chinese ramifications. We would be ready to recommend a Chinese priest who would be an admirable assistant bishop; he would be a loyal hard-working colleague; he is liked by everyone, and Synod would amost certainly accept him.

This letter brought a mixture of peace, joy and excitement to de Blank. He had earlier been asked by the Bishop of Polynesia, John Charles Vockler, to go and look after the diocese for a year for, 'as I face the future here it is very clear to me that my pastoral tasks cannot be carried out without a working grasp of Hindi and Fijian. I have tried my best but found that they cannot be learned under my present circumstances. They must certainly be learned before my numbers of indigenous clergy increase or the task of leading the church here forward will be immeasurably more difficult'.

de Blank had been unable to accept that intriguing challenge, but Hong Kong was different. It was not temporary but another permanent bishopric. He had a medical check and received an acquiescent nod rather than a clean bill of health. Bartha once again agreed to go with him even though she was quickly making an independent life for herself in London whilst still looking after de Blank. He was ignorant of the Chinese way of life and could not speak Chinese but he could learn. On 2 December, 1965 he wrote accepting nomination with the proviso that, if elected, he would appoint his own Chinese assistant-bishop within a year of arrival.

Ronald Hall had been an outstanding bishop for thirty four years and was known throughout the Anglican Communion. It was of great concern to him who should be his successor although his part in the election was to say nothing, only to answer any question he was asked. 'But' as he wrote in his Newsletter afterwards, 'my whole being has been stretched often to complete exhaustion in a passion of prayer and self offering of heart and mind and will to God for those whose duty it was to vote, and for this whole city of God of which the new Bishop must be in a sense the Chief Pastor, even though we are a minority Church, not in any sense "established".'

The work of the Nominating Committee began with a statement by an English representative, 'we want to know whom the Chinese Church wants for its Bishop'. The answer he got was 'the Chinese Church wants the best man for the job, whatever his race'. On 6 January 1966 the Diocesan Synod of Hong Kong and Macao decided de Blank was that man and the public announcement was subsequently made. de Blank could not leave England until October in view of commitments at the Abbey. Those months were full of plans and also signs of declining health again. His doctors warned him of the consequences of keeping an unmanageable appointment diary. de Blank did not ignore the warnings but felt a greater pressure to *do* things. Rest was a prelude to action. He could not accept rest as a permanent part of his future life style.

By June 1966 it was clear he would have to forgo Hong Kong. The doctors forbade him to go. Death would be the result of disobedience. With a pierced heart he said 'No' to Hong Kong and withdrew his resignation as a Canon of Westminster which fortunately was not effective until the end of September. It was probably never a realistic decision to have accepted Hong Kong.

Still, there were new endeavours. He served as Chairman of the London Conciliation Committee of the Race Relations Board. The United Nations designated the year 1968, being the twentieth anniversary of the adoption of the Universal Declaration of Human Rights, as the International Year for Human Rights. de Blank accepted the Chairmanship of the United Kingdom Committee. The invitation came with the express support of Mrs. Eirene White, M.P. Minister of State for Foreign Affairs. The aim was to dramatise universal respect for the observance of human rights and fundamental freedoms for all, without distinction as to race, sex, language or religion. This was the kind of work de Blank liked as it cut across boundaries and had to do with the elimination of restriction, discrimination and other deprivations of human rights in this country as well as overseas.

de Blank was encouraged by an invitation from Mervyn Stockwood, Bishop of Southwark, to be an assistant bishop in his diocese. This would mean opportunities for exercising his episcopal ministry. Unfortunately he was struck down before he could do a great deal in this and other spheres.

Nonetheless before his final stroke, de Blank had some good periods when he was not unlike the de Blank of an earlier period. The Westminster years were not all decline and demise. Quite the contrary. New friends were made, new opportunities were created not least by his hospitality in his home at Little Cloister. It became a place for parties and meetings. Again one saw in de Blank the capacity for drawing people of very different and sometimes opposite characteristics and personalities together. There were plenty of lunches and dinners in restaurants and clubs and often the scintillating conversation associated with de Blank. There were the remembered moments too. John Andrew, then chaplain to the Archbishop of Canterbury (Michael Ramsey) was at lunch with de Blank on the day Pope Paul was elected. He recalls 'Joost had asked the waiter if he had heard the news and if there were any results. The waiter returned with some cricket scores and Joost put him swiftly right on that one; he wanted to know whether there was a Pope or not. Back came the waiter shortly afterwards to say that the world had a new Pope and Joost immediately called for a bottle of champagne and we must have been among the world's first clerics to drink to the new Sovereign Pontiff'.

Although his health was failing he still accepted new commissions and engagements. One of them was an invitation to write the Archbishop of Canterbury's Lent Book for 1968. This was written between February and June 1967 and appeared the following Lent (posthumously) as *The Return of the Sacred*. This was his least satisfactory book, the work of an exhausted man struggling to challenge his readers to stress the sacred without rejecting the secular. He had rebukes for 'Christian pietists' who are entirely preoccupied with traditional aspects of worship and evangelism and 'Christian secularists' who think of the Church's mission solely in terms of social service.

On 2 August 1967 he suffered another cerebral thrombosis and was rushed to hospital. The severity of the thrombosis increased, his left side was paralysed but his mental faculties were not seriously affected. He spent three months in hospital and although he was given physiotherapy and speech therapy, progress was slow and recovery was partial. At the end of November he was moved to a centre where it was hoped he would learn to walk properly. A slight spark came when he was allowed home at weekends and he was able to attend some Abbey services in his wheelchair.

223

On 31 December he suffered another severe stroke. He had managed to write in his diary on that last day of the year: 'I cannot say how lovely it is to be home . . . One can ask that if one is going to die it may be through the loveliest of all environments. One can only say the same thing about getting better.''My times are in God's hands and I am glad'' — so runs one of the old Moody and Sankey hymns which I need to try and live out. If I am to be better let me improve soon for Jesus' sake'.

de Blank was removed to hospital and Bishop Mervyn Stockwood said some commendatory prayers at his bedside on Monday evening 1 January 1968. As so often happens in such cases the unconscious patient appears to have an inkling of what it happening. de Blank did, for he seemed to raise his hands as if in farewell. Less than an hour later he was dead.

The last months were wretched for him but so had been much of the Westminster period. To some of his friends he would half-hint and they would half-guess that he was undergoing a crisis, that he was losing or had lost his way spiritually. It was much more than spiritual cramp for that can often be alleviated by adjusting one's ecclesiastical position or accepting theological massage. It was not even faith diminished but faith lost or faith by a thread. Only hope remained and that was elusive. Soul-wrecked de Blank was like flotsam on a vast horizonless ocean.

In the worst times of his illness de Blank was wholly dependent on the ministrations of others. He was helpless and he hated it. In such circumstances it is important to teach humility and not administer humiliation. The hardest lesson for de Blank to learn was to kiss the rod which smote him without resenting too fiecely the discipline which it inflicted. Some notes he wrote show that he learned to be thankful for the way in which doctors, nurses and others looked after him. When he was alone with close friends it was different. They saw a completely broken man, a vulnerable man. The will to live had gone from a man who had to be active. Yet Monica Furlong is not alone in reflecting that 'his last illness was the greatest achievement of his life. A terrific holding on, a tremendous gripping of feeling and sort of strangling it. That had gone and he was not able to hold on, and he just sat and cried. It was so brave accepting this and not pushing it away. This was the hardest thing. I've never felt greater respect and love for him. The last time I saw him he just sat and cried the whole time. He was very troubled by his guilt and sinfulness. He yearned to get through'.

Before his last illness he told Monica Furlong that when he went to Greenhill he had felt that he would like to marry her but that she was 'ten years too young'. Monica Furlong, who was eighteen or nineteen when de Blank first got to know her, 'took it less at its face value than as a sign that he then, in late middle age, had come to trust me although I was a woman, and could just imagine that it might have been possible to trust me more. Earlier in our friendship I was often aware of a kind of terror which overtook him. What was so moving to me at the end was that this all went and that we used to sit and hold hands when I visited him in hospital, or I could put my arms round him when he wept. He so much needed plain human warmth, then, and at most other times in his life'.

Here, at the end of the earthly story, the subject of de Blank's alleged homosexuality must be faced. At various stages of his life and most notably in Cape Town, it caused raised eyebrows and malicious gossip. This was directed less at de Blank than at some of the people who were or appeared to be close to him. de Blank appeared sometimes like a prima donna, surrounded by young men. He seemed unaware of the offence he was giving and the rumours which were spreading. He had no peers with whom he could relax.

de Blank's homosexuality had always been there in his nature. As an undergraduate at Cambridge he was aware of his homosexual feelings. Under the influence of the Oxford Group Movement and 'absolute honesty' he thought he should tell his parents so he wrote them a letter. This caused terrible pain to them, they could make nothing of it, and could never bring themselves to refer to the letter directly to their son. Of course, there was the matriarchal figure of Mama looming over her children, binding them to her rather than releasing them.

de Blank told Monica Furlong that when he was a young curate in Bath he used to bicycle into the city every week to see a psychoanalyst in the desperate hope he could help him sexually. But de Blank came away empty.

Monica Furlong adds, 'The whole wretched climate of the times made the homosexual feelings so intolerably difficult to live with. He said that he bitterly regretted that, because of his evangelical leanings, he had resisted all the sexual temptations at Cambridge. ('I see now that it was all there waiting for me and I never took advantage of it'). At Greenhill, he told me, he had once had too much wine at a dinner party and blurted out some information

225

Memorial Tablet, Westminster Abbey.

about himself that obviously shocked his hosts very much. It always seemed to me that his valiant attempts at chastity drove him to overwork'.

For all that, it is important to state and emphasise that de Blank's feelings never resulted in any physical expression. Surely deliberate restraint and disciplined abstention is to be admired rather than criticised.

There had once been the possibility of marriage to an attractive vivacious American. Alan Lindsay, whose flair as a designer was used for publications at Stepney, in Cape Town and Westminster recalls: 'One day when we had lunch together in 1961 after my first visit to America we were walking along Knightsbridge and two beautiful young women passed. I said, "Pure Gainsborough — only England can produce such class". Joost replied, "I thought you would say that" and then referring to one of his friends in New York, added, "You know I nearly married her — it was the thought of the night shift that put me off".'

Another friend felt that the broken man at the end of de Blank's life was a far more acceptable sacrifice and a far more acceptable and greater person in the eyes of those who loved him (and perhaps in

God's eyes) than a successful figure. The old adage that nothing succeeds like success is not true when looking at the end of de Blank's life but perhaps nothing succeeded like the apparent failure.

On 3 January 1968, de Blank, vested in his robes, was taken into Westminster Abbey at dusk. The following day Eric Abbott celebrated a Requiem Eucharist attended by about seven hundred people. This was followed by a private cremation.

On 26 January the Abbey was crowded for a Memorial Service or rather a Thanksgiving Service. There was pomp, circumstance and official representation. Trumpets sounded and colour dominated the procession. In his instructions for his will de Blank had said, 'I have no strong feelings about my funeral, but, if possible, I should like the hymns : "Mine eyes have seen the glory of the coming of the Lord" to the tune of John Brown's Body, and also: "O what their joy and their glory must be ..."' All manner of people filled the Abbey as if the Market and Fair of the 900th anniversary celebrations had moved from Dean's Yard into the Abbey. The feeling of joy and thanksgiving was evident and genuine. So were the tears. If de Blank's faith had faltered there was sufficient in the Abbey to uphold and carry him and his spirit. It was a champagne ending for the congregation and a beginning for de Blank.

Bishop Wand gave the address. It was memorable, quite unlike the platitudinous unctuosities usually preached on such occasions where every dead man or woman is eulogised as a soporific for the living. There was praise of 'a born leader' but something more important:

> ... those who knew him well and intimately — his friends and relatives — will be thinking much of him this day and of the inner struggle that went on throughout his life and particularly in the latter years of it to know and understand what was God's will for him. Man, we are told, is born to trouble as the sparks fly upward. Sometimes we are tempted to try to jump off our own shadow and think ourselves in an imaginery life where troubles will cease to harass us. That is impossible. Life is not a sentimental sphere in which we can lose ourselves in happy and pleasant thoughts without fear of trouble or anxiety. We have to take life as it is — the trouble with the happiness. Sometimes we can be so happy that we become afraid of our own happiness. Sometimes the trouble is so great that we wonder whether indeed we have lost sight of God or whether He has actually forsaken us. Of all this stress and trouble

Joost had his fill. But we who knew him well knew how gallantly he faced up to this problem.

He had a great ideal. He gave himself for that ideal. Men will say that the thing that mattered most to him proved a failure in his hands. But who are we to judge that. The high that proved too high, the heroic for earth too hard, the passion that left the ground to lose itself in the sky. Surely we can add that it is enough God heard it once and we shall hear it by and by. Such a witness cannot fail of its ultimate effect. God receives it to Himself and stores it in His treasury and gives us the tangible result of it in His own good time.

During the service de Blank's ashes were interred by the entrance to St. George's Chapel near the Great West Door. It was an appropriate place, a busy place amongst the people. The memorial stone describes him thus:

INDOMITABLE FIGHTER FOR HUMAN RIGHTS

These words describe a notable and noble achievement but the man whose achievements they record and recall remains to some extent hidden and elusive.

CHAPTER SIXTEEN

Glory and Anguish

Bishop John Carter, Provincial Liaison Officer of the Church of the Province of South Africa had just been appointed Anglican Chaplain to the University of Cape Town in 1957 by de Blank's predecessor, Geoffrey Clayton. He died before John Carter took office. 'When Joost de Blank was elected,' recalls John Carter, 'I found myself waiting for his arrival with a mixture of excitement and trepidation. I had known and admired Geoffrey Clayton. What would his successor be like?

'I still don't know the answer to that question. He was a brilliant speaker, a commanding personality. He also seemed cold, aloof and somewhat intimidating.

'There were some things about the Archbishop's style that I found hard to take. He travelled in a big American car, flying a pennant. At Bishopscourt the emphasis was on the 'court'. I did not feel at ease there. There were touches of ostentation foreign to the South African situation. Yet he was a spokesman for Black people, and, to many, a hero.

'... This is the enigma: a man flamboyant and deep, demonstrative and cold, compelling in the pulpit but with no small talk, confident yet uneasy, admired — but perhaps not loved. I knew him, but what he was really like I still don't know.

'One visual image remains. The mission station at Modderpoort, in the centre of South Africa, was a place we used for meetings such as those of the Anglican Students' Federation. There you could see the cave where the first missionaries had lived, and the graves of twelve members of the Community who had left their bones in Africa.

'The Archbishop arrived at Modderpoort for one meeting, and called us to the chapel so that he could give his instructions for the celebration of the Eucharist next morning. At the back of the chapel a little black man was sweeping the floor. As the Arch-bishop continued his monologue, the little man slowly advanced, sweeping away, sweeping away. At last he reached the sanctuary. Everybody stood still, even the Archbishop. But the little man continued, sweeping away, sweeping away.'

If this man appeared to be unaware of de Blank it was an unusual occurrence. de Blank was used to being noticed. He made sure of that. Prior to South Africa his ministry had been conspicu-ously successful and news of his outstanding episcopal leadership at Stepney had spread quickly and widely. He was a confident man and, on the surface, a self assured one. He believed that he had been divinely appointed to exercise a prophetic ministry in South Africa. Like Amos he exposed the injustices and iniquities stemming from Government policies. His attacks and denunci-ations were scripturally and theologically based not politically based or biased. When he found that his admonitions were not being heeded he warned of impending doom. In his Charge to Provincial Synod of 1960 he went as far as to proclaim that the racial unrest culminating in Sharpeville was the judgement of God falling on the country.

In many of his sermons and addresses the authentic prophetic note is sounded. Prophets are not easy to live with but the danger is that they speak a concluding word rather than an initiating one.

de Blank's sense of drama, of feeling that he was acting on the world's stage was illustrated in many ways. Once, when on a visit to England he confided to more than one person that he did not know whether he would be able to get back into South Africa. In 1960 he drew up an impressive statement J'Accuse to be released in the event of his detention.

It has been said that de Blank courted martyrdom, a statement that is more glibly articulated than reasonably justified. The South African Government was not likely to be foolish enough to make a martyr of him. Sniping, ridiculing, condemning, threatening — yes: but never prison or deportation. The martyr is a volunteer sufferer. de Blank's suffering was of a different kind. However, if he had had a similar experience to Thomas à Becket, that kind of dramatic approach, it would probably have been a fulfilment for him. That was not to be. Instead history is likely to show him as one of the Church's *Confessors*, one who suffers for confessing his faith but only to an extent which does not involve martyrdom.

A fellow bishop wrote, 'He was inclined to be impetuous in his judgments of persons and situations with which he had little sympathy, and the clarity of his own views and the strength of his own convictions sometimes impaired his capacity for distinguishing primary matters, upon which it was necessary to take an immediate and uncompromising stand, from those of lesser importance upon which immediate judgment and action might conscientiously be deferred. This was wholly understandable in South Africa where so many features of social and political life are abhorrent to any sensitive Christian conscience as wholly inconsistent with justice and truth; but it meant that although he deservedly won and retained the confidence of coloured and African people, of whose rights he was always a doughty and courageous champion, he was less successful in winning the support of the Church of the Province. In consequence, the witness which he bore to his Lord was often more effective outside the country than within it'.

We have seen how the office of Archbishop ministered to something deep in de Blank. In identifying himself with his Office he also protected himself. The protective layer was also evident in the way he withdrew. He was more relaxed in a large number because he reacted to collective stimulus in a virile way. Equally, he protected himself by withrawing and this created a sense of mystique and mana about him. A man who pushes himself to absolutes and inspires others needs to keep reserves of inner resources. de Blank gave more because of this reserve.

Much of this biography has been taken up with words, works and controversies. Particular mention should now be made, in case it is missed, of de Blank's sense of fun. He was amazingly good company when relaxing with family or close friends or when on holiday. His humour was exhilarating; his wit sharp (and only devastating when deflating pomposity, unctuousness or self-conceit). The 'cares of Office' were thrust aside (or certainly removed to the interior) when entertaining or being entertained. His mind and his humour and sometimes his impulsive impishness made him the focus of attention, the centre of attraction: a man whose refreshing and bracing company one would seek.

At a small dinner party or pre- or post-theatre meal he showed himself to be the ideal host. Perhaps master of ceremonies is a better description; impressario better still. de Blank seemed to know something about everything and everything about something. He certainly knew enough about most things to be intelligently interested in them. Business man, graphic artist, economist, politician, actor, lawyer would be each and all amused and stimulated by his company and his knowledge. de Blank's vitality was matched by a many-sided and multi-gifted nature. And he enjoyed these occasions as much as the people who attended them. For many people this is the de Blank they remember for it is the de Blank they encountered. And what they encountered they both liked and admired.

de Blank is still held in awe, remembrance and affection by very many people and from all periods of his life. 'He helped me ....'. 'He gave me strength ...' 'He led us ...' 'He taught me ...' There are also many priests who owe their vocation to de Blank. He inspired them by his leadership, provoked them with his message and challenged them with stark directness, "Why not you?" God and prayer did the rest. They regard de Blank's capacity to inspire as one of his chief qualities which indeed it was.

The only way to keep one's Christianity is to give it away. de Blank did this and gave more of himself than people realised. In one sermon he said, 'Do you remember the story of the River Jordan, rising in the snows of Hermon, and rushing down into the Sea of Galilee, that sparkling and beautiful Lake, and going out through the Lake, and rushing down the hills until eventually it reaches the bitterness and the salt density of the Dead Sea — and the Dead Sea is bitter and lifeless, unable to support any life at all, because there is no outlet. The Sea of Galilee sparkles and the taste of the snow is in its waters, because the water is rushing through.'

de Blank spent a Galilean life to other people whilst suffering inwardly the torture of the Dead Sea. This was why he could inspire others yet not be at peace with himself. It was both glory and anguish.

de Blank exposed the sins of others but was always aware of the failings of his Church and was hardest of all on his own sins. He never spared himself. In 1960 he wrote '*I accuse* myself for the little I have done for Africa in the space of nearly three years. It has all been too easy and comfortable. So little has been accomplished — so much remains to be done.' Throughout his life the strains recur — so much to do, so little done, so much to do, so little achieved. History's verdict is likely to be kinder to him than he was to himself. Niebuhr's words should haunt every prophet and Confessor.

Glory and Anguish

Nothing worth doing is completed in our lifetime;
therefore we must be saved by hope.

Nothing truly beautiful or good makes complete sense
in any immediate context of history;
therefore we must be saved by faith.

Nothing we do, however virtuous, can be accomplished alone;
therefore we must be saved by love.

No virtuous act is quite as virtuous, from the standpoint
of our friend or foe, as from our own standpoint;
therefore we must be saved by that final form of love which
is forgiveness.

List of Publications

Will God Speak?	Lutterworth	1933
Is it Nothing to You?	Mowbray	1953
The Parish in Action	Mowbray	1954
Mighty River	Church Information Board	1954
Saints at Sixty Miles an Hour	Faith Press	1955
A Life Worth Living: B.B.C. 'Lift up your Hearts'	Layman Publications	
Call of Duty	Oxford Univ. Press	1956
Members of Christ	Mowbray	1956
This is Conversion	Hodder & Stoughton	1957
Uncomfortable Words	Longmans	1958
A Working Faith	Lutterworth	1960
Inter-Race Relationships: Robert Waley Cohen Memorial Lecture	Council of Christians and Jews.	1964
Out of Africa	Hodder & Stoughton	1964
The Life of Jesus: B.B.C. 'Lift up your Hearts'	B.B.C. Publications	1965
The Return of the Sacred	Faith Press	1968

Index